THE PARENT/BABY GAME

BY THE SAME AUTHOR

The Parent/Child Game

THE PARENT/BABY GAME

The Proven Key to a Loving Family

SUE JENNER

BLOOMSBURY

First published in Great Britain 2008

Bloomsbury Publishing Plc, 36 Soho Square, London W1D 3QY

A CIP catalogue record for this book is available from the British Library

ISBN 978 0 7475 8363 9
10 9 8 7 6 5 4 3 2 1

Typeset by Hewer Text UK Ltd, Edinburgh
Printed by Clays Ltd, St Ives plc

Bloomsbury Publishing, London, New York and Berlin

www.bloomsbury.com/suejenner

The paper this book is printed on is certified by the © 1996 Forest Stewardship
Council A.C. (FSC). It is ancient-forest friendly. The printer holds
FSC chain of custody SGS-COC-2061

FSC
Mixed Sources
Product group from well-managed
forests and other controlled sources
Cert no. SGS-COC-2061
www.fsc.org
© 1996 Forest Stewardship Council

Acknowledgements

It is the babies, toddlers and parents with whom I have worked who must be mentioned first of all. Their trust that I could help them resolve some of the problems which crop up over those first three fantastic years was truly inspiring. Thankfully, it wasn't all misplaced!

Next, I would like to make it very clear to my own children, stepchildren, grandchildren and step-grandchildren that they have provided me with the most wonderful and joyous times of my entire life. As they all profess to love me, I suppose I must have managed to achieve a modicum of success in my attempts at parenting.

Most of all, my heartfelt thanks go to my beloved husband and respected colleague Terry, whose encouragement of my sometimes-flagging efforts to finish this book never faltered.

Finally, acknowledgements must be tendered towards Professors Rex Forehand and Robert MacMahon on whose original Parent/Child Game research my own clinical work was based. Also to my devoted typist June, Diana Tyler and the Bloomsbury team who have been instrumental in bringing *The Parent/Baby Game* to fruition. Many thanks.

Dedicated to my darling mother, Kathy, who knew how to be baby-centred long before the term was even invented

Contents

Introduction

Let's Start at the Beginning

If you are pregnant or have a new baby or a toddler, then this book is undoubtedly for you. All parents want to give their baby the best possible start in life. Bringing up our baby should prove to be a challenge to which we can respond competently. Well, competently enough . . . or can we?

While there is a huge range of information available on infant development itself – first tooth, first word, first step and so on – there are precious few easily understood books on a baby's first emotional, psychological and bonding experiences. When these less tangible aspects of a baby's development are mentioned, it's often in terms of how sociable they are becoming. We have all seen their adorable smiles, their glistening, excited glances and noticed the extra wriggling that goes on when they are enjoying our attention. Delightful! How absolutely wonderful if all we had to do in order to create an emotionally healthy family atmosphere for our baby was to make them giggle a couple of times a day. But it's very much more complicated than that.

Until relatively recently there was an unspoken assumption in our society that knowing how to bring up babies to be self-confident toddlers was a natural part of becoming a parent, as if giving birth somehow automatically conferred on the new mummy and/or daddy all the information and talent necessary to become a shining success at parenthood. Thank heavens that is changing now, as that sort of attitude has, in the past, left many couples completely overwhelmed by the enormity of the task of being responsible, minute to minute, for the well-being of their child.

As I point out in my book *The Parent/Child Game*, published in 1999, parenting children aged three to ten years in a competent fashion involves skills that can be learned. Thank goodness the same applies to the nought to threes too! So there are answers to the important questions that many new parents ask. This is enormously comforting news when you are faced with the mysteries of how to help your tiny infant grow into a toddler sparkling with enthusiasm and secure in the knowledge that they are loved and loveable. Questions that new parents often ask are:

- What's the secret of success? Somebody must know, but whom?
- Why do I find it so difficult, despite loving my child so much?
- What am I supposed to be doing?
- Where can I find out about getting it right?

If we can't come up with satisfactory answers, a mood of desperation, hopelessness and failure can descend, making us feel depressed about becoming a competent – never mind perfect – parent. Every new parent needs clear advice on how to provide for their infant's physical needs. Fortunately, much of this is forthcoming from midwives and health visitors. However, there is much less information on the most effective route to establishing and maintaining a close, rewarding and joyful relationship with your baby and toddler.

Most of us are aware that a strong bond between an infant and its parents is crucial if, at three, the baby is to be an assertive yet responsible toddler. But exactly how to create such a bond remains rather a puzzle. Knowing it is from such early emotional security that infants start to evolve their psychological survival kit simply isn't enough. How can we make sure they develop the fabulous bubble of self-confidence that will keep them afloat in future? Receiving this gift from us can enable our baby to not only weather the storms of growing up and becoming parents themselves, but also to conjure up enjoyment for themselves and others along the way.

Some families just seem to produce amiable, active and able babies, toddlers, school pupils, teenagers and young adults. For the rest of us, despite our best intentions and huge amounts of energetic input, it can be a real struggle to succeed in encouraging our babies and toddlers to emerge as well-adjusted, constructive and happy children. Instead, all too often, infants are irritating, toddlers become tyrants and everyone ends up feeling miserable. So a book spelling out the secrets of successful parenting of newborns, infants, babies, one-year-olds and toddlers, including a special focus on how to create a loving bond with your child, would seem to be a good idea. Just as in *The Parent/Child Game* I emphasised that it was never too late to change and make positive progress, by the same token, it is never too early to start learning about how best to establish that all-important bond between you and your baby.

The major causes of unacceptable behaviour on the part of today's young people is now widely acknowledged to be the parents' failure to establish a good-enough quality of attachment with their children. A poor relationship between parent and child can lead to emotional and behavioural problems that, if not dealt with effectively, can escalate from tantrums at three to delinquency at thirteen. That such a process exists is now acknowledged across many differing ethnic, cultural and religious groups in a wide range of societies. In *The Parent/Child Game* I wrote of techniques that play a highly effective part in preventing children with this type of developmental pattern from going on to become adults who bully their partners, terrorise their own children and fail to adjust to their family's and society's expectations that they will function as reasonable individuals. The alternative is a cycle of behaviour that may be repeated across the generations and one that will become progressively more difficult to change the longer it is allowed to exist within a family.

The Parent/Child Game is not just a book; it is also the name of a technique that clinical psychologists have used to great effect in helping parents and children. Educating parents in the use of the techniques on which *The Parent/Child Game* is based can be of significant help to families who might otherwise produce disturbed, destructive and dangerous adolescents. However, *The Parent/Child Game* is aimed at mothers and fathers of three- to ten-year-olds. How much more helpful might it be to tackle things right from the beginning? In the first three years of life children's development is extraordinarily rapid and their potential for learning truly incredible. Not only do they progress from complete physical dependency to being able to rush about and feed themselves, they also extend their range of communication from crying through to intelligible speech and a comprehension of what others mean. At the same time they make fantastic headway in their journey towards becoming distinct personalities with their own particular likes and dislikes and a keen interest in everyone with whom they come into contact.

The biological background to these astonishingly fast changes is, of course, intimately linked with the formation of billions of connections within a baby's brain. It is the positive or negative quality of these links, their healthy strength or debilitating nature, that lays the foundation for our children's emotional and psychological development. An absolutely crucial factor in determining whether these connections will result in a secure, confident infant growing into a loveable toddler, as opposed to a difficult-to-soothe baby who emerges as a dissatisfied and hard-to-please three-year-old, is – you've guessed it – down to the style of parenting we provide.

Therefore an important aim of *The Parent/Baby Game* will be to detail the style of communication with infants that will give them the priceless advantage of a positive self-image and strong sense of being valued and valuable. There are definite guidelines to follow to encourage these qualities, even in a newborn. There are special things that can be done to strengthen the healthy connections in a baby's brain, just as there are particular words to say that will promote a one-year-old's sociable behaviour as well as a toddler's playfulness.

Also taken into account, when talking about being an emotionally nurturing parent, will be the problems of acclimatising to pregnancy, recovering from an exhausting labour and delivery, difficulties in infant feeding and weaning, the Baby Blues and, of course, mind-numbing fatigue. That is not to deny the steady stream of joyous moments all parents experience when interacting with their infants and under-threes. I will also be conveying useful hints on emotional and psychological reactions to childbirth, coping with post-natal depression, adjusting to infants' feeding routines, coping with too little sleep, surviving exhaustion, managing enormous responsibilities, juggling partnership issues and tackling those unresolved aspects of our other important family relationships. In fact, this book will cover every issue that you, as a new parent and/or carer, will have to cope with, whether you have a partner or are on your own. This is in addition to this book's aim of imparting guidance and suggestions on how to meet your baby's needs, respond to their demands and handle or avoid the inevitable clash of wills. I'm here to tell you that the 'terrible twos' need not end up with a parent on their knees while an apparently triumphant but secretly scared and insecure toddler rules the roost.

If you have read my previous book, you will no doubt realise that the principles behind the Parent/Baby Game are the same as for the Parent/Child Game and are based on the techniques I use in my work as a cognitive behaviour therapist. Neither of these approaches follows the traditional models for helping mothers and fathers to cope with a troubled child. Often the parents' only role in this old-fashioned style of therapy was to transport their offspring to and from the clinic once a week or more, where therapist and child would spend an hour together. Feedback from sessions was not given to the parents nor were they given any guidance on how to respond to their son or daughter's behaviour. In the 1960s this traditional model was joined by another approach, where parent and therapist spent time together discussing various methods for altering the child's behaviour for the better. The mother and/or father would then go home and experiment with the suggested techniques. Many parents welcomed this development, which was based on the same general foundations as the Parent/Child Game.

FOUNDATIONS OF THE PARENT/ CHILD AND PARENT/BABY GAME

The Parent/Child Game and the Parent/Baby Game are techniques solidly based in psychological theories that have stood the test of time.

- **Social Learning Theory** is all about how our behaviour and attitudes are influenced by the type of consequences we experience after having said or done something. These are consequences like praise, punishment or being ignored.
- **Child Development Theory** covers the different stages of growing up, and the sequence in which they usually appear. It is also about comparing an individual child's development with the very broad range of what would normally be expected of most children of a certain age.
- **Attachment Theory** centres on the fact that each person's uniqueness includes the way they think about themselves, others, the world and their future. Also included is their emotional range and the way in which they behave socially; in other words, their relationship style.

Although the Parent/Child Game and Parent/Baby Game rest firmly on Social Learning Theory, Child Development Theory and Attachment Theory, they are fundamentally different from the two approaches I described above. This is because of the innovative use of an 'earbug' hearing device and microphone link between the parent and therapist while the children interact directly with their mother and father during a game chosen by the child. I give the same advice in *The Parent/Child Game* as in *The Parent/Baby Game*, although the nature of the game is, of course, heavily influenced by the age and developmental progress of the infant, toddler, pre-school child, reception class or five-plus full-time school attendee. There will be lots of details later in the book on how to play with under-threes, so don't worry if nothing readily springs to mind.

The Parent/Baby Game is my own adaptation for babies and toddlers of the original Parent/Child Game, which was first used over forty years ago. It evolved from my ten years of work with mothers and babies who, following childbirth, had been admitted to a specialist psychiatric unit for women suffering from serious mental illness.

PARENT/CHILD AND PARENT/BABY GAME: OVER FORTY YEARS OF SUCCESS

- **USA 1965:** Professor Rex Forehand and Professor Robert McMahon are taught the Parent/Child Game technique by child psychologist Connie Kauf, who developed it while working with troubled children and their parents.
- **USA 1968:** Forehand and McMahon start research on the effectiveness of the Parent/Child Game approach. Their study group consists of one hundred families with three- to eight-year-olds who show difficult behaviour, which they compare with forty families without such problems.
- **USA and UK 1981:** The results are published in a book titled *Helping the Non-Compliant Child*. The techniques of the Parent/Child Game show that the parents in the study will, after treatment, manage their child's behaviour more successfully without smacking, establish a warmer and more satisfying way of interacting as a family and see their children in a much more positive light. The troubled children's behaviour improves. Parents are less depressed as individuals and more in tune as a couple.
- **USA and UK 1982:** The Parent/Child Game is increasingly adopted by professionals working with distressed families in the USA. I review Forehand and McMahon's book, and start using the Parent/Child Game in the Children's Department at the Maudsley Hospital in London. Two years later I begin to use my own adaptation, the Parent/Baby Game, on

the Mother and Baby Unit at the Royal Bethlem Hospital, also part of the Maudsley Special Health Authority.
- **USA and UK 1996:** Professors Forehand and Long publish an update called *Parenting the Strong-Willed Child*.
- **UK 1997:** A Government All Party White Paper from the Select Committee on Child and Adolescent Mental Health cites information showing that, unless powerful parenting training techniques are employed on a wide scale, the numbers of troubled children and problem families will increase down the generations. The Parent/Child Game's approach is singled out as being a particularly effective tool in stemming this depressing tide.
- **USA and UK 2000 onwards:** The Parent/Child Game and Parent/Baby Game with very young children continues to be used successfully in helping thousands of families to lead fuller and more enjoyable lives.

So relax! This approach to parenting is no passing fad but a soundly based method with an excellent track record that will help you meet the emotional, psychological and attachment needs of your infants and toddlers.

The aim of this book is, therefore, to spell out the ideas behind the Parent/Baby Game and tell you about the results of putting it into practice. You won't need an 'earbug' or a microphone though, as the basics of the Parent/Baby Game can be applied by mothers and fathers every day as a central strand of family life. This creates the emotionally secure environment that enables babies and toddlers to develop into self-confident, loving and loveable little personalities. You will learn how to meet your infant's need for warmth, approval, security, stimulation and sensitivity, by translating your love into a language that infants can understand right from the start. You will also find out how best to manage an under-three's sleeping and feeding problems, temper tantrums and downright disobedience, whilst preserving your loving relationship with them.

Because the first three years of a child's life see such tremendously rapid development, special information on the nought to ones, the ones to twos and the twos to threes will feature separately in every chapter.

WHAT NEUROSCIENTISTS CAN TELL US

Over recent years there has been a surge of scientific activity focused on investigating the neurological basis of bonding and attachment. Previously, psychologists and psychiatrists had relatively little to do with neuroscientists, unless they were specialising in brain disease or injury. Thirty years ago, a clinical psychologist like myself who had a particular interest in working with children and families with relationship, emotional and behavioural problems, would not necessarily have believed that the findings of brain studies had immediate relevance. That is no longer the case.

As I write neuroscientists are in the process of unearthing the brain circuits and chemicals that underpin emotions, sociability, play, attention, attachment and bonding. Not only do their results begin to suggest innovative new ways of helping children with autism or attention deficit hyper-sensitivity disorder (ADHD), they also clarify the amazing complexity, sophistication and incredibly rapid development of a baby and toddler's brain.

I'm not going to go into any of the enormously detailed information now available specifying the function of particular parts of the brain. Nor am I going to introduce lists of brain chemicals vital to the success of even the most fleeting interaction between you and your baby. Instead, if you are especially interested in this aspect of your baby's life and progress, I suggest you read *Why Love Matters: How Affection Shapes a Baby's Brain*, by Sue Gerhardt (Brunner-Routledge, 2004). I simply want to illustrate the complexity involved by jotting down some of the information from the world of neuroscience that has sparked my enthusiasm for looking at the quite marvellous way babies' brains function. First, some basics:

- The first two years of a baby and toddler's life sees the most rapid increase ever in the weight of their brain.
- The connections in the under-three's brain become increasingly specialised and streamlined as specific functions evolve.
- Stimulation from the people and places around our newborn baby, one- and two-year-olds is absolutely crucial for optimal brain potential.
- Babies' brains must be protected from disease and injury if they are to develop properly.
- Babies need to be physically well nourished if we want them to have healthy brains.
- The circuits in our babies' brains linked to sociability are strongly influenced by play activities and behaviour.
- Rough-and-tumble play with our one- and two-year-olds, or more gentle tickling with the under-one-year-old baby, is often what provokes their first delightful laughter.
- When babies and toddlers don't get enough playtime, they can develop relationship difficulties and emotional problems later on.
- Nobody yet understands what might happen in a baby's brain if they were prevented from playing.

For the moment we must acknowledge that a very great deal about the under-three's brain has yet to be explained. Meanwhile we might hazard a guess that play, which is seen in all children, must serve an important development process or it would not be so evident, or so much fun.

For youngsters of whatever family group, being close to their parents seems to be a significant factor in whether they play happily, or indeed at all. Being close to mummy and/or daddy is a calming experience for babies and toddlers and this beneficial influence leads to less stress and more play.

Learning what precise brain chemicals are activated during play is undoubtedly of interest, but it may not be the most helpful piece of information for a parent struggling to soothe an infant who is clearly not in the mood for play. Suppose your eight-month-old has taken sudden fright at meeting a new person. Or your one-year-old has successfully staggered across the room under their own steam only to fall face down and bite their lip. What about when your two-year-old is having a tantrum in public after realising that pester-power will not, at least on this occasion, bring them the treat they crave? What we need to know at these moments of high drama for our baby or toddler is *what to do*, not the formula for a brain chemical.

I suppose the really important thing that neuroscientists are showing us is that it's actually in coming up with solutions to the myriad daily challenges of meeting our baby and toddler's needs that we quite literally shape their brain connections. Babies and toddlers' brains are known to be more 'plastic' than our own, which means that the control centres for the senses, language, movement, thoughts and emotions can be switched around fairly easily if an area of the brain gets injured in any way. It's this plasticity that underpins the enormous range of patterns that can be formed in our baby's brain as a result of their experiences. Incredibly vital in this process is their interactions with their mother and father.

The type of attention that we provide during the ordinary give and take of feeding, bathing, soothing, stimulating, and talking with our under-threes is one of the most powerful factors in deciding whether that pattern will be beneficial or destructive. It's just as well that we don't have to keep all that in our heads as we listen patiently to our two-year-old explaining how muddy it was outside at playschool this morning. Or when we are putting a six- to twelve-month-old into their car seat at 11 p.m., frantically hoping that if we drive around long enough they might finally fall asleep. And certainly not as we gaze at our newborn flushed with the glory of our own success.

No, what we are focusing on is the visible giving-and-receiving aspect of our every waking moment spent in the company of our under-threes. In other words, the interaction as it happens, the parent–baby connection. What we have to ensure is that we work hard to give our children 'Baby Centred Attention' so their ever-busy, not-so-little brains receive a clear message of love from us, their mummy and/or daddy. That is what will forge the neurological connections that lead to self-confidence, a sense of being valuable and the ability to tackle every day of their life in an optimistic and positive fashion.

I realise you may not find the news that you have the power to shape your baby's brain for good or ill particularly welcome. The responsibilities of parenthood are already heavy enough, for heaven's sake! But look at it from another angle and it's plain to see that advances in neuroscience have helped to improve our understanding of emotional bonds and attachments, opening up a huge parenting opportunity not previously available even to the most well-informed mothers and fathers. See it as a marvellous chance to provide for your infant's physical needs and to play an active part in helping them form the brain patterns that can and will protect their positive sense of themselves as they go through life. And it's really quite easy!

How to Use This Book

Each chapter in the book is divided into sections, like this:

- **What this Chapter is About** is a short introduction to the topics covered in the chapter and helps you find the section you want quickly, especially if you're in a rush to sort out a problem. It uses **key words** to help you pinpoint issues of interest.

- **My Baby Needs . . .** explains those **key words** whilst looking in detail at each of the main emotional needs of babies and how they relate as infants grow into toddlers. This section introduces the concept of Baby Centred behaviours that show your infant that they are at the heart of your world and know they are wanted. There are seven principal Baby Centred behaviours:
  1. *Attends* – plus a very useful extra called *Best Guesses*
  2. *Praise*

3. *Smile*
4. *Positive Look*
5. *Ask to Play*
6. *Ignoring Minor Naughtiness*
7. *Imitation*

- **What Not To Do** looks at behaviour that is directly opposite to that of the Baby Centred behaviours introduced in the My Baby Needs . . . section. These are called Baby Directive behaviours. These are the behaviours that you should limit or – better still – avoid altogether.

So that you can get a clearer picture in your mind about these opposing pairs, here is a dual list for you with each Baby Centred behaviour coupled with its opposite Baby Directive behaviour:

BABY CENTRED AND BABY DIRECTIVE BEHAVIOURS

Baby Centred	**Baby Directive**
Attends	Questions
Praise	Criticism
Smile And Positive Look	Frown And Negative Look
Imitation	Teaching
Ask to Play	Command
Ignoring Minor Naughtiness	Saying 'No'
Positive Touch	Negative Touch

- **Echoes From Our Past** describes my own experiences as a daughter, mother, stepmother and now grandmother, drawing on past and present information about my own family. I also use my long years of professional experience with parents and their babies and toddlers to tell you how other families have managed to triumph over their problems.

- **Special Features** looks at particular problems that parents face during the pre- and post-birth period and in the first three years of an infant's life. These are:

  Chapter One: Ignoring Tantrums, Birth Fears and Coping with Fatigue.

  Chapter Two: Good-Enough Parenting, Baby Blues and Postnatal Depression.

  Chapter Three: Managing Anger and the Emotional Aspects of Baby and Toddler Feeding.

  Chapter Four: Developing Baby's Identity, How to Play With Infants and Relationships Under Strain.

  Chapter Five: Displaying Physical Affection and When Grandparents Undermine.

- **What To Do Next** is the part where I talk about the sorts of difficult-to-manage, hard-to-handle behaviours that even babies, never mind toddlers, can display. Don't be alarmed, though, as effective solutions of every kind will be spelled out! In Chapter One, crying takes pride of place. Chapter Two looks at sleep, Chapter Three at feeding, Chapter Four deals with over-stimulation and Chapter Five with disobedience.

- My **Golden Bullets** close each chapter and give you a brief run-through of the major points made in the preceding sections.

I hope you will find the contents of this book a useful mix of sense, sensitivity and reassurance, with just a touch of humour to keep us all sane. In fact, this is almost identical to the combination of elements required for really successful parenting. As parents, we can all use as much reassurance as we can possibly find, so one of the major benefits of learning about the Parent/Baby Game and then putting it into practice is knowing that you don't have to be perfect. Getting it right half the time will very adequately protect and nurture your baby's ability to make secure relationships, feel happy and optimistic most of the time, become an active and sociable personality and learn that they are loved and loveable.

My aim is to let you in on the secrets of how to speak to your baby and toddler in the language of love that shapes their brain, so that they develop a strong sense of themselves and become adaptable, sociable and successful personalities. In other words, when you play the Parent/Baby Game with your under-threes, you will be creating a truly loving family and nurturing the all-important emotional and relationship bond from which can spring a self-confident young child. Meanwhile I can assure you that I won't hesitate to let you know just what I think you should actually *do*. This includes vital information on how to avoid parenting pitfalls and how to dig ourselves out after we have inevitably fallen in!

You can make a major impact with the first of the Baby Centred Behaviours: *Attends* and *Best Guesses* that are introduced in chapter one. They will give your child an incredibly strong psychological inner balance, a store of emotional warmth and that fabulous saving grace of knowing they are wanted by those godlike figures, their parents.

When you give to your infant in this way, you in turn receive from them the smiles, touches and bright-eyed glances that tap into your own brain circuits, producing a glow of relaxation and a lowering of stress levels. Sounds good doesn't it? All you have to do to start the whole cycle of mutual, positive giving and receiving is get in there right from the beginning with your Baby Centred *Attends* and *Best Guesses*.

Chapter One

Making Your Baby Feel Wanted

WHAT THIS CHAPTER IS ABOUT

'Baby Centred' parents interact with their under-threes in a style that, from their infant's perspective, translates as un-equivocal emotional warmth and approval. This chapter looks at your baby's need for emotional warmth. Each chapter looks at one or two Baby Centred behaviours that parents can do in order to meet their baby's emotional and psychological needs. This chapter focuses on how giving your baby *Attends* and *Best Guesses* ensures that an infant feels the emotional warmth of your love and so receives the unmistakable and desperately important message that they are wanted and welcome.

Also in this chapter:

My Baby Needs . . . Emotional Warmth

Hearing my babies' cry stirred in me an irresistibly powerful desire to pick them up and hold them close. It's the same for most parents, unless they are literally unable to move because of total fatigue. Why is that? There must be a good reason for this universal reaction by parents, and there is. Comforting and soothing your baby's distress is something best accomplished by close physical contact, and while infants can't move towards us, they can provoke us to go to them. Cuddling babies is a vital way of showing them emotional warmth.

Of course, what is relevant for babies may not necessarily be appropriate for older infants. While all children need emotional warmth, the way in which parents respond has to be tailored to their stage of development. It's quite a challenge to keep up with them as they romp their way through their first three years. Sometimes it feels as though our daughter or son has only just arrived even when they are wielding a spoon and splashing their cereal all over the kitchen!

Babies and toddlers need emotional warmth from their parents in order to learn how to manage their own intense feelings. You could think of it as an essential exercise in calming the infants' emotional brainstorms. This is the first step towards doing so for themselves. One of the major tasks facing children aged under three years old is starting to learn how to soothe their ruffled feathers when something or someone has upset them.

Of course, it is many more years before they can reliably direct their strong initial emotional reactions into reasoned and socially acceptable responses. In fact, throughout our lifetime we are likely to remain vulnerable on certain sensitive issues to explosive out-bursts of feeling. Imagine how impossible it is for an infant to use their embryonic powers for rational thought in the face of over-whelming floods of emotion.

That is where *Attends* and *Best Guesses* come in. An *Attend* is when, in a loving, encouraging and approving way, you describe what another person is doing or what they are wearing or how they look or seem to be feeling. You can deliver an *Attend* about something that is happening right now, and you can also refer back or anticipate the future. *Attends* can be given to every one, whatever their age, gender, creed or culture. You could try some on a partner, sibling, friend, or colleague – not to mention your own mum and dad. It will probably feel odd at first, but persevere and you will see how much pleasure an *Attend* gives. Get them to try one on you, too, so that you get the full benefit!

This is one of the exercises I use when I train professionals in how to use Parent/Child Game and Parent/Baby Game techniques. It always ends up with smiles and laughter, plus a degree of embarrassment, of course, because there are too few *Attends* in most adults' lives. Giving babies *Attends* seems to come quite naturally, though we may not be aware that's what we are doing when we gaze at them adoringly and say, 'Oh, look at you! Waving your little arms about!' or 'You look so peaceful/awake/sleepy!' Yes, these are *Attends* and they actively promote feelings of well-being in your baby because their message is one of undiluted emotional warmth.

Best Guesses are all about providing emotional warmth at times of stress. *Best Guessing* works by demonstrating to your child your belief that they have a mind of their own, quite separate from yours. This apparently simple, everyday assumption seems to be the foundation upon which a baby and toddler's sense of being wanted as an individual is built. When you *Best Guess*, you are giving your offspring a special type of *Attend*. *Best Guesses* are warm, sympathetic statements about what you believe your off-spring is feeling, when they can't express their emotions verbally.

The sequence of steps that make up a *Best Guess* includes a finishing touch that I believe to be especially important. That's because it helps parent and offspring to move on towards a successful resolution of the potential crisis. You will see what I mean when I set out for you the pattern of each *Best Guess*. I hope you'll find them quite a best friend at the inevitable points of confrontation between you and your under-three. There are four steps:

Step 1   **Mirror** your baby's feelings, using a fairly matter-of-fact tone of voice, plus your pet endearments, of course. This diffuses the emotional temperature for all concerned. For example, you notice your baby's cheeks are rather flushed and they keep grizzling and patting their head near one of their ears. Your **Mirror** would be to say, 'You seem quite upset, my precious. Perhaps it's earache or toothache.'

Step 2   **Validate** your infant's experience by showing them you understand why they feel as they do. This maintains the emotional connection between you. Use a gentle yet relaxed tone. For example, using the same scenario as before, your **Validation** would be, 'I can see it makes absolute sense for you to be protesting like that, darling. It's because you're probably getting another big tooth through.'

Step 3   **Empathy** for your baby or toddler's feelings is demonstrated by letting them know that you, personally, understand how they feel. You can use a really warm and sympathetic voice at this point, referring to your own similar experiences. With the toothache/earache example, your **Empathy** could be shown by saying, 'Oh, poppet! Of course you're feeling miserable. Toothache makes anyone feel awful. I know just how it feels, my poor little love.'

Step 4   **Resolve** your under-three's distress and help them to return to a comfortable emotional mood. This will re-establish their feelings of security because you are showing them they are wanted, even when their whole little world is crashing around them. Sound as if you know what you're doing as it's reassuring for them to believe you have everything under control, even when you don't! For example, in terms of the earache – or indeed any other physical ill or psychological upset – your **Solution** should be put across like this, 'Right, sweetheart, first of all I'm going to help your poor mouth feel better so here's the cooler ring for you to bite on. There. Now let's see if you want a little drink and then we might check your temperature. After that it's time for our trip to the shops.'

And there you are – back on track and still close, your relationship more secure than ever. Throughout this chapter I will give you lots of tips on how to make sure you are giving *Attends* and *Best Guesses* that are sensitive to each stage of your child's development.

A parent's warm voice and supportive and understanding commentary on what a baby or toddler seems to be experiencing provide the input children need to regain their emotional balance. Without our help, they would, as far as we know, feel consigned to an unending torture of uncontrollable emotions. Sounds extreme doesn't it? But as more is learned about infants and very young children's psychological life, it becomes steadily more apparent that they cannot function unless we give them masses of *Attends* and *Best Guesses*. Even their brain structure can be influenced away from healthy to maladaptive patterns were we not to rescue and comfort them. If they do not regularly receive emotionally warm lessons from a parent in calming themselves down, then their development into personalities who can take their proper place in family and community life is put at risk.

Meeting your baby and toddler's need for emotional warmth, so they can rest assured that they are wanted, is of central importance. When a parent is unable to provide a sufficiently Baby Centred style of attention, their child often displays outbursts of anger, aggressive behaviour, self-destructive habits and their relationships are of poor quality. It is also known that babies and toddlers who are not treated as if they have their own individual thoughts, ideas, feelings and fears develop less healthy intellectual abilities. Shocking, isn't it, to realise just how huge our own responsibilities are in becoming parents? Scary too!

But don't allow yourself to be overcome by the enormity of the challenge. You can learn exactly how to provide emotionally warm

Attends and *Best Guesses*, as well as the other Baby Centred parenting behaviours, by reading on. First I am going to spell out for you the nuts and bolts of making sure your baby or toddler receives the *Attends* and *Best Guesses* they need.

For speed and ease of reference I will use the term 'parent' to mean the child's mother and/or father and/or principal carer(s), as their individual situations are similar when it comes relating to a baby or toddler. Modern families take many forms but I won't rehash all the stuff you already know about, for example, how gender roles can be swapped. Nor am I going to focus on a father's right to spend quality time with his children or a mother's prerogative to return to work within weeks of giving birth. Instead, I will present the child's perspective on the role of parent/carer and how adults can make contributions of real, lasting value to the children in their care.

When talking about parents giving their children good quality *Attends* and *Best Guesses*, it has to be acknowledged that for the baby their mother's voice is going to be the most familiar. All those months during pregnancy of listening to mummy talking, singing, laughing, complaining, groaning and moaning, means your baby knows your voice extraordinarily intimately. So, mums, you have a head start; take advantage of it when you are giving *Attends* and *Best Guesses* to your tiny tot. And dads, don't be left out. Being Baby Centred is man's work too.

Let's think about what you must do during the first twelve months to get across your message of warmth, of wanting your baby and crediting them with a mind of their own. When I say 'mind of their own' I mean quite literally their ability to think their own thoughts. The phrase as used here does not imply any contrariness of character, stubbornness or threatening degree of independence, as you will see when you read on.

Attends for Babies Under Six Months
Suppose you are sitting quietly holding your newborn baby – a blissful few moments without visitors – just you and this little miracle who has been living inside your body for nine months. The baby is

briefly awake, though not crying. Now is your chance to give them the *Attends* and *Best Guesses* you know will make a very positive contribution to their development into emotionally and psychologically healthy little personalities. Here are some actual *Attends* and *Best Guesses* you can try right from the moment of birth:

- 'You look so *gorgeous*, my little *angel*!'
- 'You're so *tiny/big*, you're a *miracle*!'
- 'At *last*! Here you *are*, in your mummy's arms!'
- 'I can see you are quite *perfect*, your little nails and *everything*!'
- 'You're so *strong*, what a *grip*!'
- 'Oh, my little *sweetheart*, your eyes are really *bright*!'
- 'You *smell* delicious, so new and *fresh*!'
- 'I can see you like being *talked* to, you do, yes you *do*!'
- 'That's *right*, poppet, you have a good *stretch/yawn/sleep/look round*!'
- 'You're *so* beautiful, so *beautiful*!'

You can also add in some *Best Guesses*. Try these:

- 'Oh darling, I can see you're quite *tired*. I would be too if I'd just been through all *that*! Let's make sure you can have a lovely *sleep*. There, there, ssshhh.'
- 'Poppet! You're all *confused*! You don't know *where* you are. Well, you're quite safe because you're with your *mummy* who loves you. Yes I *do*!'
- 'You're *hungry*, I *know* you are! Come on my love, let's get you *latched* on so you can have some of mummy's *special milk*. There, that's better.'
- 'Oh, my little *sweet*heart! You're *crying*! It's all been too much, just too *much* for such a tiny bundle. There, ssshh, ssshh.'

You see how quickly you can get going with *Attends* and *Best Guesses* that will make absolutely sure your new arrival feels your emotional warmth right from the beginning, and knows they are truly welcome.

In my examples of *Attends* and *Best Guesses* I have included lots of italics and exclamation marks. This is in order to illustrate the special intonation and emphasis that is so typical of how mothers speak to their babies that it has been given a particular name: 'motherese'. 'Fatherese' would be the equivalent for dads, but as far as I know it has yet to be studied. So, when our voices are said by some of the uninformed to be just 'gooing and gurgling', 'oohing and aahing' or even 'coochy-cooing', we can let them know in no uncertain terms that babies positively need to be treated to 'motherese' or 'fatherese' if they are to be able to form a secure attachment to their parent.

Whether you are a man or a woman, there's no need at all to feel self-conscious about raising your voice at the end of a statement when communicating with your newborn. No need at all to be anxious that you seem to be emphasising the really important words in your message. It's in this way that we can get across the message that not only do we love our baby to bits, we are attempting to understand what might be bothering them minute by minute.

And in this way we are also letting our babies know that we believe they have their own individual internal experiences, as this actively promotes their development into unique personalities. To lovingly describe your newborn baby with *Attends*, such as the ones already set out, to comfort and calm them by recognising and responding to their distress, is not at all difficult to learn. Many mums and dads seem to come up with this kind of behaviour quite spontaneously. For those of us who, for whatever reason, don't seem to be able to swing straight into *Attends*, *Best Guesses* and 'motherese' or 'fatherese', all is not lost. Far from it.

Lots of mothers and fathers who find it difficult at first, realise it can become much easier the more they practise. These are essential contributions to your baby's development as an emotionally balanced, positively attached and closely bonded little person who has a healthy sense of their own individuality. Understandably, though, it might be hard at first, particularly for those mums who are physically ill, emotionally low or just plain exhausted, and for those dads who are feeling strung out. Childbirth when compared with what you wanted, imagined or expected, can turn out to be much less of a glorious endeavour and more of an impossible mission when you actually experience it – especially towards the end of stage one labour!

I look at various difficulties and vulnerabilities such as this in the Special Features Section, focusing on two or three issues per chapter. In this chapter, the aspect of a parent's adjustment problems to be discussed will be the reaction to the birth and the fatigue of those first few months. So, if you did not emerge from the experience glowing with triumph, never fear, help is at hand and remember, you are *not* a bad mother or father simply because you're too shattered by a long labour and tough birth to cover your baby with *Attends* and *Best Guesses* – not to mention 'motherese' or 'fatherese' – immediately after their arrival.

So, supposing you are feeling groggy, weak, tearful and poorly, what can you do to meet your baby's needs for emotional warmth, even though you yourself are decidedly less than vibrant? The answer is that Baby Centred behaviours do not have to be verbal. You can use *Loving Looks*, *Smiles* and *Positive Touches* instead of *Attends* and *Best Guesses*. If you want to skip ahead and read about these non-verbal ways of communicating your love to your newborn, turn to chapter three for more details.

Now, let's look at *Attends* and *Best Guesses* for infants aged six to twelve months. These babies will be much more alert, coordinated and mobile than a newborn, of course, and so you will have much more scope for describing their many activities.

Attends for Babies Aged Six to Twelve Months
- 'You're playing with your spoon!'
- 'I can see you love banana!'
- 'Look at you sitting up all by yourself!'
- 'You can crawl so fast!'
- 'You love playing in the bath!'
- 'You've chosen your favourite colour!'
- 'You are so cuddly!'
- 'You're stroking my hair!'

- 'You're very sleepy!'
- 'You've just done a giant yawn!'

The effect of an *Attend* on any particular behaviour is to increase the likelihood that the person it's directed towards will do it again in the future because it functions as a reward. This is one of the central tenets of Social Learning Theory. But be warned. All of us, from tiny tot to granny, are heavily influenced by rewards – even if we claim not to be. So we, as parents, should only give an *Attend* to behaviours we positively want to encourage. It follows, then, that if playing with the spoon results in a level of mess that makes you irritated, don't provide an *Attend* like the first one just listed. Likewise, if the hair stroking is threatening to leave you bald, don't follow it with an *Attend*. Better to silently and gently remove your baby's hand from your hair and then wait for the next behaviour you approve of and give that an *Attend*.

When you look at the *Attends* I've suggested so far, you might think they sound a little bit short, though happily not at all sharp. This is due to the fact that most of us, when giving a positive commentary on our baby's behaviour, add on a praise of some sort. It just feels more finished if, instead of saying, 'You've drunk all your milk!', you round off with 'Clever boy/girl!' as praise. I shall be going into detail about *Praise*, another crucially important Baby Centred behaviour used by successful, sensible and sensitive parents, in the next chapter, so I will leave further explanation until then.

Best Guesses at six to twelve months are also more complex due to your baby's increasingly varied display of emotions. They are more likely to experience the frustration of desperately wanting to explore their immediate environment, only to find they cannot yet quite come up with the motor movements necessary to achieve their goal. A frustrated baby is a stressed baby, and tense six- to twelve-month-olds will need you to respond in a way that will help them to achieve inner calm once more. That's where *Best Guesses* such as the ones listed below are so very handy.

Best Guesses for Babies Aged Six to Twelve Months

- 'Trying to poke those in there seems to be making you cross, darling. I'd be fed up too, poppet, if I couldn't manage it. Let's do something else.'
- 'I can tell you're not feeling well, sweetie, and that's why you're so grumpy about not wanting your breakfast. I'm not very hungry when I'm ill either, my little love. We'd better just concentrate on milk and drinks today.'
- 'You look as if you're trying to reach those interesting things in the corner, sweetheart. But you're going backwards instead of forwards, my darling. It's frustrating, yes it is. Let's pick you up and move you closer.'
- 'You're just desperate for your lunch, angel, I can see by the way you are banging your tray. I'm hungry too. Let's get you started right away.'
- 'You're tired, my little star is really sleepy. I could do with a bit of a nap myself because it's been a busy day, so I'm going to settle you down.'
- 'Oh, you're not comfy, darling, something isn't quite right. Something might be too tight, and nobody likes that. Just let me see so I can sort you out.'

These *Best Guesses* will help your six- to twelve-month-old feel secure in the knowledge that, however frustrated, poorly, hungry, tired or plain uncomfortable they feel, you have noticed and sympathised with their predicament. Not only that, but you are immediately going to do your very best to solve their problem. No matter that to us grown-ups wanting our food right this minute is something we usually manage to cover with a veneer of civilised behaviour. After all, we have had decades in which to learn to hide the evidence of our mouths watering at the mere sight of our favourite food, be it curry or custard, mangoes or mince. But six- to twelve-month-olds are pretty much consumed by their experiences of the moment and have yet to learn anything effective about waiting calmly for food, sleep or a snugly fitting Babygro!

At that age, when faced with these overwhelmingly intense and frightening feelings, you still need lots of help in calming down. That's where giving a *Best Guess* works wonders because you are actively reducing your baby's anxiety and stress levels. Babies can easily be in a state of frantic panic if they aren't rescued by a familiar adult who can signal that they are going to do what's necessary and aren't at all afraid themselves. The most scary situation for six- to twelve-month-olds – and indeed all babies and toddlers – is to be in the care of a grown-up who is themselves scared about their ability to rise to the challenges posed by a baby.

It's likely that a frightened parent's interactions with their young offspring could lead to unhelpful connections being laid down in the baby's brain. These in turn undermine the security of their attachment to their mother and/or father which leads to later emotional problems. These can include feelings of being unwanted. Altogether bad news.

But what are we supposed to do when we are at a loss as to how to respond to our baby's fury, tears and fears? How are we going to give our infant a message of emotional warmth when we ourselves are feeling highly anxious, uncertain and stressed?

Well, at least part of the answer is to give them a sensitive yet soothing acknowledgement that you understand what's happening to them and why. Adding on a calming description of your solution as you swing into action further reduces the emotional storm that's swamping them. I'm not saying it's always easy, but I am saying it works. There's a benefit for us, too, as while we are *Best Guessing* our baby, our own anxiety levels can decrease. 'But,' I hear you say, 'suppose I guess wrong and, instead of contentment and peace, we both end up in a state!' Well, that can happen of course, but there are answers to be had and I'll be going into some detail on how best to settle a distraught baby or toddler in the **What To Do Next** section of this chapter. Meanwhile I would advise repeating the whole *Best Guess* sequence with a second try at spotting the real trouble and responding with a suitable solution. Have a third, fourth and fifth go if necessary! You are pretty sure to strike it lucky if you persevere for long enough.

Let's have a look now at some *Attends* and *Best Guesses* for one-year-olds. As you are now more familiar with the ideas involved, I'll concentrate on the differences in content that you will need if you are to keep up with your child's rapid development. You should give one-year-olds an *Attend* only when they are doing something that earns your unalloyed approval. You will find there are *Attends* for every area of their startling progress.

Attends for One-Year-Olds
- 'You're walking so well now!'
- 'You can get up all by yourself!'
- 'You look fabulous in that hat!'
- 'I think you're the smartest boy/girl I've ever seen!'
- 'You're concentrating on your book!'
- 'Yes! You've done a lovely red scribble!'
- 'You want to cuddle your teddy!'
- 'You're making a lovely noise on your drum!'
- 'You can say Dadda and Mama and baby!'
- 'You're really talking now, telling me you want more biccies!'
- 'Aah, you're loving your daddy and giving him smashing kisses!'
- 'Mmm! You've given me a gorgeous squeeze!'
- 'You're giving your biscuit to your little friend!'
- 'Oh! You've noticed that other baby is crying!'
- 'Yes, darling, you're laughing and dancing with the bunnies!'

Feel free to indulge in a sing-song kind of delivery as this seems to be, literally and figuratively, music to your children's ears. So, while a vocal style like this would undoubtedly be inappropriate if used with other adults, I would urge you to be unabashed when interacting with your infant.

And just as the *Attends* for this age range are more complex than earlier because your one-year-old is surging forward developmentally, so *Best Guesses* cover a different type of stressful situation, one much more likely to contain an element of confrontation and challenge between you and your child. In situations like this, the four steps of Mirror, Validate, Empathise and Resolve are specially important.

Best Guesses for One-Year-Olds

- **Mirror:** 'Darling, I can tell you're cross because you don't want to get dressed. I know it's more fun to run around in just your pull-ups because sometimes I quite like prancing about in my underwear, too. I can see how annoyed you must feel. No wonder! Now, let's make it into a little game instead of falling out. I know! I'll pop a piece of grape into your mouth every time you put something on. Right, away we go! Socks first . . .'
- **Validate:** 'I know you're fed up with sitting in your high chair. I expect you want to come and sit up next to me. You do! I know, poppet, it's miserable for you. I guess I would feel the same, rather left out. Ah, poor little sweetheart. I suppose we could move you much nearer to mummy or daddy and give you one of our spoons. We'll try that . . .'
- **Empathise:** 'Now darling, I can see you'd love to stay in your bath until midnight, but you do have to come out. Yes, it's clear you are terribly frustrated, I would be too if I had to abandon my fun time in the water. Of course you're furious! Out you come. I tell you what, let's roll you up in the towel and then I'll try to find you . . .'
- **Resolve:** 'Darling, I can tell from those big tears of yours you really don't want to put the Play-Doh away. It's horrid to be interrupted, I know I don't like it either. I'd probably cry too if I had to stop my best game. Poor sweetheart. But guess what we're going to do now! Yes! Splash in the sink – one of your favourite games . . .'

You can see how much more sophisticated your language can be now. Even though one-year-olds don't understand every word they will still delight in your musical intonation. Let's look at another *Best Guess*, this time with the highs and lows of your voice written in: highs in CAPITALS, lows underlined.

- 'I can see you're getting rather grumpy because you're ready for your LUNCH. Lots of people feel like that when they're HUNGRY, including me! Your tummy is probably rumbling, oh, poor little <u>love</u>. I <u>know</u>, let's have a quick snack of BANANAS, mmm, YUMMY!'

It doesn't always swing along like that, though. There will be times when your patience is so tried that your teeth are locked together in exasperation. At those moments it's difficult to make yourself speak reasonably at all, never mind with a lilt in your voice. Probably best to stay silent at those particular flashpoints. More on that in chapter five when we talk about *Ignoring*.

It's important to remember that there are two main methods of getting a message across to the under-threes: verbal and non-verbal. As babies develop into children, parents invest more and more in the verbal aspects of communication. After all, use of language is one of the great defining features of being human. But we should also make sure that we properly value the non-verbal messages we constantly give in any and every interaction with a child.

Just think about it. You are tired, they are tired. What had been a lovely afternoon is rapidly descending into a vale of tears. None the less, you are trying to sound chirpy and upbeat as you announce that you'll soon be home when you can both have a snack. Let's face it, at moments like that you could almost kill for a coffee! So, your words are optimistic, but what about those tell-tale non-verbal messages that let your child know the real state of affairs? You know, the droopy mouth, the leaden steps, the laboured breathing, the tension in your shoulders when one of the super-market bags breaks and six eggs are transformed into a slimy mess. The baby or toddler does not respond cheerfully to our positive-sounding words. Instead they hook into our negative non-verbal language and start to bawl inconsolably. It seems they are very sensitive to our emotions right from birth. I will be talking about how to soothe your baby using Baby Centred physical affection in chapter three.

Meanwhile, I would strongly advise you to get home as soon as possible, where your child can be reassured by more *Best Guesses* that you really can keep them safe when they have scared themselves into a panic by the intensity of their feelings. Every time you manage this positive parenting trick, you will have helped your child forge an even more secure attachment with that all-important, magical person: you. The child will also be learning that they are so special, valued and wanted that you would never abandon them to their suffering. I know this all sounds rather dramatic, but the fact of the matter is, from birth onwards, our children are on a painful learning curve as they begin to develop the ability to subject their strong emotions to the influence of their intellect. This skill is barely present in the under-threes, as is often demonstrated at their third birthday party when even a minor incident of frustrated desire can escalate into a sobbing tantrum of mind-boggling magnitude. Just because at three they can talk in proper sentences, feed themselves and entertain adults with refreshingly unselfconscious song-and-dance routines, it does not mean that the brain circuits that allow rational thinking about stormy feelings are in place and functioning.

Despite the incredible speed with which a baby's and toddler's central nervous system increases in complexity during the first three years, the potential to override emotional responses through the exercise of reason remains – quite literally – in its infancy.

Now on to *Attends* and *Best Guesses* you'll want to use with your two-year-old. Baby Centred behaviour by parents of this age group is particularly important because your toddler will be testing out their independence from you in no uncertain terms. We have all heard of the 'Terrible Twos' and are right to expect our authority to be challenged several times a day. This isn't a sign that you have failed to meet your child's need for emotional warmth, nor that they feel unwanted. It is simply a necessary developmental phase when, as part of exploring their world and relationships, they find they cannot wait, do not want to share and are all too often overwhelmed by their feelings of frustration and anger.

This means it is even more crucial to keep the *Attends* and *Best*

Guesses at optimal level. As ever, of course, you might find yourself knowing that an *Attend* would be helpful just when it's most difficult to deliver, because you've already waded through six *Best Guesses* in three hours and, frankly, you'd like nothing more than half an hour in a toddler-free zone!

Don't give up, though, as *Attends* are often especially powerful when they are hard to produce. To give yourself heart, remember that every time you give your child an *Attend* following an acceptable/welcome behaviour, you increase the likelihood that your relationship with them is secure. You also increase the chances of them coming up with something similar in future. This is because *Attends* are a reward and when children (and adults) experience something good immediately after they have performed a particular behaviour, a strong connection is made in their brain and they think, 'Mmm! I'll try that again.' You can almost see their minds whirring away as they discover the upside of being good.

Attends for Two-Year-Olds

- 'I can see you're making a lovely biscuit with the Play-Doh!'
- 'I can tell you're enjoying your colouring. You've done a big blue bus!'
- 'I see you are swinging really high!'
- 'I love the way you're digging in the sand!'
- 'I think it's great how you're concentrating on your book!'
- 'I believe you are the best swimmer in the group!'
- 'I'm really impressed you know so many words now!'
- 'I can tell you are getting dressed all by yourself!'
- 'I know you're a kind person because you shared your sweeties!'
- 'I love the cuddles you give me!'
- 'I think your smile sparkles!'

These *Attends* are slightly different in format from the ones I've suggested so far. That's because they contain an 'I/you' combination that is particularly potent in making children feel the welcome heat of your emotional warmth. It also makes crystal clear that you, as an individual, have not only noticed what they're up to, but have also approved! For the under-threes, and indeed older children too, parental approval equals love. Not just that, it's love expressed in a way that is meaningful to your two-year-old. Under-threes do not know we love them unless we show them by Baby Centred behaviour such as *Attends*, especially of the 'I/you' type.

How many *Attends* should parents be giving their under-threes? Well, if I tell you that successful mums and dads give their two-year-olds around forty to sixty Baby Centred behaviours *every ten minutes*, would you be flabbergasted, horrified or just plain disbelieving? Alternatively, you might be nodding your head sagely and saying that sounds about right. If the latter, you are already a better parent than I was to my three children when they were in their twos! I had no idea about Baby Centred *Attends* then.

Fortunately for my children, my own parents showed me a great deal of emotional warmth and approval during my first three years and so I had that to draw on, albeit subconsciously. *Attends* are only one of the seven Baby Centred parenting behaviours, so if we were to be giving our two-year-old equal amounts of each, we would deliver approximately nine in the ten minute period, that is, about one per minute. The thing to hold on to in the face of this rather challenging news is that each *Attend* takes only a second or two. You don't even have to think them up first, you simply have to make sure you notice all your toddler's positives and comment on them out loud. Saying to yourself or whispering to another adult, 'He's so brilliant!' or 'She's a real star!' will have no direct impact on them. They must be able to hear what you say in order to learn to trust that you mean what you say. And just think of the rewards you will reap! Anything from a cooperative two-year-old to a lifelong truly close and secure relationship with your child.

Parents who fail to show enough approval and love by being Baby Centred are likely to cause problems in day-to-day life because their baby and toddler will find it more rewarding to be naughty than good. Playing up often attracts more attention from a parent or carer, and it's attention – any type of attention – that they crave above all else.

In my work as a cognitive behaviour therapist, time and time again the angry, anxious and depressed adults I see did not have sufficient expressions of approval from their parents when they were children. As a result, each one has failed to develop that essential component of their psychological survival kit: self-confidence. Few, if any, mothers and fathers wish a life of emotional pain for their children, and one very effective way of ensuring your own baby and toddler avoids such a miserable fate is to give them lots and lots of *Attends*.

These simple statements are almost magical in their power to create and then extend the positive neural connections and pathways in your offspring's brain. The message carried is one of trust in you, the parent, as the under-three bathes in the emotional warmth of being noticed, approved of and wanted. Seems silly not to cram in as many *Attends* a day as humanly possible, doesn't it?

Now some *Best Guesses*, which will help to keep your bond with your two-year-old through even the most stressful incidents. I will put in the four steps of Mirror, Validate, Empathise and Resolve again, just to remind you of the sequence.

Best Guesses for Two-Year-Olds

- **Mirror:** 'You seem to be feeling rather clingy today, darling.'
- **Validate:** 'No wonder, when you've got such a nasty cough. I would feel the same.'
- **Empathise:** 'You poor little sweetheart. Your chest must really hurt.'
- **Resolve:** 'Now, I'm going to give you a lovely cuddle, then it will be time for your delicious pink medicine and afterwards we'll do some handprint painting. There. Snuggle up, I've got you.'

- **Mirror:** 'I can see you're really upset because we can't find your favourite teddy.'
- **Validate:** 'That makes sense, poppet, it's like when daddy can't find his wallet. I'd feel upset and worried too.'

- **Empathise**: 'Never mind, sweetheart. Oh, look at those big tears!'
- **Resolve**: 'I know what will help you feel better! Let's go and fetch your dear little toy rabbit and give her a nice shampoo. I know you love doing bubbles. Off we go, let me wipe your nose. Aah! My little star.'

- **Mirror**: 'You look fed up, I can see you're frowning. I expect you're cross.'
- **Validate**: 'It's really annoying that we can't go to the park because it's raining so hard. I don't like staying indoors either.'
- **Empathise**: 'I'm so sorry you're not a happy bunny, darling.'
- **Resolve**: 'What about finding something exciting to do at home! We could make a camp under the table and have a picnic dinner inside. Come on! Let's get a throw and some cushions. Would your toys like to come too?'

Of course, we have to do most of the running when we are *Best Guessing*, but the reward is nearly always worth the effort. When you are treating your child to a steady diet of *Attends* and *Best Guesses* you are strengthening the bond between you and showing your love for them in a way that gives the clear message: 'you are loved and you are wanted.' No parent can do more to make a unique contribution to their baby and toddler's need for emotional warmth (except, of course, to add in some of the other Baby Centred behaviours I will be talking about in the other chapters!).

It may be comforting for you to know that once you have learned how to do *Attends* and *Best Guesses*, they will serve you loyally throughout your baby's childhood. You can use my first book *The Parent/Child Game* for details on the three- to ten-year-old age group.

What Not To Do! Don't Interrogate Your Child

In this section I talk about the opposite of each Baby Centred parenting behaviour discussed in the 'My Baby Needs . . .' section.

That is, its paired Baby Directive behaviour. In other words, **What Not To Do!** The main aim of the Parent/Baby Game is to significantly *increase* the number of Baby Centred behaviours we use when interacting with our child, while simultaneously reducing the rate of Baby Directive Behaviours.

So, the opposite of *Attends* is to *Question* your toddler like an inquisitor. You should make every effort to bump up the *Attends* and limit the *Questions*. To ensure that your baby and toddler are emotionally nurtured, for every ten minutes of your attention there should be at least forty *Attends* (plus twenty *Praises*) and not more than about ten *Questions* (or *Commands*). Sounds a bit weird doesn't it? We aren't used to thinking that questioning an infant is wrong. Almost the reverse in fact!

How many times have I found myself trying to engage a toddler in conversation by asking them question after question: 'And how do you like preschool?' 'What are you asking Santa for this Christmas?' 'How old are you now?' 'What have you been up to today?' And – heaping coals on their undeserving heads – 'What do you think of your baby sister/brother?' To get answers from one- and two-year-olds can never be relied upon, as quite rightly they often view our questions as unwelcome and confounding intrusions into their world. In truth, the only person being emotionally nourished during my rather banal attempts to prise some answers from these poor unfortunate toddlers was myself!

Grown-ups find it enormously rewarding when, as a result of our probing queries, the very young object of our unsought attentions pipes back with even a faintly intelligible reply. Why? Well, I think it's probably because we see asking questions of someone shows them we are sufficiently interested in them to try to find out more. Also, when they answer we can feel extremely satisfied with our powers of communication.

In order to appreciate more closely your toddler's likely reactions, pepper a friend with lots of questions about their day, their hopes and their fears. Get them to do the same to you and then ask yourselves whether it would have been more pleasurable if each of you could have offered the same information spontaneously instead. Pushy questions put people off, often because we feel our personal space has been violated in some way and that has led to our wanting to put a distance between us and our interrogator. I have noted at the local preschool that two- and three-year-olds particularly disliked being asked their name. As it's a fluctuating group I sometimes find myself interacting with a toddler whose name I don't know or can't immediately recall. If I ask the child themselves, their reaction goes something like this:

- They stop talking
- They look straight into my eyes, but briefly
- Next, they avert their gaze and turn their head away or look down
- They might go rather still for a few moments
- And finally they carry on doing whatever they were up to . . . *as if I hadn't spoken!*

I can't think of a clearer way of showing someone they are being ignored because their behaviour is unwelcome! On the other hand, if I ask their peers, the silent one does not object to their name being disclosed or my then immediately starting to use it. Should I then go on to lavish *Attends* on them or *Best Guess* any little problem they are having, we become firm friends in a matter of minutes. My conclusion is that very young children can resent adults' questions and as a direct consequence lose their spirit of cooperation, whereas if we offer them *Attends* they feel noticed and approved of, which makes them readily communicative and more compliant.

I'm not suggesting you give up questions altogether when interacting with your under-threes. What I am saying is you should concentrate on giving *Attends* rather than make demands on them by asking too many questions. Parents often say to me their friendly interest on collecting a toddler from nursery or play school, phrased as questions, frequently goes ignored. In fact I can remember worrying about my children's hearing, so oblivious did they seem to my maternal enquiries at the school gates. I finally twigged that I got more out of them if I allowed them to comment on their day's highs and lows at their own pace. By the time I became a grandparent, I had learned that to offer *Attends* speeded up no end my grandchildren's confidences about the dramatic incidents they had just experienced.

So, instead of putting the query, 'What did you do today?' or, 'Have you been good?', try saying to your one- or two-year-old when greeting them after a few hours apart, 'You look as though you've had a busy time, sweetheart' and then *wait*. Chances are they will decide to let you in on the glories of their time in the Home Corner or tell you about who was really noisy during story time. Take a chance. See if it works for you. My bet is it will!

Of course, if we were only motivated to ask questions because of a desire for a chatty response, we wouldn't be asking babies questions at all. Or would we? When you think about it, the sorts of queries we put to babies are often our addition to the *Attend* we've already given or the *Best Guess* we are about to try. An adult's conversation with a baby often sounds like this:

'You're looking so cute, aren't you, my poppet?'

'My, you've grown! You're a whopper now aren't you, darling?'

'Why are you crying, sweetie? It's that nasty wind, isn't it?'

See what I mean? The big difference is that when we talk to babies we do not expect or demand any specific response from them. With toddlers, however, they know they are supposed to come up with a reply using language which they themselves have only just begun to learn to speak. Probably the most constructive thing you can do as a parent/carer is to continue to practise with your toddler the *Attends* you were already using when the child was a baby. At the same time you should hold back the questions unless you are honestly giving them a real choice. You know the sort of thing: the red top or the stripy jumper, or the choice between an outing to the park or the river, while you would be telling them they would be wearing their wellies wherever they decided to go!

Please try to remember my point about keeping the rate of questions low when you are interacting with your tiny tots. It really makes them feel the warmth of your love when you give *Attends* instead.

Echoes From Our Past: Feeling Wanted

I'm hoping some details of my own experiences with nought to threes, both personal and professional, will help you to see how our rather scary power over our baby's brains has featured in other parents' lives, even if they didn't, like me, realise it at the time. It is in this section of each chapter that I will be letting you in on some of my own experiences as a daughter, mother, stepmother, grand-mother and step-grandmother. Plus I shall mention, without break-ing confidentiality, families with whom I have worked over the last thirty or so years. I will carry through the chapter's main focus by concentrating on emotional warmth, being wanted and how *At-tends* and *Best Guesses* can be powerful ways of getting that message across to your baby and toddler.

My own first three years were played out against a background of the early part of the Second World War. I was a much longed-for baby as my mother and father had spent seven years 'practising'! In those bygone days there was little high-tech professional help with the issue of apparent infertility. Couples were instead urged to 'relax' as the tension of wanting to conceive seemed to be an obstacle to success. And to have lots of sex, of course. In my mother's case, an acute appendicitis requiring surgery also seems to have been a factor.

I was therefore welcomed into the world with special joy, I am told: my bemused father called me his 'Golden Girl'. It seems I was quite jaundiced, which the poor man interpreted as my having this golden glow. So, from my very first hours, I grew up believing that in his eyes I was very much approved of and wanted. He often called me 'My Golden Girl' as I grew up – a first-class *Attend* if ever I heard one. My father, Harry, came from a rather undemonstra-tive family where feelings were neither shown nor discussed. What a dreadful psychological burden that must have been, when a parent, particularly a father, was believed to 'spoil' their children simply by saying words and phrases of approval for their little ones. I am so thrilled to see the enormous expansion of a father's role in giving their babies and toddlers emotional warmth so they can grow up knowing they are wanted.

And what about Kathy, my mother? Well, she came from a family where, very unusually for that period, her parents openly kissed and cuddled each other in front of their three daughters. The sisters therefore grew up with a rare advantage as they had vicariously learned about adults showing each other emotional warmth. My mother seems to have been the sibling least favoured by her own mother, Ada, though thankfully she was a favourite of her father. During my childhood, I was frequently told of the joy she experienced when she set off with her father on what seemed to her to be exciting adventures. In actuality they appear to have spent a good deal of time on his allotment or walking by the River Thames. So, my grandfather Caleb's emotionally warm behaviour towards my mother fortunately seems to have offset any disapproval she experienced from my grandmother and allowed Kathy to develop sufficient self-esteem to carry her successfully through her childhood and adolescence.

When she gave birth to me, her eldest child, it's said she was at once exhausted and elated. Know the feeling? I do! Those first hours after delivering your baby are a very strange mixture of apparently contradictory emotions even when everything has gone brilliantly. My mother said she had determined there would be no favouritism between her own children and I seem to have been given lashings of baby *Attends* similar to the ones already described in this chapter.

Providing *Attends* for newborns, babies and toddlers who can't talk actually seems to come naturally for most parents. I suppose it's to compensate for the inevitably one-sided nature of our conversations with them during these very early months and years. Mind you, that's no excuse for dropping *Attends* from your repertoire when your child starts to talk. Really, we should keep them as a permanent feature of all our interactions, whatever the nature of the relationship involved.

As a direct result of my good fortune in having openly approving parents, I was able to develop a pretty healthy bubble of self-confidence. However, this took a significant knock when, for no reason that I could understand at the time, my father was no longer there to call me his 'Golden Girl' as he was called away to war. I sometimes think I have subconsciously spent a good deal of my life ever since trying to be pretty enough, clever enough and good enough to prevent a repetition of this trauma. We all carry so much baggage around with us, it's positively scary, isn't it? Though more about that in the next section.

Meanwhile, the *Best Guessing* part of my parents' input continued, or so I gather from what I remember of their behaviour towards my sister Elizabeth and brother Jonathan. It's quite difficult to actively recall your mother and father's exact words to you from those early days. I personally have much clearer memories of Liz and Jon, three and eleven years younger than me respectively, being *Best Guessed* than I do of myself receiving this particular type of attention from either parent. For instance, Liz, a vibrant redhead then and now, used to hold her breath until blue in the face when frustrated. I can still conjure up the image of my mother sitting Liz on her lap and saying words to this effect: 'I can see you're really cross because you can't have a drink right this moment. I know you're thirsty and thirsty girls can feel furious if they don't get a drink when they want one. But I can't take you to find a drink until you start breathing properly. There, that's it, gently now . . .'

You can see that, without realising it, my mother was *Mirroring*, *Validating*, *Empathising* and proposing a *Resolution*. When that sequence is carried out countlessly during an under-three's life, the cumulative effect is to provide reassurance that however much *in extremis* the baby and toddler may feel, however difficult their behaviour and mood, you are not going to abandon them. Instead you are taking the time to notice they need help and stick around until things are sorted out and peace restored. My brother Jon was a notoriously fussy eater as a toddler, so I have enduring memories of my mother's efforts to *Best Guess* him at the kitchen table. They went something like this: 'Jonny darling, I know you're not keen on egg and spinach. You just don't want it, do you? The thing is you need your lunch and that's what there is, egg and spinach. What about if Mummy sprinkles some grated cheese on top and you only have to eat half? Let's try that . . .'

Of course, my mother wouldn't have called it *Best Guessing* or what psychologists call 'intentional dialogue', though in effect that's precisely what she was doing, which proved to be a huge bonus for myself and my two younger siblings when dealing with the troubled times that characterise life as an adult.

Just as there are families where freely expressing emotional warmth is part of everyday life, so there are those where the only feelings shown regularly are anger, scorn and hurtful criticism. Often parents who behave like this have been treated that way by their own parents, who were distant as well as cold and a source of fear. Thankfully, it is quite possible to break this damaging cycle as long as we want to be more emotionally warm to our baby and toddler than our parents were to us. We can all too easily dwell on the past injustice of our own upbringing, mean to do better, and then if we have no model of positive parenting, fail to make the changes we have sworn to achieve. This is where I hope this book will come in useful.

I have worked with numerous families where parents recognise their style of interacting with their child might not be warm enough. Without wanting to, we can end up like this:

- Finding little time for our under-threes
- Giving priority to work and other activities
- Having difficulty in showing warm feelings to our children
- Saving our energy for ourselves
- Regarding our baby or toddler as simply a burdensome responsibility
- Finding parenting all duty and no fun.

At the same time it may be that the soft-focus dream of life with a baby and toddler featured in so many adverts across the media bears little or no resemblance to the realities of fatigue, anxiety, burped-up milk or spat-out apricot cereal. What if we notice we are failing to give enough *Attends* and *Best Guesses* to ensure our children are feeling so loved and approved of that there can be no doubt that you really and truly want them? Later on, I look in more detail at experiences that can get in the way of delivering these vital ingredients, and suggest how you might spring out of being a distant parent. For now, though, I'll remind you of your baby's perspective on the situation. It's what we all wanted from our own parents in the way of emotional warmth, even though we might not have received it, through no fault of our own.

The main problem from a baby and toddler's point of view is that it seems to them there is almost nothing they can do to guarantee emotional warmth or approval from those all-powerful figures, their parents. Our under-threes are desperate for our attention, indeed they depend upon it for their survival. They cry, scream, choke, sweat, wriggle and go rigid, limp, red or blue in their attempts to gain that precious commodity. Meanwhile, they are struggling to believe, in view of their parents' cold and distant style, that they are wanted or loved at all. Babies and toddlers of parents who cannot show them enough emotional warmth, acceptance and approval can develop problems such as:

- Feeling unsure of their place in our affections
- Believing they are somehow failures
- Longing for warmth and approval
- Learning to be afraid of emotional intimacy
- Experiencing destructive anxiety about whether they are wanted
- Behaving 'badly' to attract our attention

Naturally, loving parents don't want their under-threes to suffer in this way, so how can we best offset any tendency in ourselves to repeat our own parents' mistakes? Well, the first step is to look back with an adult eye on those very childhood experiences that were the most painful. That is not the same as heaping blame on the previous generation, rather it is a necessary first step in making any real progress towards a point where you yourself can begin to change things for the better. Maybe you had difficult feelings like the ones listed above. Perhaps our parents weren't able to allow us to be emotionally close enough to give us the certain conviction that they loved us with all their hearts. We may have felt we were somehow not good enough to deserve emotional warmth from the people who mattered to us most. Actually, we might still feel like that, unable to shake off those doubts about being truly loveable. Perhaps our mother or father was unable to reach out with the degree of emotional warmth required for us to feel securely embraced in their love.

I have, in my role as a cognitive behaviour therapist, met so many adults who recall times when they:

- Felt unsure of their place in their parents' affections
- Believed they were somehow failures in their parents' eyes
- Longed for approval and warmth from their parents
- Learned from their parents to be afraid of emotional intimacy
- Behaved badly to gain parental attention, even rebukes
- Felt emotional anxiety about whether their parents loved them

Case Study One

I remember one young woman, who I will call Gemma, who had just had her first baby, a girl. She could not stop herself from being highly anxious about what opinion her own mother, now dead, would have of her early weeks of motherhood. Gemma's mother had always been very sparing in her approval of her daughter and had found it difficult to demonstrate any emotional warmth although she was a dedicated parent. For Gemma, this led to a self-perpetuating situation where, though she constantly strove to earn her mother's admiration, she viewed her every success as a failure because the maternal warmth and approval she so craved as a child was never available. In fact, Gemma was an intelligent twenty-five-year-old with a promising career in market research. It took several months of helping Gemma to challenge the Negative Automatic Thoughts (see pages 116–18) that undermined her self-confidence before she was able to recognise her many good points as a mother. As Gemma learned not to give any weight to illogical negative automatic thoughts like: 'I'm a hopeless mum, I can't even get the ironing done. My mum always had the ironing up-to-date. She would be ashamed of me', so her self-image improved, her anxiety faded and her baby thrived.

Case Study Two

And dads? Yes, they can suffer too, though finding services tailor-made for new fathers who are having trouble showing emotional warmth to their baby or toddler can be a challenge. I remember one man in his thirties who felt so completely overwhelmed by the sheer weight of responsibilities involved in becoming a parent that he was missing out on the joyful parts altogether. Brian, not his real name of course, very much wanted to be an emotionally available dad, especially as his own father had been cold, distant and highly critical. Brian had suffered a great deal as a child and adolescent because of his father's emotionally frigid parenting style so that when his baby boy was born he became extremely anxious about not repeating history with his own son. Thankfully Brian was able to respond to cognitive behaviour therapy aimed at helping him to realise he could now, as an adult in a supportive relationship with his partner, take the chance to become close and warm towards their infant without harming him. Brian's positive automatic thoughts such as, 'I *can* be a loving father' slowly but surely began to outweigh the negative ones left over from his childhood. He was able to challenge successfully the effects of his own father's coolness towards him and learn that he need not be defined by the criticism and lack of approval he had received as a child.

If you are a parent whose mother or father gave you little or no sign they approved of you, did not use cuddles to express their love for you and gave you no opportunity to feel the flood of pleasure which comes from being a child who is told 'I love you', take heart! There are things you can do to help yourself become more self-confident, both as an individual and as a parent. Here are some ideas on how to move forward that have worked for other people in your situation. Start giving yourself positive messages about becoming a warmer and more demonstrative parent. Try these examples of self-instruction, or your own special version would be even better:

- 'We can be a happier family if I open up and show the love I feel for my baby or toddler.'
- 'I can say "I love you" to my one-year-old even though my parents never said it to me. Nothing terrible will happen so I will just give it a try.'
- 'I can be proud that I've managed to make a link between my own childhood experiences and how I am as a person and a parent.'
- 'I want my child to grow into a self-confident and communicative adult so I must make sure I show them approval and warmth.'
- 'When I'm warm towards my under-three they will feel good inside and want to please me. It will be much more fun to play with them and we'll all enjoy each other's company more.'
- 'My baby loves me and approves of me, so I'll learn to approve of myself.'

The more often you give yourself these instructions and reminders, the better your chances of feeling confident about openly expressing your approval of your toddler. But of course you won't really know the joys of emotionally warm parenthood until you have taken a shot at using lots of *Attends* and *Best Guesses* with your baby. Try talking to other grown-ups about the situation and your plan to do things differently from your own parents. Start with these:

- Choose a friend or relative you trust and tell them that you are going to do whatever it takes to get emotionally close to your under-three, including telling your child on a daily basis that you love them masses and masses.
- Talk with a sympathetic person about the experiences in your childhood and adolescence. You will find very often that they want to return the favour and confide in you.
- Find someone you feel at ease with and tell them you have begun to make links between the way your parents brought you up and your own style of parenting.

Remember, even though this might all be a bit scary, and you obviously wouldn't stop strangers in the street and share your innermost thoughts and feelings with them, talking to other people about emotional issues is an integral part of becoming a more open person. After you have spoken to someone about these pretty heavy topics, you will find giving your infant, one- or two-year-old frequent *Attends* and *Best Guesses* will be an absolute doddle!

There are also practical steps you can take to help swing you away from any difficulty you might experience in being emotionally warm and available to your under-three.

- Take a quiet half hour to write out a list of the benefits of showing your loving feelings. Next, put down the disadvantages of hiding them from your baby or toddler.
- Tell your child, at least once a day, that you love them. Say those three words, 'I love you'. It can transform your child's view of themselves, their parents and their place in the family.
- Plan fifteen to twenty minutes each day when just you and your baby or toddler can spend time focusing on each other whilst doing an activity you both enjoy.
- Make sure you use lots of *Attends* and *Best Guesses* with your under-three so they are left in no doubt that you are not only noticing them but approving of them too.
- Give yourself a little treat every day for working hard at becoming a warm and loving parent. And while you're eating your choccie or choosing your video, say to yourself, 'Well done! You can do it!'

Don't forget, changing your behaviour is a good way to kick start your feelings. Even if you aren't very keen on setting time aside for one-to-one play, you will find taking the risk of becoming emotionally close to your baby is rewarding both minute by minute and in the longer term. Give that powerful phrase, 'I love you' an airing, even if it's something you tend to avoid. A couple told me recently that life with their two-year-old twins had become so much more fun since they had started to make moves towards being emotionally warm with their children. A double dose of challenges from twins can swamp parents with the drudgery of nappy changes, food routines, soothing two babies at a time – the list goes on. So remember, taking practical steps towards shifting your focus from the mundane physical tasks to the exciting opportunities for building emotional bonds can lift everybody's mood.

But supposing you are slowly sinking beneath the unending deluge of daily demands of being a parent, and you want to give yourself a quick jolt about not distancing yourself as a way of coping. What can you do? Well, what I suggest is you buy a couple of sets of alphabet fridge magnets and spell out this emergency self-help message:

BE BRAVE – BE WARM – BE HAPPY

Repeat it to yourself like a kind of yoga mantra, as you proactively decide that your partner, sibling, best pal or nana or grandad will have to get the shopping today/tomorrow/for ever, because you are going to spend the time otherwise eaten up at your local super-market concentrating exclusively on your under-three. Blow bubbles, sing songs, make mud pies and blue paint footprints. Whatever makes you both feel the priceless glow of sharing emotional warmth with your baby or toddler. You will both feel wanted, approved of and loved.

Whatever our style of parenting, too distant, domineering, inconsistent, passive, intrusive, or evenly balanced, there are always echoes from our past which we have to deal with in order to be the parent our baby, toddler, one- and two-year-old needs. Don't let these shades from the past rule you. Tackle any tendency towards a lack of emotional warmth by adopting the suggestions just set out. You really have nothing to lose and lots to gain. Don't worry if you think your parenting style is one of the others mentioned. I deal with each one in the following chapters.

Special Feature: Ignoring Tantrums

Suppose your toddler wants their little friend's Bob the Builder hat or Fairy Princess tiara. Wants it so much that when the little friend refuses to part with their treasure, your child throws themselves on the floor. They wail. They scream. They thrash about. In short, a temper tantrum of Mega proportions ensues. What to do? We certainly don't want to encourage such displays. Should we try to distract them? Should we give them a cuddle and try to soothe them? What about persuading the little friend to share their prized headgear with your toddler, who by now has a face bright pink with frustration and glistening with tears?

Well the answer to all three suggestions is 'No'. The best way is to help our toddlers learn that when they can't get what they want, throwing a wobbly does not work. What we must do is ignore the tantrum, difficult though this might be. It's especially tough to do this when the pair of you are an object of intense interest to every passer-by.

Removing something the child likes and wants – in this case adult attention – results in the toddler having fewer tantrums in future. Expect the tantrums to get worse before they get better as our toddlers make strenuous efforts to manoeuvre us back into giving them our attention. Never the less you must be consistent. It's no good ignoring a tantrum one day and scooping your child up for an ice cream the next. This only ensures that they learn to persist with their outbursts of frustration because they know that at least some of the time they will wangle a reward out of you – the return of your attention during an explosion of toddler temper. Though it is very easy to advise a mum or dad to ignore their child's tantrums or pestering behaviour, putting it into practice can be tough. So here are a few tips on what you should and shouldn't do when successfully ignoring.

Dos and Don'ts of Successful Ignoring

- **Do** stop looking at them, except out of the corner of your eye
- **Do** avoid any physical contact
- **Do** walk away – but not too far
- **Do** keep your face calm and neutral – much easier said than done!

- **Do** stop talking altogether
- **Do** make your voice a little louder than usual as you say – 'I'm pleased you're quiet now'
- **Do** be consistent

- **Don't** put your face close to theirs and lock your gazes
- **Don't** wrestle, haul, push or shove
- **Don't** chase or play hide and seek
- **Don't** look furious, frown, grimace or cast your eyes up to heaven
- **Don't** say, 'I'm ignoring you'
- **Don't** shout, scream, mutter, or spit out words between clenched teeth or make sarcastic remarks
- **Don't** give in, even occasionally, to tantrum terror or pester power

Ending your ignoring should be reserved for that moment half a minute after the tantrum behaviour has ceased and peace once more prevails. You need to let your child know that by being quiet they have achieved the return of your much prized attention. You can say something like: 'I love it when you are calm. Now let's get on with putting your socks on/mashing the banana/feeding the cat. Off we go!'

But what should we do when our under-three behaves in a way that cannot be safely ignored as it risks harm to life and limb? These behaviours can include aggression, dangerous daredevil pranks, wanton damage or experiments with matches and household appliances. Some parents think a smack or a good telling off are appropriate punishments, but they simply don't work. Why? Let me explain.

Most people's view of punishment is to make someone suffer as a consequence of breaking the rules of our society. In social learning theory it's about achieving the situation where our child is less likely to repeat their dangerous or destructive behaviour in future. The punishment itself should be boring, not painful. Keep in mind that smacking and shouting make your child believe you don't love them and this can spur them on to even greater bad behaviour as they feel they have nothing to lose any more.

Picture the scene: your toddler is found teetering on the arm of the sofa, dangerously close to the sharp edge of the coffee table should they fall. You can't ignore it. Indeed, even before thinking out a coherent plan you have stepped in and saved the day by sweeping them into your arms. Your biggest temptation is then to do a little rant about how naughty they were being and how you are likely to have a heart attack if they should ever do anything like that again. You might even give in to temptation to smack your toddler, on the basis that they have scared you half to death.

Unfortunately all these responses spell out loads of adult attention which, as we have already seen, has the opposite effect to the one we are looking for. In other words, we are inadvertently encouraging the child to scale further heights in the future. So, suitable punishments for our toddler mountain climbers? Stay calm and state clearly that CBeebies is off the TV menu this morning. Or sit them on the Magic Chair or Magic Step and withdraw your attention for half a minute. This is a mini-version of Time Out, a popular punishment amongst parents, which will be fully described and discussed later. As you have gathered, my own view on punishing children is that we must avoid smacking and shouting, and instead withdraw attention, privileges or use Time Out.

That leaves us with the last of the strategies: negative reinforcement. Here, removing a disliked consequence of a behaviour means it is more likely to occur again. Make a note that this is not 'negative attention' or physical punishment. A classic example, and one I've definitely fallen into, goes like this:

I was in the final stages of preparing Sunday lunch. My one- and two-year-old daughters, little blonde angels with cherubic smiles, had escaped from their father and were now crowded into the tiny galley kitchen of our modest 1930s terraced family home. Via a mixture of fractious requests, 'Mummy, up!' and 'I want a cuddle!' I was rapidly made aware that my attempts to get the Brussels sprouts into the vegetable dish were to cease forthwith. Muttering, 'Not now, darling, Mummy's busy', I managed to tip out the Brussels and dump the pan in the sink. Now for the carrots. Well, that was my intention. Not to be! The girls had by now glued themselves to the hem of my skirt and were beginning to sound tearful. So guess what I did!

Yes! I put the carrots down and picked my little girls up. By doing this, giving in to pester-power, I was negatively reinforcing myself by getting rid of something I didn't like, the tearful entreaties, whilst simultaneously rewarding my daughters for their persistence. Brilliant! And did it all happen again and again and again? Of course!

No one had explained to me clearly about how giving in to pleading under-threes would just lead to more of the same, with the stakes getting higher all the time. Eventually I reached my limit – you know, the 'I've had it right up to here!' moment – and made an unbreakable house rule: only Mummy in the kitchen during dishing up and Daddy to entertain our two girls. So, learn from me: giving in just makes things worse.

Special Feature: Birth Fears

No matter how many antenatal classes we attend and irrespective of the numerous discussions on becoming parents we might have had with those already in the know, nothing but first-hand experience really tells it like it is. Immediately we are hit with emotional shock waves that the experience of pregnancy has failed to properly prepare us for. You may have been eagerly awaiting the birth; you may have been dreading the whole prospect. Whichever way your feelings have been tending, by full term most mums- and dads-to-be can't wait to get it over and done with!

Even if you have both been serenely confident, you would be most unusual if you hadn't been trying to counteract the anxiety-provoking items on your pregnancy Scary List. A brilliant nurse specialist and tutor in cancer treatment and care gave me the idea of Scary Lists (thank you, Audrey) when I was on holiday with her sister in Corsica (thank you, Pia). Anyway, I've since elaborated on the theme and I think that two levels of Scary List probably cover the scope of our very natural fears about our baby's birth. See what you think. First the Official Scary List, the one you own up to when confiding in your closest friend.

Birth

THE OFFICIAL SCARY LIST

Mum	**Dad**
The pain will be unbearable	Her pain will be unbearable
The labour will be interminable	It could go on for days
Something will go wrong	Something could go wrong
A Caesarean will be necessary	She might need an operation
The baby won't be normal	There could be something wrong with the baby

I'm sure you have extra ones, or different ones altogether, so you might like to jot them down now and compare them with the labour and delivery that you actually experienced. The point of writing down your Scary List as opposed to trying to squash it out of your consciousness is that putting pen to paper means you are distancing yourself from your fears and getting a more reasoned perspective. Try it with the Unofficial Scary List too. That's the one you barely admit to yourself, let alone to anyone else.

Birth

THE UNOFFICIAL SCARY LIST

Mum	**Dad**
I won't be able to cope	I won't be able to cope
I will make a fool of myself by shouting, screaming and swearing	I will make a fool of myself by fainting or being sick
I won't be able to stand the pain and they won't give me enough drugs to make it bearable	I won't be able to stand watching her being in a lot of pain
My baby's heart will weaken if I'm in labour too long	The baby could die before it's born
My baby will be born deformed	The baby could be handicapped
My baby will die	The baby might die
I will die	She might die

All these fears, however overly dramatic they might look in retro-spect after the birth has gone swimmingly, are shared by millions of mothers and fathers awaiting the birth of their child. Of *course* you worry about the things it seems rather pathetic to voice to anyone else, we all do. So, rather than bottle it all up, try sharing even your most secret fears with someone who you trust to listen without judging your perhaps overactive imagination as some sort of weakness. Giving birth is the most dramatic life event we are ever likely to go through, and while pregnancy is not a medical con-dition as such, the birth itself can feel a little like a medical emergency, even when everything is going to plan!

I have purposely left off both Scary Lists fears of the real biggy – and it's about love. I know many parents-to-be are almost tortured by anxiety and apprehension that they will not love their baby immediately or, indeed, at all. However long we have waited for our baby, however much time we have spent gathering together dinky little outfits for our darling, and however intensely we long to hold them in our arms, that doubt often lingers. And right up there with it is that other show-stopper: will we be a 'good parent'? My position on this last point, as already mentioned in this chapter, is that successful parenting of your newborn baby can be achieved by being Baby Centred, and you can learn how by reading this book, so press on!

The other worry, about not being overwhelmed with love for our infant the moment we set eyes on them, is in some ways more complex. The fact of the matter is that, for all sorts of reasons, you may not immediately fall in love with your newborn. It is quite common for a new mother who is exhausted by a hard labour, distressed by surgical intervention or zonked out by the necessity for serious medication, to feel a flood of relief rather than love as her major reaction after the birth. Sometimes the new dad is the one with the energy that enables him to launch straight into the adoration stakes. On other occasions, as a father you might feel a degree of antipathy towards your baby for causing your beloved partner pain and suffering. Or maybe it all went well and yet you somehow don't feel properly connected. Whatever the cause, please don't put yourself down for being an 'unnatural' mum or dad. The whole process of pregnancy and childbirth is both wondrous *and* taxing, a miracle *and* a serious challenge, eagerly anticipated *and* viewed with some dread. So, it is no big surprise if we emerge looking and feeling rather less rosy than we had hoped. Being in the same boat as loads of other new parents, knowing you're not alone is always a comfort isn't it? Fortunately you can also tell yourself that there is a tried-and-tested route for reaching those dizzying heights of baby infatuation that seem for the moment to have passed you by. And I'm going to tell you about it right now.

Bridging a bonding gap is within the grasp of every 'semi-detached' parent. You just have to know something of how mums and dads become attached to their babies and how newborns build up their relationship with their processes. These two processes, although intimately linked, are not mirror images of each other. That's because parents become bonded with their infant through caring for them, while babies thrive on the emotional, social and psychological aspects of being looked after by adults.

Notice I put 'adults' there, as newborns will happily respond to the attentions of their primary carer, whatever the genetic link or lack of any blood tie. A pretty fortunate arrangement when you come to think of it, otherwise millions of babies would have been denied the love and devotion given to many by non-biological parents. As both a natural and adoptive mother myself I can say without reservation that bathing, feeding, dressing and stimulating a nine-week-old newcomer to our family was an extremely rapid route to forming the loving bond with my adopted son that still exists to this day.

Here are some hints on how to make sure that changing nappies, bottle and breastfeeding (more on that in chapter three), putting on babygros, cleaning tiny fingers and faces, brushing little wisps of hair and generally being in physical contact with your baby, can lead to the emotional closeness of a blossoming bond between you and your newborn.

- When you are changing nappies, look closely at your beautiful little baby. Stroke them gently with your fingers and give your newborn an *Attend*. Say 'I can see your lovely little body and your wonderfully strong legs'. Continue to give *Attends* throughout nappy changing and avoid making any noises of disgust even when your infant is particularly wet or messy. Focusing out loud on the positives helps to create emotional warmth from parent to child.

- When you are bottle feeding in a situation where you can relax comfortably with your baby, take off your top and bra, if you're wearing one, and hold your little one close to your skin in the position you would be using if you were breast-feeding. Looking down at the unique configuration of your newborn's head against your breast can trigger strong emotions of attachment towards the recent arrival. And dads! You can try it too! Think of all those posters of semi-naked fathers and their tiny babies. There's a reason we all go gooey at that sight. This is your chance to simultaneously protect and nourish your own creation. Go for it, though probably not in a coffee shop!

- When you are a breastfeeding mum, all of the hints already mentioned for bottle-feeding parents apply too. Newborns who have skin-to-skin contact when latched on to their mother's breast can set off a flood of warm, protective emotions, so you could take off their clothes, too, for a double dose of bonding potential. Now dads, we know you don't produce breast milk, but that doesn't leave you out of the loop. Bare your manly chest while you give your infant son or daughter some expressed breast milk in a bottle. It really is a good tip to take up if you want to increase the warm bond with your newborn.

- When feeding and changing your baby, remember that from their perspective it's not really the type of milk that is of burning importance. They are much more focused on whether their tummy feels comfortingly full or distressingly empty. It's not the leak-proof quality of their nappy nor its snugness of fit that occupies them most. No, it's whether their little nether regions feel soft and smooth or sore and uncomfortable. But, in the context of bonding, more important than all of this is your ability to use every occasion of physical caregiving as an opportunity to strengthen the bond between you.

- What you need to do is to come up with as many Baby Centred behaviours as possible when you are changing, feeding, bathing and dressing your infant. Use lots of *Attends*. Slot in *Best Guesses*, should your newborn become fractious or distressed. Not forgetting the *Praises*, *Loving Smiles*, *Imitations*, *Ask to Plays* and *Positive Touches* that make up the rest of the Baby Centred parenting behaviours we will be looking at in the chapters to come. You won't need to *Ignore Minor Naughtiness* at this age though, as, quite simply, newborns are incapable of intentional mischief. We might well find them demanding, but that's another story!

- When feeding, your *Attends* would include ones like these:
    'Oh! You're looking straight at me!'
    'What a powerful suck! I can see you're going to grow fast!'
    'I love to see you looking so full-up.'
    'Oh!, you're desperate for milk!'
    'You're going to sleep now, aah, sssh . . .'

You will also want to add in lots of endearments and pet names too, even if at first you have to remind yourself that any effort you make now towards being Baby Centred will pay off huge dividends in terms of emotional closeness in the years to come. Add in some fingertip stroking of your baby's head and face, grip their little hand in yours, and you are undoubtedly on a winning streak.

- Similar input from you when you are trying to squeeze their rather bendy limbs into their Babygro, washing their tiny fingers, bathing them or doing their hair, will ensure that while you are bonding with them by looking after their physical needs, they are becoming attached to you because of your Baby Centred *Attends*.

So, even when you are not feeling especially close or warm towards your newborn, remember that going through the motions of being Baby Centred when you are catering for your infants' physical needs will help you to get closer to them, not least because, of course, they will respond to your input with a rewarding reaction. Love between a parent and their newborn can come in several guises including the lightning strike of love at first sight, and the slower to start but none the less deep and enduring type of love that can creep up on you while you are nourishing, nurturing and protecting your baby.

Being Baby Centred towards your recent arrival will enrich your bond with them no matter whether you two get off to a flying start or a more sedate beginning. Just remember that the very act of repeatedly giving your newborn *Attends*, *Best Guesses* and other Baby Centred input will, in time, bring on the warm feelings slower starters find a little difficult to develop at first. So don't give up! You too can confidently expect to establish a precious and unique relationship with your baby, even though it may take a little more energy than that expended by those parents who immediately fall in love with their newborn. One day you'll realise it's all happening without you making any conscious effort at all. You have nothing to lose and everything to gain!

Naturally, we all have days when we are firing on less than full power. We may be unwell, worried about money, coping with elderly relatives or thinking wistfully of those days pre-baby when we could simply decide on an outing and go! Not any more! By the time we have assembled all the necessary baby paraphernalia, and some of the unnecessary 'just in case' items, our original motivation for the trip can have decreased to vanishing point. So, when you know you are not at your best but your newborn still needs you just as much, make sure to give yourself treats for managing to get through the afternoon without going entirely crazy.

A spoonful of honey in your tea, ten minutes deciding what television programme you will record for later viewing, a waft of your favourite perfume or aftershave, four tracks from your all-time-favourite album, and a short moan to your best friend about how looking after one tiny mortal is so much more exhausting than the job you previously thought stressful – any or all of these tactics can help lift you sufficiently to cope with a difficult day. A final really important plan to have in place for those 'off' times is an arrangement that, in the evening, someone else – co-parent, partner, relative or friend – takes over responsibility for the baby for two to three hours. After all, they need opportunities to bond too, so think of it as doing them a favour.

Special Feature: Coping with Fatigue

Parents have needs too. We must make sure that we aren't so preoccupied with baby bonding that we forget to look after each other. So let's talk about post-birth fatigue. It's certainly a universal problem.

Some people are lucky enough to be able to call on grandparents or other adults who can take on responsibility for baby care when a parent is so bone-achingly tired they are no longer sure of their own names. This is a trusted someone who will continue to be a positive feature in your baby's life and who makes sure the new parent gets the requisite eight hours' sleep a day, or night. Maybe not in one solid stretch, but still – eight hours! Wow!

Sadly, for most of us this will remain a dream. This is a huge shame because we *all* function so much better when we are not sleep deprived. I know some 'superheroes' claim to be incredibly active, alert and on the ball despite a regular diet of no more than three to four hours' sleep a day. Well, lucky them! It's not a state I have ever achieved, especially after giving birth. So let's just assume you are not a superhero and that you are suffering from fatigue. You can barely drag yourself around because you aren't getting more than two to three hours' sleep at any one time. First of all, a look at the official Scary List on fatigue.

Fatigue

THE OFFICIAL SCARY LIST

Mum	**Dad**
Once I drop off I will not hear my baby cry	I'll probably sleep through the baby crying because I'm on my knees with tiredness
I am so tired I will make mistakes and not realise	I'm so exhausted I could fall asleep at the wheel
I will resent my baby because they are keeping me awake when I'm exhausted.	Nobody told me it would be so tiring being a dad
Being utterly tired is making me irritable and tearful	I could snap if this goes on

Let's spell it out loud and clear. Despite all the concerned predictions, the sensitive warnings and the anticipatory glee of all those who highlighted the fatigue problem for you during your pregnancy, nothing, but *nothing* can prepare you for the

MIND-NUMBING
KILLING
UNIMAGINABLE
UNRELENTING
CRUCIFYING
HIDEOUS
UNBEARABLE and plain old
ENERGY-DRAINING nature of chronic sleep deprivation

That's not even the whole story! What about the other list? The one we feel we can't reveal to even the most sympathetic listener: the Unofficial Scary List.

Fatigue

THE UNOFFICIAL SCARY LIST

Mum	**Dad**
Because I won't wake up when my baby cries, they will choke to death	I sleep so deeply my baby could die and I wouldn't know
I'm so flattened by sleep deprivation I will accidentally burn my baby with hot tea or coffee	I could be killed in a car crash because of exhaustion and then my baby would never know me
I will end up hating my baby because they won't let me sleep and that makes me a terrible mum	I'm so tired I'm beginning to really dislike that baby It's ruined my life
I will get so cross through tiredness that I will injure my baby	I could easily get so frustrated at being kept awake that I could hurt someone

Of course, for most of us the Unofficial Scary List rarely appears at a conscious level and then only for a few nanoseconds. If you become preoccupied with any of these items, you should confide in not only your best friend but also your health visitor or GP. At the end of this book I list the names and phone numbers of organisations that can help, often anonymously or confidentially, when you have reached breaking point because of sleep deprivation.

I think it's important, though, to acknowledge that even the sanest and most balanced amongst us can be transformed into gibbering wrecks when our sleep quota is reduced below a bearable level. Having Official and Unofficial Scary List thoughts and feelings does not, and I emphasise *not*, make you a monster mummy or devil daddy. On the contrary, you belong to a parenting club with millions of members!

But what to do? What steps can you take to minimise the chances that you will be rendered so groggy by wakeful nights that you could end up putting the nappies in the microwave and the baby's bottle in the washing machine? Let me give you a few tips:

Practical Ideas

1. **Sleep when your baby sleeps**
   It doesn't matter what time of day it is. It doesn't matter what jobs you were supposed to be doing. It doesn't matter that you haven't even got dressed yet. Just take the phone off the hook, snuggle down near your baby, and snatch some catch-up shut-eye.

2. **Take the night off**
   Once or twice a week, arrange to let your partner – or someone else you can trust – take complete responsibility for the night shift so you can sleep through the night. It doesn't matter if you are a breastfeeding mum because you can express some milk beforehand for your partner or friend to give to the baby while you're asleep, or you can make up some suitable formula to tide the baby over until morning.

3. **Invite a trusted relative or friend to take over**
   If you are at home with your baby while your partner, who barely stirs during the night when you are up and about with your infant, goes out to work, phone a friend. Ask – all right, beg – them to come over every other afternoon for a week so that you can nap for three or so hours while they take the strain.

Small Expectations

1. **Hang the housework**
   It is not vital to wipe down the worktops. Chaos will not ensue if the carpet is not cleaned. No one who loves you will mind that there's a layer of dust on the TV. Your priority now is nourishing and nurturing your newborn, and they couldn't care less if the kitchen floor is dotted with crumbs.

So give yourself permission to focus on your baby and let the housework go hang.

2. Go for comfy clothes
    Spending those first few weeks in your giant T-shirt or pyjamas is perfectly OK. Loads of new mummies and daddies find that somehow getting dressed in proper clothes becomes a dream of Before Baby Life (BBL). That's absolutely fine. I'm not suggesting you don't change your comfy clothes on a daily basis, but I am saying that your baby will not notice if you haven't washed up in case of company. Anyone who has been through similar experiences will be all sympathy and understanding.

3. Choose quick and easy food
    No need to even try to keep up your creativeness in the kitchen. It's not reasonable to expect to be able to prepare exotic cuisine when you are sleep deprived. Ready meals are perfect for those early weeks and months, and you and yours won't die of scurvy because the broccoli is frozen not fresh.

4. Rope in your friends
    Very often friends do not quite know how best to show their interest in your dramatically altered status from BBL (Before Baby Life) to ABL (After Baby Life). So they visit and bring gifts. Meanwhile, you are expected to make them a drink or snack while they, understandably, gaze at the wondrous new addition to your family. Then they leave you feeling even more exhausted! So, pre-empt this by ringing round and telling them what you need them to bring from the shops – nappies, baby lotion, baked beans or more giant T-shirts – and let them do the leg work. When they arrive say, 'It's marvellous to see you! Put the stuff away anywhere, and then get us both a cup of tea and one of those biscuits I see poking out of your bag.' Do *not* go into the kitchen, instead say, 'I don't know what I'd do without you.'

5. Ask for help
    There is no valid reason why you should expect to sail
    through the arrival of a baby without missing a beat. There
    is no reason to believe that you will not be totally wiped out
    with tiredness. In other words, it's really rather silly to think
    you should not need to ask for help, now isn't it? So, instead
    of trying to battle on against overwhelming odds, admit to
    yourself that no one can cope if they don't get enough sleep,
    and tell friends and relatives exactly what help you need.

Everything changes when you have a baby. It was certainly an
exhausting process for me, adjusting to the new sleep regime. Two
of my own babies seemed to be mostly awake from the word go,
though the third was much less taxing and slept through the night
from comparatively early on. So I know how crippling fatigue and
sleeplessness can be. But give some of my tips a chance to work and
you may feel just that little bit more energised. And remember, this
is only a phase and you will one day emerge vibrant and quivering
with vitality . . . although I just can't tell you when that day will
actually arrive! Meanwhile, sleep when your baby sleeps, take
nights off, invite a trusted relative or friend to take over, hang the
housework, wear comfy clothes, choose quick and easy food, rope
in your friends and, above all, say you need help – we all do! In
chapter three I look at how breastfeeding, while having many
benefits, seems to increase fatigue levels for mothers.

What To Do Next: My Baby Keeps Crying!

In our focus on what can happen when your baby or toddler cries, I
think it will be helpful to include parents' emotional reactions to
their under-threes' crying. We'll then look at some guidelines for
dealing competently with the situation. We can sort out the feelings
into those that we are likely to be capable of handling with ease,
ones that undermine us, those that stir up discomfort and the group
that may frighten us. I see them like this:

Easy To Handle
Tenderness
Desire to soothe
Protectiveness
Attentiveness
Loving Concern
Urge to comfort
Wanting to identify the cause
Wanting to find a solution

Uncomfortable
Irritation
Anger
Embarrassment
Frustration
Need to quieten

Undermining
Confusion
Powerlessness
Incompetence

Frightening
Panic
Fear
Alarm

So, you can see why the Easy-to-Handle emotions fall under that heading – simply because they are pleasant to experience, even if we are startled by their intensity. Babies do that – evoke very strong reactions from the grown-ups around them when they cry. Obviously there's a powerful biological reason behind our Easy-to-Handle responses to crying. They allow us to give our child the comfort and the help that they have signalled they need.

On a surge of tenderness and driven by a desire to soothe and protect, we focus our attention on our baby or toddler, showing loving concern. Our urge to comfort them impels us to seek out the cause of their distress and then provide a solution. The result? Our under-three is once more content, as shown by the fact that he or she has stopped crying. And us, the mummy or daddy? We feel triumphant, capable, relieved and ever so slightly smug! All this is on a good day of course, though we should still give ourselves loads of lovely *Attends* for our success.

But, what about the bad days? Those days when we are confused about why our baby is crying? Those days when we feel powerless to soothe them, when none of our tactics work? Those times when we feel useless and incompetent as a parent because we cannot get our under-three to stop crying? And everybody has those days.

You aren't alone by any means. Plus, it's all made so much worse when you finally hand them to someone else who works their magic and reduces the frantic tears to gentle sobs. Talk about undermining! You are left feeling even more confused, powerless and incompetent – a horrible situation.

What are you going to do with these negative emotions? Ignoring them could mean that they are more likely to zip back the very next time your infant cries. That can eventually lead to you developing a set picture of yourself as a useless mum or dad – even when that's a million miles from the truth. So tackling these undermining feelings, and the thoughts that go with them, is a must.

What I suggest you do is this: *Best Guess* yourself! You remember *Best Guessing* don't you? Mirror, Validate, Empathise and Resolve. Well, it can work on us too as long as we put into it the energy we would otherwise use up on undermining thoughts, feelings and behaviour.

Suppose you had just fed your newborn, or put your infant down for a nap because they seemed sleepy. Maybe you've just picked up your one-year-old from nursery, or your two-year-old from pre-school. However, they won't stop crying! Instead of feeling like a failure:

Mirror yourself: Say to yourself: 'I notice I'm feeling really useless at the moment.'

Validate yourself: Say to yourself: 'Lots of other mums and dads feel like this when their under-ones, twos or threes won't stop crying. No wonder I feel undermined.'

Empathise with yourself: Say to yourself: 'Feeling useless is a real pain. It's unpleasant, no doubt about that.'

Resolve: Say to yourself: 'I will feel much better if I DO SOMETHING, so:

- 'I'll check my newborn for wind.'
- 'I'll see if my eight-month-old really is sleepy or is just bored.'
- 'I'll find out if my one-year-old had an upset at nursery.'
- 'I'll check whether my two-year-old has had an argument with their new best friend.'

If your various ploys don't work and your baby or toddler is still crying, try distracting him or her – more about that later on. Until and unless we own up to some of the negative feelings we experience when our newborn, one- or two-year-old cries, we are unlikely to be able to move on to dealing effectively, calmly and affectionately with finding a helpful solution to the cause of their distress. Thankfully, acknowledging an undesirable emotion is not the same as acting it out, though if we don't consciously recognise a potentially destructive feeling then we are more likely to find ourselves dumping it on others. What I'm trying to highlight is that *all* these feelings are a perfectly normal part of our reactions when our baby or toddler cries. Some are less constructive than others, granted, but the best way to deal with them is to start by acknowledging their existence *without guilt*.

Moving on to the Uncomfortable group of reactions to a crying baby or toddler, it's important to realise that one of the reasons for being irritated, angry, embarrassed, frustrated or experiencing an urgent need to quieten them, is that our level of physical arousal significantly increases when they cry. Now, if you were about to go out to a party or attend a job interview, your body would probably rev up in a similar fashion. We would label those feelings as excitement or apprehension though, not irritation or any of the other uncomfortable emotions stirred up by our under-three when they are crying. So what's in a label? Well, lots actually! In this case, a more useful term might be 'stressed', a concept that's taken firm root in our society. Being 'wound up' is also an accurate description of how the additional arousal is usually linked to a physical state of muscular tension. You know, that knot invading your neck and shoulders, when you feel tempted to scream, shout or throw something simply to relieve the build-up of stress inside you.

So, what to do when we have acknowledged our heightened stress level? Supposing your newborn has been crying in the middle of the night for what seems like an eternity, or your ten-month-old has been whingeing all day, non-stop. Maybe your eighteen-month-old has pushed their lunch away for no apparent reason and is now red in the face as a result of squealing for a quarter of an hour? Or what about your two-year-old flinging themselves to the floor in the frozen food aisle of the supermarket, yelling, crying and writhing about? Will *Best Guessing* yourself work in this situation when you feel you will snap any minute, or should you try another strategy? Let's test it and find out.

Mirror yourself: Say OUT LOUD: 'I'm so stressed I think I'm losing it!'
Validate yourself: Say OUT LOUD: 'Any other parent could feel the same. I've tried everything and nothing works.'
Empathise with yourself: Say OUT LOUD: 'Feeling so wound up is dreadful. It makes me terribly uncomfortable.'
Resolve: Say OUT LOUD: 'I will feel better if I do something', so:
  • 'I'll just lay my newborn safely in their cot and go and make myself a hot drink.'
  • 'I'll pop my ten-month-old into their high chair and give my face a nice rinse with some cool water.'
  • 'I'll put out some finger foods and a drink where my eighteen-month-old can easily reach them and then go and sit in the next room and decide which TV programme I'd like to see tonight.'
  • 'I'll leave them on the floor, walk away several paces, almost turn my back and focus on reading a food label.'

Yes, it does all sound as if you could be found in public muttering to yourself in what might seem an ever-so-slightly deranged fashion! So what? It's the bond between you and your little one that's crucial, not what censorious strangers might think. Instructing ourselves, out loud or under our breath, is a powerful psychological technique used a great deal in cognitive behaviour therapy. It's used a great deal because it works, it really works. It sounds so simple, though, that we may be inclined to brush it aside. Don't. Self-instruction for moderating our emotions is one of the most useful psychological tools around, plus it's easily available and absolutely free! What more could you ask?

But what you should also notice is that, for Uncomfortable emotional reactions to a baby or toddler who just won't stop crying, we must actively plan to remove ourselves from their immediate environment. If 'losing it' and 'snapping' are rough equivalents to becoming so suffused with anger that you worry you might 'do something I'm ashamed of', in other words physically punishing your under-three, then distancing yourself is a very effective way of allowing cool-off time and space. Your baby or toddler will also have a chance to wind down to hiccuping sobs. From your perspective, keeping your baby safe from the harm you fear you might cause them should you explode, means moving away so they are literally beyond your reach. In effect you are giving yourself the space to come off the boil, simmer down and retrieve a sufficient amount of your cool to deal with your baby and toddler in a more serene fashion. Anything that relaxes you is a good idea, though a two-hour soak in a hot bath may be going over the top. Save that for later!

There is no need to put yourself down as a wicked parent because you have these Uncomfortable emotional reactions to crying. The vast majority of parents of under-threes experience similar feelings at one time or another. One of the major distinctions between a good mummy or daddy who nurtures a close relationship with their nought- to three-year-olds and a parent who is undermining their bond instead of building it up, is that the former does not act out their Uncomfortable emotions on their baby or toddler. There is a world of difference between having an emotion and acting on it.

Take my tip: *Best Guess*, move away and relax whenever you reach your stress ceiling. Then you can congratulate and treat yourself for having successfully weathered the storm. So, don't feel guilty about having Uncomfortable emotions, just learn how to manage them without making your infant suffer in any way.

Next, let's look at the Frightening emotions that can be provoked in us by a newborn's, six- to twelve-month-old's, or one- or two-year-old's crying. You can view these feelings as an extreme version of the same set of biological reactions described in respect of the Uncomfortable category. When we experience panic, fear, alarm and an overwhelming impulse to escape our situation, it is really that old favourite, fight, flight or freeze. We often experience these Frightening emotional reactions to the kind of crying all parents dread because it's associated with possible emergencies. You know, that sudden screaming cry that raises the hair on the back of any caring parent's neck. We are instantly in high alert mode, the frightening feelings being driven by involuntary biological changes designed to optimise our ability to either cope with, or run away from, a crisis.

This isn't a first-aid manual or a medical reference book, so I won't be dealing with information on how to respond to the – thankfully rare – serious emergencies you might be unfortunate enough to encounter. Instead, I'll focus on those times when, even though our palms are sweating and our mouths dry with panic, the problem turns out to be relatively minor. Like a two-year-old who has managed to bend their own fingers backwards momentarily, an eighteen-month-old who has bumped their head on a sandpit surround or a one-year-old who has their leg jammed sideways in their high chair as you go to lift them out.

With your newborn, you are much more likely to feel panicked for no good reason other than your own as yet untried prowess as a parent. That said, a screaming newborn with a sudden high-pitched cry should always be taken seriously and an immediate medical opinion obtained. Much better to be labelled unnecessarily anxious than to risk some hurt to your tiny infant going untreated. I know we often want to avoid thinking of ourselves, or being seen by others, as 'neurotic' parents. In my opinion we need to stand alongside our under-threes, ready to act as their champion and interpreter in whatever trials and tribulations might face them, however panicky, fearful or alarmed we might feel. Just remember, although those emotions are not at all comfortable, they can be brilliant at galvanising us into action, just exactly when our baby or toddler needs our help most. Heart pounding, stomach churning and eyes wide open, we rush to the aid of our under-three and do our damnedest to rescue them from whatever has threatened their safety.

Not much time for *Best Guessing* yourself then! But here's what you can do, either during or after the emergency, real or imagined. And boy, do we imagine! My heart rate is up just recalling some of the shrieks I've responded to in the past. Fingers slammed shut in doors, lips split from falling off swings, egg-shaped bumps on heads in sharp contact with hard edges, and, my personal best *and* worst, being six months pregnant, carrying a one-year-old and being menaced by a group of wild wolf-like dogs halfway up a mountain in the Himalayas!

Step 1: Assess the situation. This means using our brains to augment and/or override our heightened emotions. Tell yourself to THINK as well as FEEL.

Step 2: Decide what to do. At this point you have grasped what's wrong with your under-three, or at least made a pretty informed guess about what's happened. Tell yourself to ACT as well as THINK and FEEL.

Step 3: Take action. This is where your frightened emotions and sensible thoughts come together to provide the power and direction for your RESCUE and REPAIR actions.

All this can happen in milliseconds, the big thing is to use your panic, fear, alarm and impulse to run away to jolt you into action, rather than paralysing you. 'Headless chicken' reactions can and do happen, of course, as I remember all too clearly, but we must do our utmost to allow them only a couple of heartbeats. It is a truly amazing experience to find yourself instantaneously responding to and coping with your baby or toddler's frightened and frightening cry. When the emergency has been contained, lots of *Attends* and *Best Guessing* are in order for both of you, plus some soothing stroking all round, if at all feasible.

Well, that about rounds up the different emotional reactions we can have to our baby or toddler's crying. It's good to know that even some of the less admirable responses and feelings are quite normal as long as they aren't present all the time, and we don't act them out at our infant's expense. Crying is meant to trigger us into paying attention to our under-three and it's right that we should experience a variety of emotional reactions as we move in to soothe, comfort or rescue the child.

I finish off this chapter with my Golden Bullets. These act as a sort of memory jogger for when you know you want to do lots of *Attends* and *Best Guesses*, but can't quite remember how they went!

GOLDEN BULLETS

- **No. 1. My Baby Needs . . . Emotional Warmth!**
  Here I discussed making sure your infant is given the emotional warmth and sense of being wanted they need from their parents. Giving your child lots of *Attends* and *Best Guesses* instead of bombarding them with questions improves the parent–baby bond. *Attend* means describing in positive tones how your new arrival, baby, one- and two-year-old are looking, what they are doing, and when they are pleasing you. Use often. A *Best Guess* is when you Mirror, Validate, Empathise and then Resolve to make things feel better for your infant when they are upset, tired, hungry, frustrated, in pain or unwell. Use often.
- **No. 2. What Not To Do! Don't Interrogate Your Child**
  Avoid questioning your child with interrogatives starting with 'who . . .?', 'what . . .?', 'when . . .?', 'where . . .', 'how . . .?' or 'aren't you . . .?', 'didn't you . . .?', or 'won't you . . .?, or ending with an upward inflection. Use as sparely as possible. Try to use six Baby Centred parenting behaviours for every one Baby Directive behaviour. This is your optimum Baby Centred to Baby Directive ratio. Aiming for a six to one ratio like this will make your bond warmer and closer – although a ratio of one to one or even one to two will do quite nicely. However, one Baby Centred parenting behaviour to three or more Baby Directive parenting behaviours will leave your baby and toddler unsure

about your emotional warmth towards them and whether they are really wanted and loved.

- **No. 3. Echoes From Our Past: Feeling Wanted**
Even if you were brought up by a distant or emotionally cool mother or father, you can learn to be the close and warmly expressive parent to the needs of your baby and toddler in order to form a strong bond with you. Giving *Attends* and *Best Guesses*, plus added physical closeness with your baby and toddler, will help you to realise that showing your love and approval will bring you the reward of an intimate and mutually rewarding bond with your child.

- **No. 4. Special Feature: Ignoring Tantrums**
When you start to ignore your toddler he or she may test you out for a short while but you will soon notice a change in their behaviour. You don't have to take my word for it – give it a try. You won't believe how effective it can be and you'll be thrilled with the decrease in those tense, embattled moments that can sour your relationship with your precious infant.

- **No. 5. Special Feature: Birth Fears**
Childbirth is a momentous event and can leave everyone feeling a bit shell-shocked. It can take time to develop a bond with your newborn, so don't despair if you don't immediately 'fall in love' with them. Giving lots of *Attends* and *Best Guesses*, even if it just feels like going through the motions at first, will gradually bring you closer to your baby. Your emotions will become warmer, while meanwhile your newborn will flourish because of your Baby Centred behaviour.

- **No. 6. Special Feature: Coping with Fatigue**
Fatigue from disturbed sleep can leave you feeling exhausted. Chronic tiredness because of broken nights can be an almost unbearable burden. Share the load with trusted relatives and/or friends and sleep when your baby does.

- **No. 7. What To Do Next: My Baby Keeps Crying!**
A crying baby or toddler stirs up a variety of strong emotions in their parents, some of which can be quite uncomfortable, although they are all a natural part of being a responsible mother and father. Managing your own emotions, recognising whether your reactions are positive, undermining, uncomfortable or plain frightening, will ensure you deal with the tears, howls and screams of your little one in the Baby Centred way they need.

Chapter Two

Making Your Baby Feel Loved

WHAT THIS CHAPTER IS ABOUT

This chapter focuses on how to meet your baby's need for approval, thereby giving them the certain knowledge that they are loveable. As we saw in chapter one, being Baby Centred in your approach to your infant enormously enhances the closeness and mutually rewarding aspect of your relationship with them and their attachment to you. Many of the points made in the previous chapter regarding your baby's need for emotional warmth also apply when looking at approval, although there are some important differences. I will try to include these as we tackle the links between love, loveability and being loved from our baby and toddler's perspective. We will be looking in detail at *Praise*, a Baby Centred behaviour of enormous importance.

Also in this chapter:

My Baby Needs . . . Approval

Think about the last time you recall being praised. Unless you're very lucky it's likely to have been a while ago because in our society we are very grudging in our acknowledgement of others' prowess, rarely offering praise for achievements. What about being praised by your own mother or father? Approval from that quarter is always especially rewarding isn't it? Even when we are adults and parents ourselves, we yearn to hear that our efforts have been noticed and acknowledged out loud with love and affection. I know that even as a grandmother, I still found it hugely pleasurable when my activities found favour with my own mother. I am fortunate enough to have had lashings of *Praise* all through my life from my parents (though more about that in Echoes From Our Past). But do babies really need *Praise*? Surely they know we love them? Surely they know we find them loveable? Surely they are aware that our hearts are positively bursting with pride, joy and approval? Well, as a matter of fact they don't, not unless we have shown them through our behaviour.

Babies urgently need our *Praise* if we want them to grow into self-confident little personalities whose positive image of them-selves enables them to deal with life's unavoidable challenges in an assertive yet caring fashion. It's really very good news indeed that most parents find their newborn baby and toddler unutterably delightful. It's sometimes quite difficult to stay on the right side of totally foolish adoration, isn't it? This applies not only to mummy or daddy, but also grandad, grandma, aunts, uncles, cousins, friends, neighbours, and the lady in the Post Office, of course! *Is* it enough just to 'Ooh' and 'Aah' though? Not really, as we need the words as well as the emotional warmth.

When we give our baby or toddler *Praise* along with an *Attend*, they immediately experience a flood of sensations that leaves them with a warm glow inside, because although *Praise* and *Attends* are pretty powerful stuff when used separately, together their strength is awesome. Awesome in that when we give them frequently enough to produce a six to one ratio when compared with the number of *Questions* and *Commands* we are using, the message conveyed to our tiny tot is one of such unalloyed approval that they inevitably come to see themselves as loveable. Remember, loving our infant from nought to three-year-olds must be shown in a language that has meaning for them, and that means adopting a Baby Centred rather than a Baby Directive style of attention.

So, what is *Praise*? I expect we all think we know exactly how to identify *Praise* when we hear it: 'Well done!' 'Good girl!' 'Clever boy!' It's true that when these familiar phrases are delivered in ringing tones of enthusiasm, their emotional impact can equal or even outshine any number of 'Brilliant's and 'Fantastic's given on a dying stress. The words alone are not enough if we want to convey to our under-threes the unequivocal message that they are both loved and loveable. Even the tiniest infants are sensitive to variations in their mummy or daddy's voice, and as they develop into toddlers this exquisite awareness increases.

A *Praise* is therefore more clearly defined as verbal approval given in an emotionally warm manner. The verbal and non-verbal parts of good quality *Praise* are of equal importance and we should never allow ourselves to 'damn' our babies and toddlers with faint praise. You know the sort of thing: 'Oh marvellous. Thanks very much', someone tells you in a heavily sarcastic voice after you've somehow managed to crash your trolley into theirs, sending their groceries skidding across the floor of the supermarket. Sadly, while we know it's uncomfortable to be spoken to like this, we can none the less find ourselves using a similarly deflating approach with our under-threes, especially when we are feeling stressed ourselves. Therefore, in order for our babies and toddlers to grow up with a strong sense of their own value to those very special people – that's you, their parents – we must always use a loving tone of voice when we *Praise*. Equally, we must be completely genuine in what we say and allow our enthusiasm to colour our words.

Your baby and toddler can never be given too much *Praise* if you want them to become individuals who are able to love themselves and therefore be caring and generous towards others. Your *Praises* for your tiny tot's progress in sorting shapes, sifting sand and sticking stars are part of the foundation of their personal growth. Being shown by our parents that we are loveable is one of the single most emotionally, psychologically, socially and personally beneficial experiences a baby and toddler can have. It sets the stage for a healthy attitude towards oneself and others and it would be difficult to over-emphasise its importance.

Without approval from mummy or daddy, those luminaries in an under-three's world, babies can feel unnoticed and unloved. Toddlers can have tantrums in order to attract your attention because being disapproved of is better than being ignored. We have all seen under-threes accomplish some new marvel – another red brick on the tower, another fat bead on the string, another feat of domestic mountaineering – and look immediately to us for signs of approval. They urgently need us to *PRAISE, PRAISE* and *PRAISE* again. Don't disappoint them!

When you are holding your newborn, smiling with your six- to twelve-month-old, moulding Play-Doh with your one-year-old or singing with your two-year-old, you will, of course, be conscious that they are either your delicious little daughter or your gorgeous little son. We may, though, hear ourselves saying that we would love them just the same whatever their gender. It's about that outpouring of protectiveness, approval, nurturing and sensitivity that we can barely contain when we gaze at our very own under-three. Those sorts of fundamental emotions are experienced by all loving parents. But is our behaviour towards our infant similarly unbiased, irrespective of whether they are boys or girls? Do we, for instance, praise them with the same words? Praise them for the same activities? Use the same intonations and inflections? The short answer is a resounding 'No!' So what is going on?

Well, close observation shows that not only do mothers hold babies in a different fashion from fathers, they use different positions for babies they believe to be girls – compared with those they regard as boys. Boy babies are more likely to be held so they are facing out to the delights of the world around them, while girl babies are the ones cradled and protectively folded in close to our bodies. It's not much of a surprise is it, that dads are prone to expose their little sons to stimulation while mums tend to nestle and soothe their baby girls? After all, none of us are simply a 'parent', we are either a mother or a father. No matter how much we might interchange our childcare responsibilities on a daily basis, it remains a fact that all dads are male and all sons are boys. Just as all mums are women and daughters girls. These biological determinants of our gender naturally play a huge role in how we perceive others and them us, including each and every under-three. So, not only do our baby sons and daughters seem interested in lots of the same activities, they can also be seen to show preferences for boyish or girlie toys and play themes.

For example, at preschools up and down the country, as in the one I visit weekly, two-year-olds of either gender can be seen clustered round the sandbox, busily filling and emptying containers, burying plastic elephants and feverishly sweeping up spilled sand with such boundless enthusiasm that very little finds its way into the dustpan, despite their intense concentration on their self-appointed task. Similarly in play groups across the land, there are huge numbers of girls tottering round in full princess get-up, often with additional fairy wings and soft toys in tow. Meanwhile, the boys have adapted a twig into a weapon of some sort and are charging about in small gangs uttering warlike whoops. Of course, there are bound to be exceptions to these observations. Only a few days ago I had the pleasure of watching Sam, a boy of almost three, tenderly tucking in a knitted scarecrow doll he had previously clutched haphazardly round the neck when flying around the playground at an alarming rate. In contrast I had also witnessed the angelic Eleanor, beribboned curls bobbing, repeatedly trying to smash her plastic pedal play car into dear little Daniel's legs.

So, just as we must acknowledge that under-threes, whether girls or boys, share many characteristics, we should also remember that our daughters and sons are different on several important scores. The same principle applies to *Praise*, so let's be clear then, when we are praising our child – whether newborn or three-year-old – we should not be afraid to celebrate their being either a boy or a girl, nor should we shy away from highlighting features which these tiny tots have in common.

I want to let you know about the various kinds of *Praise* there can be. If we think of *Praise* as synonymous with being given a reward, it becomes immediately apparent that there is enormous scope for age-appropriate rewards, just as there are rewards that wouldn't do. For example, newborns would not relish a scooter as an early present for sleeping through the night. Nor would a one-year-old drool over the prospect of a pack of Happy Family playing cards, though they might well cover them in dribble if handed them to look at. One-year-olds are not keen on money and two-year-olds adore purses and tiny rucksacks.

But whatever might be your under-threes' special favourite *Reward* at any particular given point in their development, the same categories of *Reward* and *Praise* apply. They are:

- Rewards given only after a specific behaviour has occurred: 'Labelled Praise'.
- Rewards given irrespective of behaviour: 'Unlabelled Praise'.

TYPES OF REWARD

Primary rewards
Food
Drink
Physical warmth
Physical comfort

Social and emotional rewards
Praise: labelled and unlabelled
Attends and *Best Guesses*

Secondary rewards
Smiley faces
Stars
Stickers

Material rewards
Money
Toys
Games
Equipment

Activity rewards
Singing and music
Dancing
Swinging
Story reading
Stimulating games
Interesting outings
Painting, gluing, building and dismantling

The last category shown in the box could go on for ever, as the permutations are truly limitless. But for the purpose of this chapter I am going to focus on the social and emotional group of rewards, with *Praise* as the main object of our attention. First of all, your newborn. What *Praise* can we give, in those early weeks of life, that will make a rich and durable basis for that all-important lesson we want to teach them: that they are loved and loveable? A good start would be where it is their little personality rather than their behaviours that are highlighted. This would be an example of *Unlabelled Praise*. I'll be saying more about *Labelled Praise* in a minute.

Here are a few examples you could try. Remember, Baby Centred behaviour tells your very recent arrival that you find them loveable. They won't understand the words as such, but they will certainly grasp your message of love.

Praise for Babies Aged Under Six Months
- 'You are so cute! I adore you.'
- 'I think you are good enough to eat! I love you so much.'
- 'You are the most marvellous baby in the world! I think you are gorgeous.'

- 'You are the most wonderful, beautiful baby! I love you every minute of every day.'
- 'I know who the bestest baby is! It's you, sweetheart!'

These are *Unlabelled Praises* that can be given irrespective of behaviour. Don't forget to *Praise* yourself, too. After all, you are the creator of the most magical bundle of all – your baby. Buy yourself and/or your partner a little memento of these early weeks. Perhaps sit together holding hands while you congratulate yourselves on giving birth to such a gifted little individual, or have a bubble bath, alone or with your partner. It's about celebrating your rightful place as miraculous baby producer(s), so don't stint on giving yourself and each other at least a few of the honours.

Next, the six- to twelve-month-olds. In the second half of the first twelve months, it is just as important to continue with the same style of baby-focused *Unlabelled Praise* and really you should try to use this type of *Praise* every day of your child's life. There's plenty of time for them to learn that we are deeply impressed by their latest achievements. Meanwhile you can be driving home the one lesson that it is never too early to take on board: that mummy and/or daddy love you to distraction!

Praise for Babies Aged Six to Twelve Months

- 'You are my most darling baby! I love you so much, I'm going to give you a really scrummy kiss!'
- 'Mmmm! You are so cuddly . . . let me snuggle up. Oooh, I love you millions.'
- 'Let me give you a little kiss because you are so delicious and I love you to bits.'
- 'You are so precious to me, my angel, and I love you with all my heart.'
- 'You are my star, my brightest star. I'll love you for ever and ever.'

You'll notice the constant presence of the three most magical words in the entire world: 'I love you'. Don't underestimate the awesome power they wield and how their absence can breed uncertainty, longing and loss. Fortunately, lots of parents find themselves overflowing with warmth, wonder and generosity towards their babies, so it's easy to let this bubble up into the actual words 'I love you'. Even if you are taking time to warm up to your infant, still make sure you are saying the words several times a day. It only takes a millisecond and the benefits are lifelong. Build it into all your Baby Centred behaviours because it functions as a hugely important strand of the bond between you and your baby.

You in turn will be enormously rewarded when your one- and two-year-old throws their arms round your neck saying, 'I love you, Mummy' or 'I love you, Daddy'. I challenge anyone and everyone to deny experiencing total meltdown of the heart at those fabulous moments. For instance, at a recent nursery concert I saw several parents and grandparents, utterly disarmed by their apparently rocket-fuelled under-threes launching themselves into a close embrace with the beloved grown-up, clasping sticky little hands around Mummy, Daddy, Nana or Grampa's necks while saying, 'I love you'. The joy was so evident on their faces, and if adults can experience this, think of the emotional impact on a six- to twelve-month-old on hearing those same three words!

Even if you were brought up in a family where it was extremely rare to hear these amazing words, it is never too late to start changing your behaviour and become more emotionally expressive of your tender feelings. This goes for dads as well as mums, grandads as well as grandmas. We all know we can't alter the past, but we *can* change the present and therefore the future. Our babies' brains can be encouraged to develop positive and constructive neural networks as a result of the *Praise* we give them, so don't hold back even if it feels uncomfortable at first. As I may be at risk of becoming a bore on the 'I love you' topic, I will move on to '*Labelled Praise*' for one-year-olds.

Praise for One-Year-Olds
- 'Great try! I can see you're a fantastic walker!'
- 'Wow! Fabulous digging. I think you're king of the castle.'

- 'Ace steering! You're the best bike rider I know!'
- 'Brilliant hand printing. I think your painting is the best in the whole wide world.'
- 'What marvellous swimming! You are the fastest water baby I've ever seen.'
- 'Stupendous dancing! I can hardly believe my eyes, you're such a wonderful little mover!'

Unlike *Unlabelled Praise*, these *Labelled Praises* are given for specific behaviour – no matter that their 'walking' is at first a mere totter, their 'digging' a sort of sideways swipe with the flat of the hand, their 'steering' more wishful thinking than actual going in the direction they want to go, their hand prints the result of patient effort on your part alone, and their 'dancing' being jiggled up and down on your lap. We should always *Praise* effort as well as achievement, which we can sometimes forget to do. There is a fine line between encouraging our under-threes to move on to the next phase of whatever skill they are busy trying to develop, and becoming prey to unrealistic notions of what they should be managing. Our one-year-olds need us to demonstrate how loved and loveable they are by giving them genuine and unstinting *Praise* for their own individual rate of progress.

We must steer away from ending up with any implicit message that they are doing well, *but . . .*' In that 'but . . .' lies the difference between our under-three knowing they are approved of and fearing they do not match up to our standards of success. It may not seem terribly important at the time, just another little example of how they are lagging behind in comparison to our expectations. But ask yourself this: 'Do I want my child to be secure in the certain knowledge that they are beloved or am I so concerned with pushing them on to the next step that I am willing to sacrifice their self-confidence and damage our bond into the bargain?' The answer is 'of course not!', and an important aspect of preventing such an unwelcome outcome is *Praise*, *Praise* and *Praise* again. *Praise* their liveliness. *Praise* their sleepiness. *Praise* their cheeks. *Praise* their fingernails. *Praise* their gentleness. *Praise* their strength. *Praise* their smile. *Praise* their frown of concentration. And, most of all, *Praise* them simply for being themselves, because the real message is *spare the praise and you'll spoil the child.*

When talking about using *Praise* with two-year-olds, we should not forget that the first three years of our tiny tot's life sees a pace of development that surpasses even the tremendous changes in the surge towards adolescence. We need to keep up with their latest attempts at mastering how to put their shoes on the right feet, their gloves on the right fingers and their hats on at an angle that doesn't entirely blind them. It's all too tempting, isn't it, to laugh indulgently at our two-year-old's antics with an ice cream, a handful of currants or a cup full of juice. They look so cute and adorable don't they? Ice cream up to their eyebrows. Currants inside their tops and juice everywhere except in their mouths. However, our smiles and laughter, no matter how loving from our point of view, might not always be welcomed by our two- or three-year-olds. To them, soaking a sheet of paper with glue and then lovingly placing a single piece of glitter in the bottom left-hand corner is a serious business. Their concentration can be so complete that they hold their breath momentarily. Our laughter can be felt as a kind of put-down by two-year-olds, so it's best to smile behind your hand while you *Praise* their Herculean efforts and delightful personality.

Of course, there will be delicious moments when your two-year-old clearly enjoys being the focus of parental glee and will repeat their actions until you are quite smiled out! We are often the ones who tire first, aren't we? Of course, at times they are genuinely funny and we can't help giggling at their antics. But watch out for those tell-tale signs that they are feeling unsure, embarrassed and confused by your reaction, because those signals indicate that your enjoyment is not matched by your under-three. You know the kind of signals:

- lowering their eyes
- breaking off eye contact
- averting their gaze
- hanging their head

- becoming motionless and speechless
- walking away
- pushing someone
- kicking their foot out and saying 'Stop it! Don't laugh!'

In extreme cases they may burst into tears. The best way to make sure that your laughter doesn't undermine their new-found courage in attempting to make you some yummy dinner – out of Play-Doh or sand usually – is to give two-year-olds Baby Centred *Praise*, throw in an *Attend* and finish up with 'I *do* love you'. OK, here are some examples:

Praise for Two-Year-Olds

- 'I think you are a very, very, *very* good cook, darling. Fancy you making me this lovely chocolate cupcake at play group. Thank you, sweetie. Mmmm, I'm going to eat it all up. Mmmm, I could eat you too because you're so delicious. I love you.'
  This is when you pretend to wolf down the rather stiff, strangely shaped brown goo you have proudly been offered. We have all done it and survived, so be brave!
- 'You have put your own boots on, sweetheart. What a clever little poppet you are! I love my poppet I do!'
  This is when you let them walk around with their boots on the wrong feet for a bit, looking like a complete clown whilst you try to stifle your laughter. Don't worry, even though it feels as though you might choke, most parents live to tell the tale!
- 'Darling one! I can see you are really swinging all by yourself. Brilliant. You are so grown-up these days. I love you millions.'
  This is when you realise that despite much waving of legs, it's you who is putting 98 per cent of the physical effort into their movement on the swing. In between gasping for breath and trying to avoid being knocked down, remember how delicious that sweeping motion is, and call out 'Wheeeee!'

- 'You sang the Christmas Pudding song all the way through by yourself! Fantastic singing, precious! I love your singing and I love you!'
  This is when you have sat, truly awestruck, through three verses of the seasonal song, with only the words 'Christmas Pudding' at the end being at all audible. All you are required to do is clap wildly and call for more – on your own head be it!
- 'What a top star you are! You have read that whole book to me, sweetheart, just like a big two-year-old who will be going to play group soon. I love having a big girl/boy and so I love you.'
  This is when, although you are looking forward to two mornings a week free of childcare responsibilities, you also have a distinctly sinking feeling about launching them into the big wide world. The tug can be really painful, but we have to be brave!
- 'Brilliant painting, darling! You have made a beautiful picture of a . . .' (Flower? Boat? Potato? Car? Princess? Sword?) 'It's magic! I love your painting and I *love you too!*'
  This is when you have spotted that instead of happy scribbling, your two- to three-year-old has obviously attempted to draw something. But what exactly? Hence the wisdom of holding back on your own probably off-target guesses, instead leaving a judicious pause during which they can enlighten you with their very own notion.

Well, that's it on *Praise*. Now I'll talk about *Criticism*, the Baby Directive behaviour that is the direct opposite of Baby Centred *Praise* and how we can protect our child from its emotionally damaging influence.

What Not To Do: Don't Criticise

I realise, of course, that none of us sets out to be critical towards our under-threes. Perish the thought! The trouble is that, like all our other good intentions, they can fall by the wayside when we are faced with the rigours of everyday family life. One of the ways we can strengthen our resolve is to try to put ourselves in our child's little shoes. Another is to think back to how we felt when our own parents were uncomplimentary towards us. A further exercise, if you are feeling brave, is to swap a couple of pretend put-downs with a friend.

So exactly what is it that makes a *Criticism* so hurtful to us? Well, perhaps if we look at some examples it might become clearer. Let's put ourselves in our two-year-old's place. Suppose they have just made a painfully tense effort to pour milk from a jug into their plastic cup, but inevitably spilled some on the table. What would we, as a two- to three-year-old urgently wish would happen next? Obviously, to be forgiven, tenderly reassured that everything is all right, the puddle mopped up and all restored to pre-accident light and harmony.

But what might actually happen? Take your pick from these:

- 'Oh no! Not again! I *told* you not to try that!'
- 'Look at that *mess*! I've only just cleaned up!'
- 'You're so *clumsy*! You're not to be trusted!'
- 'You did that on *purpose*! You're just trying to make me angry!'
- 'Clear that up at once, you *mucky* little thing!'

Pretty crushing to be on the receiving end, wouldn't you agree? And not likely to improve your child's attachment towards you, nor yours to them. Do you recall being criticised by your parents when you were a child? Or do you remember being praised? Or both, at different times? Which gives you, still, a warm glow and which a cold shudder? It's not hard to predict. The memories that can undermine us for the rest of our lives probably include some examples like these:

- 'You'll *never* manage that in a month of Sundays!'
- 'You're *completely* useless!'
- 'You are *so* totally stupid!'

- 'You're *bound* to mess it all up!'
- 'It's *all* your fault!'

Do you notice the emphatic nature of the words used in these examples? Each italic word is like a nail being driven into the heart of any individual's self-confidence. When parents repeatedly use *Critical* phrases like this they are slowly but surely eroding their infant's chances of developing into a vibrant, self-confident and well-adjusted child, teenager and adult. Our children can be such easy targets. They are, after all, quite a lot younger and smaller than us. *Of course* they can't manage the same tasks as us. *Of course* they will fail at first when learning a new skill. *Of course* they don't know as much as us. *Of course* they make mistakes, though it is rarely all their fault!

So what is the point of voicing out loud our illogical *Criticisms*? Will overt censure improve the situation? The short answer to that question is no. The plain fact is that *Praise* builds up the positive connections in our brains that provide the basis for an upbeat self-image, while *Criticism* has the opposite effect. That's a clear message for all of us as parents and grandparents, not to mention our other roles of partner, pal, colleague or simply day-to-day member of society.

Just put yourself in touch with the difference in your own reactions, even as an adult, to *Praise* versus *Criticism* and you will immediately realise how energising it is to be verbally rewarded and how utterly deflating to be devalued. So hold back! Button your lip! And . . .

WAIT UNTIL YOU CAN SAY SOMETHING POSITIVE INSTEAD

In other words, use the *Attends* technique (pages 18–19), not because I say so, but because it works!

What about taking the courageous option? Swapping pseudo-*Criticisms* with a friend. It must be a best friend, otherwise feelings could easily be hurt during the exercise, however mature and sophisticated you had planned to be! Be prepared to laugh, joke, even fall about, as role play can be enormous fun. However, you must also listen out for those inner voices that will be telling you your 'Ouch Factor' is taking a bit of a battering. These are just a minor version of what our under-threes experience when we use *Criticism*. This is what they are feeling when we see them:

- Drop a quivery lower lip
- Splash some tears down their cheeks
- Take in a few sobbing breaths
- Open their mouths to howl

Naturally, as our babies and toddlers become schoolchildren, adolescents and grown-ups themselves, they learn to hide their bruised and battered egos – at least some of the time – but the damage can be deep.

Let's be realistic, though. On occasion, each one of us can be taxed beyond all reason and there will be times when our normally loving attitude evaporates and a spontaneous *Criticism* will escape. If and when this happens to you, try out these tips for a constructive resolution of your emotional outburst:

- Forgive yourself for being only human.
- Apologise for having been unkind and unjustified.
- *Praise* your under-three for making a good effort to:
     Bring up their wind
     Feed themselves with a spoon
     Sit still on their chair
     Pat the baby gently
     Talk quietly
     Share the biscuits
     Be chatty

The list could go on and on. We have to keep in mind that as our infants attempt to do virtually anything and everything, things will go wrong sometimes. The best focus for our energies at these times is to *Ignore* the mistake, *Praise* the attempt, and swallow the *Criticism*. That particular little sequence of Baby Centred parenting is undoubtedly an important part of the route to a closer, warmer and more secure attachment between you and your under-three. So, in brief:

MAKE SURE THAT FOR EVERY CRITICISM YOU SUPPLY SIX PRAISES

It's one of the biggest favours you can do your baby or toddler as their unique personality begins to emerge.

Echoes From Our Past: Feeling Smothered

In this section, I am going to focus on how, despite the best of intentions, we can sometimes turn out to be over-involved and therefore unrewarding as parents. But first something on my own childhood experiences of being praised, plus a little on why being in my father's good books brought me such great joy. As you might have gathered from the 'Echoes From Our Past' section in chapter one, my father's family were much more tight-lipped than my mother's on the topic of love and relationships. They were also pretty demanding and quick to criticise rather than praise or reward. Maudie, my paternal grandmother, was particularly keen on sneering at romance and other 'lovey-dovey stuff'. No wonder that her two sons grew up to be men who only become effusively affectionate after a few drinks.

Not that my father was cold or unrewarding, rather his praise was often quite difficult to attain, even for his 'Golden Girl'. Of course, I had a heavy emotional investment in seeking out his approval because, looking back, I can see how his absence during the Second World War left me uncertain as to his love for me.

Hence my treasured pencils and dolls that my mother bought locally but pretended had been sent home from my father in Egypt. His praise, certainly as I was growing up, was 'Labelled' and depended on the success of my achievements.

My father's generation of dads had often been brought up by emotionally cool parents and therefore found it difficult to express their approval unless it was to congratulate them for coming first, being best or carrying off top prize. Meanwhile it seems mothers of that era were allowed more emotional leeway with their children, though this was often seen by the males in the family as foolish over-fondness.

So, does *Unlabelled Praise* equal being over-involved? Well, I don't think so, although there may well be professionals around who claim *Unlabelled Praise* should be rationed as too much can interfere with a child's personality development. Other professionals such as myself are of the opinion that everyone, including the under-threes and their parents, function much better on a regular diet of both forms of *Praise*, Labelled and Unlabelled. My own childhood was a mixture such as this, with my father delivering more Labelled and my mother more Unlabelled – a gender bias that still exists today. For example, when I was still quite young, though aged over three years, my father focused on *Praise* for the following:

- Tidying up toys
- Painting and drawing
- Reading
- Climbing a tree
- Riding a bike

As I grew older, the list changed somewhat, as it should, to:

- Completing school homework
- Getting up to do a paper round
- Coming in on time
- Passing exams

And my mother? She had a gift of somehow melding together the two types of *Praise* in one sentence, rather like this, 'You are such a sweetheart, Suzie, really generous. Look at the way you have tidied up all the toys. Well done, darling. What a great little helper you are, thank you, precious.' or, 'Suzie my love, you have done an absolutely terrific job of painting that picture of a bus, a lovely yellow and orange bus. Good choice of colours, poppet. You really are my bestest Suzie, you have been concentrating. Clever, that's what you are, my pet!'

The result of my parents' differing styles of *Praise* was that I was much more secure in my mother's love than my father's. I believe to this day that had my dad been more forthcoming with *Unlabelled Praise* we could have enjoyed an even closer relationship.

So how can we tell if our efforts at parenting our children are over-involved? What I suggest is you run your eye over the bullet points below and see if you recognise as your own any of the features set out:

- Too close emotionally
- Interfering
- Over-protective
- Intrusive
- Anxious

When we are over-involved parents, we are pretty good at justifying our behaviour to our child. Distant parents rationalise their style of interaction with their children as good, because being emotionally close to anyone threatens them, not their child. Similarly, over-involved parents claim that it is necessary to be perpetually on their offspring's case in order to keep them safe, while it is actually the grown-up who is the anxious one. I know it may seem a bit rich to be urging you to be closer one minute and the next to beware of crowding your little one, but that's because it's all a matter of balance. Never easy, is it?

When we are over-involved the difficulty from our baby and toddler's perspective is they almost literally have no space to become an individual with their own personal sense of identity. Even under-threes can feel that their parents are almost living their lives for them and problems can develop, problems like:

- Fragile sense of identity
- Feeling smothered
- Fearfulness
- Resentment
- Frustration
- Problem behaviours
- Emotional explosiveness

Of course, we don't want our children to experience these uncomfortable sensations, quite the reverse. So why are some of us lured into an over-involved style of bringing up our babies and toddlers? Well, no doubt it won't come as any surprise if I suggest that a glance back at our own childhood might be enlightening. Take a look. Did you feel smothered to the point of exploding with frustration? Were you afraid to do much at all unless your parents were close at hand? What about chronic resentment towards your mother and father because nothing, not even your thoughts and feelings, were yours alone? If any of this rings a bell, then it's likely that your parents found it difficult to give you enough room to breathe, let alone develop as a separate individual in your own right!

Over-involved parents often overprotect their children, so you could have memories of desperately wanting to do things for yourself, only to become frustrated by your parents' unwillingness to let you venture into the unknown without their constant supervision. Perhaps you struggled to make and maintain friendships with other children as teenagers because, before you could even get to know them, your mum or dad had become a key member of your little gang. Even though you probably understand now, that it was your parents' own anxieties about your safety and welfare that drove them to remain literally and figuratively close to you, this does not necessarily free you from the implicit message that you can't manage on your own, however big you've grown.

It might seem odd to talk in the same breath about over-involved parenting and issues of loss that can persist right into our adulthood as the two concepts superficially seem polar opposites. Not so. If I were the child of an intrusive parent, I would be losing my personal space, I would be losing my chance at independence. But most of all I would be losing the opportunity to develop a strong sense of self identity. These losses, if we can't restore them sufficiently, will hang around and actively interfere with all our relationships, including the Parent/Baby bond. Horror of horrors, we can sometimes watch ourselves turn into the same kind of overanxious and unnecessarily protective parent we swore we would never be.

So there we are, truly wanting to give our children the love that will encourage them towards self-confidence, when the message that comes across is our extremely undermining conviction of their inability to cope. Over-involved parents don't praise enough, they are just too anxious.

Case Study One

I remember one young mother whose anxiety levels had reached phenomenal heights in the wake of her first baby being born. She became so preoccupied with the notion that her newborn would catch an infection and become seriously ill that she went to enormous lengths to protect him from all possible sources of contamination. Bella, as I shall call her, allowed no one to kiss baby Liam, not even herself, for fear he would contract herpes. Nor would she take him to Mother and Baby groups, for similar reasons.

Her own interactions with her baby son were, by the time we met, characterised by such anxiety for his health that she was hardly able to enjoy his company and had herself become quite isolated. Fortunately, Liam's daddy realised that his wife's reactions were outside the normal range of worries that all new parents feel, and contacted health-care professionals.

Bella's own mother was a doting but overprotective grandmother, and Bella herself was helped to see that by transferring their fears on to Liam, they were actually doing much more harm than good. Of course, it's not easy to move away from an ingrained style of interacting with others, though after approximately six months of working with the family the two women were able to challenge their thinking about the dangers to Liam – at least for much of the time. Liam had an easy temperament and so soon adapted quite happily to calmer, less intrusive and anxious attention from his mummy and nana.

Case Study Two

Charlie, not his real name, was overjoyed at the birth of his baby daughter Nadia after some years of struggling to start a family with his partner Joanne. Successful at last, the couple quite naturally regarded Nadia as a priceless treasure. However, while Joanne was able to maintain a balanced level of loving interest in Nadia, Charlie's attitude bordered on the obsessive. He would ring at least once an hour during his working day and insisted on Joanne giving him a minute-by-minute rundown on the minutiae of Nadia's progress since his previous call.

Joanne understood Charlie's anxieties but began to feel that he did not trust her to look after their baby girl properly, and became resentful. Charlie's mother, known in her family as a fusspot, made matters worse by siding with her son. Little Nadia could barely take a breath without an ensuing debate on how it was to be categorised. She was becoming difficult to soothe and settle whenever her daddy was around. Eventually Charlie realised that his adored baby seemed to be very much more happy and relaxed when he did as Joanne advised and literally took a step back from Nadia.

The couple were helped to arrive at an understanding of how their own childhood experiences were influencing their parenting style with Nadia. In Charlie's case, it was a family where anxious tensions were a permanent fixture. Slowly but surely, Nadia's father learned to use the energy he had spent in doom-laden prophecies of disaster to regularly give his little girl a wide variety of *Praises*. Nadia is now a buoyant three-year-old who is settling into playgroup very well.

Supposing you began, like Charlie, to become aware that you were burdening your baby or toddler with anxieties that were to do with your own family history rather than giving them the space to develop into individual personalities with hearts and minds of their own? What could you do to help achieve a more balanced parenting style? Let me give you some ideas on the subject. A good starting point is to use self-instruction. Verbal is good, but verbal-plus-written is much, much better. So, take the time to jot down and recite these reminders repeatedly on how to become a more balanced mum or dad:

- I *can* learn a new, more balanced way of parenting.
- I know there are links between my own childhood and the kind of parent I am now, and that is a very important step in the right direction.
- My under-three needs me to give them more space to be themselves so they can develop their own special identities.
- When I give more space to my child, I will also be giving more space to myself.
- I can learn to be myself. There is nothing to be afraid of.

We can all change our behaviour so long as we move forward in tiny steps. Think of yourself as building up inner strength for progress every time you self-instruct. It's a lot more positive than the self-destruct button we sometimes go for!

You can also try another avenue of support in your efforts to be a more relaxed and less intrusive parent: talking with relatives and friends. When you decide to put some energy into your venture, include things like:

- Discussing with your partner the changes you intend to make so you can become less anxious about your child.
- Confiding in your best friend your plans, hopes and fears about trying to avoid burdening your baby and toddler with your own as yet unresolved issues of loss.
- Talking to a trusted individual about how you believe your

childhood is linked with your over-involved parenting style and why you want to change.

Always be ready to listen in your turn as, when we open up to others, they often feel able to share some of their own thoughts and feelings, plans for the future and experiences from their past. There are, of course, practical steps you can take. See if any on my list suit you:

- Work out what small and very safe things your baby or toddler can do alone or with another trusted adult and take the plunge of allowing them to go ahead. However, I cannot stress enough that this is not about risking your tiny tot's safety even for a second. It *is* about you sometimes taking a tiny step back emotionally.
- Learn to relax by using a recording made for that purpose. When you can reliably make use of your relaxation training, use the techniques when you feel panicky about letting go of your baby and toddler.
- Make progress by gradually increasing the degree of separateness you give your little one so there are no shocks for anyone involved.
- Tell your baby and toddler about love and togetherness. You can never start having a family dialogue on emotions and relationships too early, but don't expect any sophisticated responses from your little ones just yet!
- Make yourself a star chart spelling out your short-term and final goals. Reward yourself for the progress you make with stickers that can be converted into treats at the end of each week. Or each day, at first, if it makes you feel better.
- *Praise* yourself in no uncertain terms for each step you make towards giving your baby and toddler the room they need to develop their own personality.

When we change our behaviour we are inevitably having an impact on our thoughts and feelings. A family I know of were not at all convinced of this idea and were pretty resistant about even trying to disentangle their own unresolved issues of loss from their baby's need for space of their own. After some considerable persuasion on my part, the two parents agreed to give the practical tips I've listed above a one-week trial. The young father found relaxation training a great help while the baby's mother went for the praise and star-chart tactics. When I caught up with them a couple of weeks later, they both said how pleased they were with their progress. The mum had earned a manicure session as a treat and the father claimed to be able to relax and de-stress at the drop of a hat.

Naturally, things do not always work out so well. Suppose you were feeling particularly anxious and emotionally distressed at the mere thought of your baby having to be cared for by a friend for two hours? How best could you help yourself to separate from your tiny tot if you hadn't time for thorough de-stressing? Well, try giving yourself the following emergency helpline message:

I CAN LET GO AND GIVE MY BABY THE SPACE THEY MUST HAVE TO DEVELOP THEIR OWN IDENTITY

Or what about a more punchy version?

I CAN KEEP MY BABY AND TODDLER CLOSE BY LETTING GO

Or even,

RELAX – LET GO – BE CLOSE

I know letting go and staying close sound contradictory, but in this case, where we are dealing with the overspill of your yet-to-be resolved emotional fallout from childhood on to your under-three, then one really does follow the other. That's because you are letting go of the smothering anxiety you feel. This very act sufficiently frees up the quality of your bond with your tiny tot to allow them to emerge as unique individuals who actively want to be in close psychological contact with their now more relaxed mummy and/or daddy. Don't let the fears and uncertainties that many of us drag around, courtesy of our own parents' over-involved style of attention, prevent us from being relaxed and confident enough to bring up our under-threes in a more balanced manner.

If you try the self-help suggestions in this chapter, there is no reason why you shouldn't succeed in your quest to give your baby and toddler the best possible opportunities of becoming the sort of personality who is at ease with themselves and the people and world around them.

Special Feature: Good-Enough Parenting

However comprehensive our grasp on parenting principles and child development theories, we should *always* be aware that perfect parenting, just like the ideal marriage, simply does not exist. Never has and never will. So where does child development theory feature in our attempts to become adequate parents? First of all, though, what is it? I suppose it's best described as the body of knowledge that encompasses the sequencing of children's progress across all their different areas of functioning. Physical, motor and sensory, cognitive, language and play, social, attachment, temperament and personality, behavioural, emotional and psychosexual, as well as their responses to education. When I am preparing a report on an individual child's developmental profile, I always include observations and/or test results on each of these areas. Of course, I am not medically qualified and so any comments on physical health included are based only on my own observations.

But how would I know what inference to give an observation that at six months a baby was unable to support their own head? How would I react to a one-year-old who was speaking two languages as fluently as most five-year-olds? What should I make of a six-month-old who can walk and a two-year-old who is still shuffling round, albeit pretty rapidly, on their bottom? Does it matter that some two-year-olds are brilliant at inset puzzles while others would rather mess around in a sandbox? In essence, how do we know what to expect? What is normal, and does our under-three qualify as a slow, medium or fast developer?

Child development theory attempts to answer such pressing questions by providing clear descriptions of what most children do and when they start doing it. The information used comes from an ever-growing body of research studies that aims to chart the developmental profiles of large populations of children. Various nations carry out their own investigations and then cross-cultural comparisons are made, highlighting similarities, divergencies and new data.

Professionals involved in such work come from a wide range of disciplines such as obstetrics, neurology, psychology, sociology, education, psychiatry and community health. One of the aims is to establish the normal range of development so that the children who fall outside its parameters can receive special provision to compensate for any difficulties. Another aim is to provide parents with information on what to expect from their offspring from birth onwards, taking into account all the areas of development mentioned above. So child development theory gives us valuable insight into how our under-three is developing compared with other babies and toddlers of similar age.

As parents we naturally hope for our little ones to be not only normal but supernormal! Not only walking and talking, but also ahead of their peers. Not only drawing but doing potato people while others are still scribbling. *Not only* able to count to ten, but far in advance of the rest, put ten – and only ten – bricks in a heap or, even better, a tower. Not only . . . I could go on for several pages like this, so eager are we to see our child triumphing over the competition! But I won't. I know you get the message that child development theory should give us a rule of thumb for use in encouraging our child towards the next step in their progress, not a rod with which to beat ourselves or our precious infant.

Child development theory is much more focused on studying via observation how we grow and mature rather than hypothesising about invisible psychoanalytical process. My advice about how to incorporate child development theory is this:

- Focus on your baby and toddler's uniqueness, it is a treasure beyond price. Your relationship will flourish.
- Avoid making comparisons with other children as much as possible, they can be damaging to your bond with your child.
- Once you have assured yourself that your under-three is within the normal range of development for their age, relax, enjoy their company and strengthen your attachment.
- The broad normal range really is quite wide, so do not worry unnecessarily as unfounded anxiety on your part could harm your relationship with your child.
- You can encourage your baby and toddler to move on to the next stage in their development, but never push. If you do, the quality of your bond with them could be put at risk.
- Make sure you realistically align your expectations of your tiny tots with their individual potential. Misjudged expectations can seriously dent the security of your little one's bond with you.

Special Feature: Baby Blues and Post-natal Depression

Contrary to the myth of joyous early parenthood, a substantial percentage of couples experience Baby Blues. I say couples because when this low mood strikes it affects everyone in the baby's life. That includes dads, siblings, grandparents, relatives and best friends. One of the major problems with Baby Blues is closely related to our unwillingness to admit either to ourselves or to others that we are feeling so overwhelmed and down. We also tend to imagine that every other mother or father of a new baby is managing famously, making us the odd ones out, the failures, the bad parents. Though it's clear that the whole family is involved when Baby Blues descend, the main sufferer is almost exclusively the infant's mother.

New mums, after the euphoria following a successful delivery has waned somewhat, can find their mood deteriorating quite rapidly. All sorts of anxieties related to the huge responsibility of parenthood gatecrash the cosy scene, aided and abetted by a swift change in hormonal levels. We are more aware now of the influential role hormones play in our lives. What needs to be understood by everyone involved with Baby Blues, excepting the baby of course, whom we would hope to escape unscathed, is that anyone who over a nine-month period has developed four hundred times the normal level of a particular hormone will have been significantly if temporarily altered by the experience.

To then undergo over a very few days a crashing fall in those levels is extremely painful. But this is what happens to every woman during pregnancy and immediately after giving birth, and when you think that some psychiatrists have called oestrogen, the substance in question, the 'happy hormone', then it's no wonder that Baby Blues are so common. It seems that at least half of us experience something of this sort around three days after our baby has been born for about two to three weeks. It appears that if our oestrogen levels don't take this severe dive, our breast-milk production can be seriously hampered, though more on that when we talk about post-natal depression.

I remember only too clearly the physically and emotionally agonising simultaneous occurrence of oestrogen draining away as breast milk surged in! On the third day following the birth of my first baby, large tears plopped down on to my newborn's head as I encouraged her to latch on to my painfully milk-engorged breasts! Isn't nature wonderful, I thought, as I gently sobbed in time with her vigorous sucking! This went on for a couple of weeks, with my young husband desperately trying to be supportive towards me as I cried and said how happy I was really, all in the same breath. The poor man became so distracted that arrangements were made for me to visit his parents on the coast, until I'd settled in to being a mother. It was a long, long train journey but at least I managed not to weep over my baby daughter's head in front of the closed, packed carriage of assorted travellers.

No such tear control was in evidence in the lonely, windswept front bedroom of my in-laws' isolated home. However, over the next week I gradually began to feel more optimistic and less like a wet tea towel. If you have been in that situation you will know exactly what I mean.

One of the important things to remember about Baby Blues, apart from the fact that it's so frequent it could be called normal, is its limited duration. I assume this is because we adjust reasonably quickly to our much-reduced oestrogen levels (which, by the way, is still higher than it would have been pre-pregnancy). Luckily it's one of those situations where you really can say with complete confidence, 'And this too shall pass.' Everyone in the family needs to be aware of the transitory nature of Baby Blues so they can respond in a measured fashion. This will help you to maintain a positive perspective on your future even when your feelings seem to be running out of control.

But what to do? Given the high proportion of new mums who suffer Baby Blues, what can be done to ease the situation? We know it's temporary and comparatively short-lived, but that doesn't mean we shouldn't try to alleviate the suffering of ourselves and our dear ones. Here are a few suggestions for you to try if you find yourself becoming blue just after giving birth to your baby:

Dos and Don'ts of Coping with the Baby Blues

- **Do** tell your husband/partner, siblings, parents and friends
- **Do** accept their help and commiserations
- **Do** arrange to get more sleep (see tips in chapter one)
- **Do** keep a star chart of all the things you do in a day
- **Do** give yourself praise during these activities
- **Do** treat yourself to a bonus prize for simply getting through the day
- **Do** listen to others when they say you are doing fine – you are
- **Do** tell your nearest and dearest that all gifts for the new mum – that's you – will be very welcome
- **Do** tell yourself, 'I'm doing my best and that's good enough'

- **Don't** keep your feelings to yourself, spit them out
- **Don't** push away offers of help: relax and gracefully receive
- **Don't** battle on single-handedly: it's all hands to the pumps
- **Don't** tell everyone in irritable tones 'I can cope! I can cope!'; own up instead
- **Don't** secretly tell yourself you are a rubbish mother: you are not
- **Don't** push yourself to complete all the things you used to manage pre-baby: there's no need
- **Don't** tell yourself you are a failure because other new mums don't feel like this; lots of them do

So what about dads? Once upon a time it would not have been considered their business, but that's no longer the case, thank heavens. These days there is a widespread expectation that fathers will participate in antenatal classes, be present at the birth, take paternity leave and be sensitive to the emotional needs of their partner. As with so many relationship issues, the practical aspects mostly look after themselves, it's the emotional side of things that can get decidedly sticky. Of course, new dads have their own feelings to deal with, ranging from joyful pride through calculated indifference to bitter resentment and anger. In the normal run of things, it is only when there have been serious medical complications for the new mother that the latter shows up. Attachment problems between the parents often account for the distancing, indifferent father, while for most it is simply a matter for celebration of the creation of a new life.

One of the reasons why men can experience tears of joy but not the Baby Blues is, of course, the fact that their equivalent hormone, testosterone, has remained level, unlike the switchback ride experienced by their pregnant and then lactating partner. Dads can therefore find the first few weeks after birth a much less emotionally demanding time than the mother. That's why fathers must support their partner while they battle the Baby Blues.

Mind you, that's not to say that only new mums have Scary Lists about the Baby Blues. See if you recognise any of the items I've listed below:

Baby Blues

OFFICIAL SCARY LIST

New Mum	New Dad
I feel really down	She doesn't seem very happy
I don't seem to be able to cope	It's all a bit too much for her
I'm exhausted	She's overtired
I didn't realise it would be so much hard work	A baby really is lots of work
I didn't expect to feel like this	Other new mums seem to be OK
It's not how I thought it would be	It's not how I thought it would be

So, not only are the hormones playing up, there's also the sinking feeling brought on by the widening gap between your expectations of family life and the less rosy reality you find yourself grappling with. And it's when you become aware of the sheer size of the discrepancy that the Unofficial Scary List can kick in. You might well recognise some of these points:

Baby Blues

UNOFFICIAL SCARY LIST

New Mum	New Dad
I feel depressed	She seems really down
I simply can't cope	She's completely overwhelmed
I will collapse if I don't get more sleep	Perhaps having a baby was a mistake
I'm the only one in this state	Maybe she should see the doctor
I might be going round the bend	She'll make herself ill at this rate
I'm a failure as a mum	Perhaps she needs a break

Any of this sound familiar? Yes, I thought so! But don't despair, as long as you acknowledge that this is Baby Blues and put into action the list of **Dos** I suggested, then you will find that in two or three weeks you are beginning to feel decidedly brighter and more able to cope with your new role. Meanwhile dads, friends, grandparents and other relatives should feel free to offer help and support and insist that you avail yourself of their loving generosity. And stay away from the **Don'ts**! Lots of women have found these tips on beating the blues really helpful, but of course they only work if you put them into practice. Give it a try and find out if it makes a difference for you. I suspect it will. You can also make use of the suggestions on how to deal with the shock, however delightful, of your infant's birth, which I set out in chapter one, along with ideas on how to beat fatigue.

Baby Blues don't happen for every new mum, and you may be one of the lucky ones. I was talking recently to the blooming first-time mother of a three-month-old baby girl, admiring her little angel and generally enjoying myself. I do love babies! When I asked about Baby Blues she shook her head and said, 'No, nothing like that luckily! But my friend . . .' and then went on to describe how she had been involved in supporting this other new mum through several weeks of the blues. We were able to end our chat on an upbeat note because, as ever, the Baby Blues had only lasted a short while and everything was now going swimmingly. Apparently friends, family and, to a certain extent, health professionals had all rallied round during these few crucial weeks with the result that no lasting harm had occurred to the new parents or their baby boy.

I suppose one of the things we fear about Baby Blues is that our bond with our newborn will be impaired in some way. It's an understandable worry, which is all too easily puffed up to enormous proportions when we are stuck in the middle of a low mood. Remember those ideas I talked about in chapter one when we were looking at bridging the bonding gap?

Well, they all equally apply to the situation where Baby Blues feel as if they are interfering in our becoming attached to our little darling. If this is happening to you, turn back to pages 57–8 and plug yourselves into all the daily parenting activities in a Baby Centred way, only this time you can add in *Praises* along with the *Attends* and *Best Guesses*. It's really important to keep in mind that going through the motions of being Baby Centred, even when you are struggling with the Baby Blues, will tide you and your newborn over what can be a difficult, but thankfully short, period of hormonal and emotional adjustment to parenthood.

But supposing it doesn't end? Supposing you feel extremely depressed? What if you are having thoughts of ending it all? This is what is known as post-natal depression, something most of us have heard about and sincerely hope to avoid if at all possible. However, ignoring it is the last thing we should do, so let's look at what it is, where it comes from and what to do if you suspect yourself or your partner may be suffering from this unwelcome condition.

Post-natal depression (PND) is very much less common than Baby Blues though decidedly more frequent than a mother's psychotic breakdown following the birth of their baby. The most severe form of psychological disorder in new mothers used to be called post-partum psychosis, though when I was working on a specialist psychiatric mother and baby unit (MBU) it was known as psychosis in the post-partum period. In the ten years I spent on the MBU as principal clinical psychologist, professional under-standing of this serious condition grew apace, with special reference to the role of post-birth hormonal changes as a causal factor.

I want to make it clear that psychosis in the post-partum period is very rare indeed and significantly different from PND in that the sufferers can experience delusions, hallucinations and extreme changes in mood, including hypomania and mania as well as catatonic depression. Mania means an abnormally high mood while catatonia is where someone is so depressed they cease to move voluntarily. Just to help you recognise how PND and psychosis in the post-partum period differ, here is a quick rule of thumb to refer to:

Post-natal depression	Psychosis in the post-partum period
Depression	Extreme, totally debilitating depression
Mostly rational thinking	Irrational ideas
In touch with reality	Contact with reality lost
No elevated mood	Extreme and debilitating elevated mood
Insight about depression	Little insight into condition
Ability to function in an apparently normal fashion	Loss of ability to function in an apparently normal fashion
Baby seen as normal	Baby can be seen as having special powers for either good or evil
Professional help needed	Specialist professional help needed
May have suicidal ideas and feelings	High risk of suicide and infanticide

This is all pretty heavy going isn't it? PND and psychosis in the post-partum period are conditions that must be taken seriously and will definitely involve professional medical and therapeutic intervention in order to be resolved properly. The good news about psychosis in the post-partum period is that with the proper treatment, which might involve time on a specialist unit, new mothers who experience this condition can return to normal, usually within a few months. However, particular precautions are necessary if a repeat problem is to be avoided when the next baby is born. Mothers who have experienced a psychotic breakdown after giving birth would of course be properly monitored when they next became pregnant. It is partners, husbands, fiancés, grandparents, siblings and friends who need to be the most aware in terms of picking up the signs of a maternal psychotic episode because the new mother herself would have little insight into her condition, particularly if she were to be manic.

The major advice for anyone who suspects the new baby's mother is becoming psychotic is to immediately involve your GP as they are the gateway to all the specialist care that will be needed over the next few months. It's a tough situation for everyone involved, though fortunately in recent years much more attention is now being paid to the emotional and psychological needs of the parent who is left often literally holding the baby – that's dad!

When we focus on post-natal depression, it is clear that while the situation is not as serious as psychosis in the post-partum period, it is no less of a trial for the depressed mothers themselves. However, a post-natally depressed mother has the ability to reflect on her own experience, realise that something is wrong and then take steps to get help, while a sufferer from a psychotic episode does not.

If you look back at the lists relating to these two conditions, you will see that PND is in some ways like an extreme form of Baby Blues that does not fade away but persists and becomes worse as the months pass by. Some women suffering PND have even said that wanting to kill themselves seemed at the time an entirely matter-of-fact thought. This could happen because most post-natally depressed women are so busy getting on with their numerous parenting tasks that suicide just seems like another item on the long list of jobs to be done. Additionally, the depressed new mother is likely to be aware that her thoughts feature what can be called Typical Thinking Errors, a key feature of PND.

In order to give you a clearer idea of clinical depression, that's the kind where you're so down you can't kick-start yourself into a brighter frame of mind and really do need professional help, I think it would be useful to explain a little about the characteristic symptoms and thinking errors seen in depressed people. Let me first set out another list, this time of the changes that you or those around you would notice:

SYMPTOMS OF DEPRESSION

Increases	Decreases
Sadness	Concentration
Feelings of failure	Appetite
Dislike of self	Decision-making ability
Feeling punished	Sex drive
Guilt	Interest in others
Ideas of suicide	Restful sleep
Being discouraged about your future	Energy
Crying	Pleasure
Self-criticism	
Feeling worthless	
Restlessness and tension	
Irritability	
Fatigue	

There are some other symptoms featured in PND that can either increase or decrease, and amongst these are appetite and sleep. It might also come to a point where you feel like crying but simply can't.

Next, the thinking errors. I have, over the years, worked with many post-natally depressed mothers, all of whom showed some kind of Typical Thinking Errors. These patterns of thought serve to drive our mood down even further, which in turn affects our feelings and behaviour.

If you picture each human being as made up of three realms of functioning, thought, emotions and behaviour, it is abundantly clear they all interact. I don't think anyone these days would try to pursue the past belief that mind and body are separate. So there we are, our thoughts influence our feelings and vice versa; our feelings influence our behaviour and vice versa; and our behaviour influences our mind and vice versa. All inextricably mixed.

Cognitive behaviour therapy (CBT) is often the approach used when the frequency or intensity of an individual's Typical Thinking

Errors is seen as maintaining a clinical level of depression. For PND to resolve properly, the depressed new mum has to learn to recognise these distorted thought patterns, challenge their exaggerated negativity and then substitute more realistic, positive ideas.

CBT is now firmly established as an effective therapy for depression, though when I first trained in the early 1980s it was regarded by some as a bit of an upstart! Professor Aaron T. Beck and his colleagues in the USA were the first to propose that depression was first generated and then maintained by what they termed Negative Automatic Thoughts. These are the result of the thinking errors I have mentioned, and now I want to let you know just what these errors are and also give you some examples of the different types.

TYPICAL THINKING ERRORS

Errors	Examples
All or nothing thinking	If I don't do it perfectly there's no point in doing it at all
Over-generalisation	I never get anything right.
Discounting the positive	I didn't have a moment of pleasure today. OK, so I got my work done. So what? It's only what's expected of me.
Jumping to conclusions by mind-reading and crystal-ball gazing	I'm depressed again/still. Everyone is fed up with me. I'll never get over it.
Catastrophising	The worst will happen and there's nothing at all I can do about it.
Global judgements	Another mistake. I'm totally useless.
Personalisation	It always rains when I go on holiday.

Each of these examples is a Negative Automatic Thought, or NAT for short. CBT says that if you want to lift your mood you must challenge your NATs by looking for positive alternatives and therefore outlawing the thinking errors that are at the core of depression. If you find yourself frequently thinking in a negative, error-laden fashion or notice a new mum who is coming out with statements like the ones above and who is also experiencing some of the changes I listed as symptoms of PND, *get professional help at once*. I cannot stress that enough.

Whether you go to your GP, confide in your health visitor or contact a cognitive behaviour therapist is a matter of individual choice. What you *must not do* is keep your worries or concerns to yourself. There is no shame in becoming depressed after having a baby and you will be doing yourself, your baby and your family a great disservice if you try to hide it.

You can also work towards feeling more in charge of your mood and your life by taking a few simple steps. These would be the equivalent of some of the initial aspects of undergoing CBT which are well known to lift a depressed mood. Of course, when you are going through post-natal depression, activating yourself to get on with tasks like this is difficult, so only have a go at these self-help exercises *in addition* to seeking professional input.

First of all, you can do a little test for yourself to see approximately how depressed you might be. Look back at the symptoms we saw just now and rate each one in terms of the last two weeks, including today, according to a scale like this:

Score	Mood
0	No change from usual pre-birth feelings.
1	A minor increase or decrease in the symptom.
2	Noticeable changes in feelings.
3	Significant increase or decrease in the symptom.

If you score mostly 0s then, unless you are lying to yourself and others about your depression, you are fine, even if occasionally you feel like giving up the ghost. Should your scores be mostly 1s, first of all you would need to put into place the dos and don'ts suggestions I have already set out when talking about Baby Blues. See how you feel in a week's time and if there is no improvement, contact your GP or health visitor. But if you are scoring mainly 2s, you must contact the professionals at once, and even sooner if you score mostly 3s. This is only a very rough guide, so my major recommendation is, if you or your loved ones believe you might be experiencing post-natal depression, do not hesitate to seek the help of the relevant health professionals. Trying to go it alone once you have PND is not advisable.

Secondly, you could begin to try and challenge the Negative Automatic Thoughts you manage to catch hold of as they pop into your mind again and again and again. The sorts of NATs that women with PND have told me about, go something like this:

- 'I am a failure as a mother.'
- 'They would all be better off if I was dead.'
- 'I am putting my baby at risk.'
- 'I will never be a good-enough mum.'
- 'I can't even cry anymore.'
- 'I'm an unnatural mother.'

They are reminiscent of the Baby Blues Unofficial Scary List aren't they? Much more intense, of course, and lasting much longer than two to three weeks. So how exactly would you challenge these depressed and depressing thoughts? Well, here are some tried and tested methods of knocking the NATs for six and re-establishing positive thinking patterns.

Challenging Negative Automatic Thoughts

Ask yourself these questions and challenge those NATs:

1. Ask yourself, '*What is the evidence?*'
    - 'What is the *evidence* to disprove my thoughts?'
    - 'What *evidence* do I have to support my thoughts?'

STICK TO THE FACTS = EVIDENCE

2.   Ask yourself, '*What alternative views are there?*'
   - 'How would someone else view this situation?'
   - 'How would I have viewed it before I got depressed?'
   - 'What evidence do I have to back up these alternatives?'

3.   Ask yourself, '*What is the effect of thinking the way I do?*'
   - 'Does it help me or hinder me from getting what I want?'
   - 'How does it help or hinder me?'
   - 'What effect would looking at things less negatively have?'

4.   Ask yourself, '*What thinking errors am I making?*'
   - 'Am I thinking in all-or-nothing terms?'
   - 'Am I condemning myself as a total person on the basis of a single incident?'
   - 'Am I forgetting my strengths and focusing on my weaknesses?'
   - 'Am I blaming myself for things that aren't my fault?'
   - 'Am I expecting myself to be perfect?'
   - 'Am I taking personally something that really has little to do with me?'
   - 'Am I concentrating on only the negative side of things?'
   - 'Am I operating a double standard? Would I be more understanding if I was looking at someone else in my situation?'
   - 'Am I exaggerating the chance of disaster?'
   - 'Am I assuming there is nothing I can do to change my situation?'
   - 'Am I overestimating the importance of the event?'
   - 'Am I concentrating on the way things ought to be instead of accepting and dealing with them as they actually happen?'
   - 'Am I predicting the future instead of experimenting with it and trying out various options?'

5.   Ask yourself, '*What action can I take?*'
   - 'What can I do to change my situation?'

- 'Am I overlooking solutions to problems because I'm assuming they won't work?'
- 'What can I do to test out the truth of my challenges?'

Talking about PND is not a particularly cheery affair, but I want to reassure you that if you have this condition the sooner you get professional help, the more quickly you will feel like your old self again. Those who tell post-natally depressed mums to 'pull themselves together' simply do not know what they are talking about. So you can, you *must*, ignore any such ill-informed comments and approach the health professionals who will know only too well that PND needs to be actively treated, possibly with a combination of medication and therapy.

Don't become one of those families where the mother says, any number of years on, she is still depressed. These sad souls are the ones who weren't able to access the very necessary professional help after their first experience of PND and have continued to struggle on alone ever since. Once more I urge you, do *not* suffer in silence. Reach out for the help you need, you most definitely deserve it. You are not a bad mum or an uncaring dad just because PND is casting its shadow over your family. And be aware that a small number of dads can become depressed after childbirth too, usually if they feel they can't bond properly with their baby. All the NAT information applies to men as well.

PND can and does happen, irrespective of people's personal and parental strengths or weaknesses. So do yourselves, your families and your baby a truly big favour and tell it to the professionals just like it is. You will then be in a much stronger position to deal with the challenges your children sometimes present.

What To Do Next: My Baby Won't Sleep!

There are many similarities between our emotional reactions as parents to our children crying and in getting them to sleep that you should look back at the previous What To Do Next: My Baby

Keeps Crying! (page 65) to remind yourself how to handle under-mining, uncomfortable or frightening feelings you may experience when all your efforts at soothing your infant to sleep seem to have failed. The advice to *Best Guess* yourself applies equally to sleep problems in children, especially as being unable to settle is, for babies and toddlers alike, quite often associated with crying spells – as I'm sure you've already noticed! However, as the actions that would help you to make yourself feel better are a little different, I will spell them out for you.

Also in this section I tackle the often emotive topic of the dummy as part of a sleep routine with babies and toddlers. Some recent research suggests that sucking a pacifier may even help to protect against Sudden Infant Death Syndrome, so expect further devel-opments on this one. Plus I pop in some practical tips learnt from the successes of the parents I have worked with over the last thirty years. Finally, I discuss how *Praise* can be an important aspect of helping your baby to gradually establish a sleep routine that will meet their needs and keep you sane!

So, what do you do when your baby or toddler won't go to sleep? Here are some likely scenarios. You have *Best Guessed* yourself as a response to being undermined, uncomfortable and frightened by your feelings because of your inability to get your little darling to sleep. Remember: Mirror, Validate, Empathise. Now you need to Resolve the problem.

Scenario One: Babies Under Three Months Old

It's 8 p.m. You haven't eaten since midday. Your baby, who slept for two-and-a-half blissful hours in the latish afternoon, is still wide awake and quite happy *so long as you don't put them down*. Once out of the comfort of your arms they start to howl. What to do next?

Practical tips:
- Make sure your baby is not poorly, hungry, overheated or otherwise uncomfortable
- Give the baby to the other parent (or any other responsible person at hand) saying, 'I'll fix us something quick to eat'

- Alternatively, use a baby sling to keep them close to you while you fix something quick to eat
- Meanwhile, make yourself some honeyed tea or have a sip of wine.
- Switch on some of the music you played to your baby prior to their birth
- Sing or hum or la-la along with the melody
- Sway or dance gently, holding them literally close to your heart and pat their back rhythmically

Bond building:
- Use your best Baby Centred *Praises*, voiced softly and repeatedly against the sides of their head, near their ears. Try:
  'You're my darling little angel.'
  'I love you, sweetie pie, you're my special girl/boy.'
  'You'll be fine, poppet. You're so delicious I will always be with you.'
  'Oh, my little treasure, my precious jewel. I'll love you for ever.'
- Rhythmically and very softly stroke the sides of their forehead with your fingertip.
- Be Baby Centred and *Best Guess* your baby out loud, but in a soft, sympathetic tone. Try:
  'You seem to be windy/wet/hungry/a bit hot/a baby with tummy ache.'
  'I know I'd be fractious if I felt like you.'
  'You poor little darling.'
  'Now let's try and make you more comfy.'
- Give your baby some Baby Centred *Attends*. Try:
  'It's all right, poppet, you're safe in my arms.'
  'Don't worry, my little pet. I'm here to look after you.'
  'There, you're feeling a bit better now, I can tell.'
  'You like being close to me and I love it too.'

Put all of these practical and bonding responses together, or try different combinations, some more than once, and your baby will probably settle. But don't leave yourself out! Food and drink are natural relaxants, so you must remember to nourish yourself during stressful periods, physically and emotionally. I found it was quite possible to sing, dance, whisper praises to my babies *and* eat two shortbread biscuits all at the same time! These early weeks and months are a time for getting to know your baby, for establishing your bond and if a couple of biscuits help to keep you calm during tough times, my advice would be to go ahead. You will be more emotionally available to your baby the more relaxed you are.

There is, of course, another solution to consider, the 'dummy', 'pacifier' or 'magic plug'. There were times in the past when using a pacifier to soothe an infant off to sleep was frowned upon by the baby-care experts of the day. News circulated that it was a nasty habit that would later be difficult to break, or that babies and toddlers' teeth would suffer. However, it now seems to be agreed that most six- to twelve-month-olds are able to give up their magic plug without too much trouble and that no harm comes to their oral development when the dummy is withdrawn from their routine by the time they are one year old. Another criticism of dummies is that they have an adverse impact on a mother's supply of breast milk. Received wisdom suggested that babies used to sucking on a 'num num' as well as their mummy's nipple become confused because the techniques needed differ in terms of the tongue and teat arrangements required. However, if a dummy is not introduced until a breastfeeding mum has established good breast-milk production, then this risk is very much reduced. So if you are breastfeeding, don't introduce a pacifier until your baby is at least four weeks old. Of course, the most common reason why tiny babies cry and won't settle is because they are hungry, so always check this possibility first.

My own breastfed babies and grandchildren did not seem to need dummies, though my bottle-fed son and grandchildren loved them. It doesn't seem to have dramatically influenced their development as individuals either way. What I do remember, though, is the bliss of putting my baby son, plus 'dum dum', down for the night knowing he would gently slide into a deep sleep. My daughters' sleep routines were much less predictable! There may perhaps be a link with the type of feeding, and I'll look at that in chapter three when we concentrate on infant nutrition. Meanwhile, if using a pacifier eases your newborn off to sleep then use it regularly, making it part of their daily sleep routine.

Scenario Two: Babies Aged from Three to Six Months

It is 2.30 a.m. This is the middle of the night for you, though your baby seems to believe it's playtime! You have offered them a little snack of breast milk or formula milk and know their tummies are comfortably full. They actually seem quite happy, gurgling, smiling and playing with their hands. But they are definitely, almost defiantly, awake, while you desperately need to sleep. What to do next?

Practical tips:
- Decide whether you will stick with your policy of returning them to their cot, or take them into bed with you hoping they will fall asleep and then you can put them into their cot later on.
- Remember, it is your and your baby's decision. Millions of babies across the world sleep with their parents as a matter of course and come to no harm, so you might want to give the cot a miss in any case – either just this once or on a regular basis.
- You could use the baby's dummy, keep the lights very low, cut any noise right down and hope the lack of stimulation will edge them towards sleep.
- You could instead employ the relevant practical tips for under-three-month-olds already set out.
- Put lots of effort into avoiding the temptation to join in with their playful mood, however delightful the prospect. (Or perhaps not *that* delightful at 2.30 a.m.!)

Bond building:
- Very softly, *Praise* your 'little star' for being just that.
- *Best Guess* your baby as quietly as possible, this will help to calm you both down.

- *Best Guess* yourself if you are irritable and make yourself feel better by having the soothing hot drink you wisely prepared earlier and put in a vacuum flask.
- Remember, you must look after yourself if you are to be a successful bond builder with your baby.
- *Praise* yourself for coping as well as you can and promise yourself that tomorrow, when your baby naps, you will too.
- Use fewer *Attends*, as waking up in the middle of the night and wanting to play is *not* a behaviour you want to encourage in your tiny tot, so keep the Rewards to a minimum. Remember, this does not make you an uncaring parent, just really sensible and good at being fond and firm at the same time.

Helping your three- to six-month-old learn the difference between night-time and daytime routines and activities is a really important part of the socialisation process that all babies and toddlers must undergo if they are to become happy and well-adjusted members of their community. And guess who the main architects of this project are! Yes, none other than those stalwarts of every little one's life – their parents!

Sadly, I have known some chaotic families where, even by seven years old, the children have not been helped successfully to learn this basic lesson. As a result they are up until all hours watching TV, wrecking their bedrooms, arguing, fighting, and raiding the fridge, only to tip the contents over the floor and then stamp in them! I'm sure you can only too easily imagine the scenario the next morning. Everyone in the family irritable and excessively tired. Not a good way to start the day!

Once more, it is important to work at getting across the day/night business pretty much from the beginning. Just don't expect much cooperation from your baby initially!

Scenario Three: Babies Aged Six to Twelve Months

It is 6.30 p.m. You have just completed your entire wind-down routine: bath, supper, story, song, kisses and 'nighty nights'. You are almost asleep, but your baby is wide awake and apparently ready for anything! As you carry them to their cot they pat your face and smile at you with loving eyes. So far so wonderful. But settle in their cot? You must be joking! Lay them down, they pull themselves back up! What to do next?

Practical tips:
- First, you will probably want to try any or all of those techniques that have worked for you and your baby before, including perhaps some of my previous suggestions on sleep or crying.
- Maybe by now you have decided that your policy will be to do your baby's bedtime routine once and then leave the room, determined not to respond to whatever crying and screaming might ensue.
- Alternatively, it could be a family decision that at this young age babies should not be left to cry, even if they should be ready to drop off to sleep.
- So, you could take them to lie on your bed with you. You could sit by their cot and sing to them or you could take them back downstairs and try again in an hour.
- Perhaps now might be the time to start using the approaches outlined in one of the manuals for parents who find their babies won't settle down to sleep at an appropriate time.
- Or try the wonder dummy as a regular part of your bedtime routine.

Bond building:
- As well as trying the relevant bond building suggestions from the under-six-month scenarios, focus on *Praises* and treats for yourself. This will be a positive contribution towards a secure relationship with your infant because you will be attempting to manage a challenging situation with a feel-good factor for yourself. This isn't to imply that you are self-indulgent. Not in the slightest. Rather it shows that you have learned that both partners in a relationship – you and your child – need to feel appreciated if a loving balance is to be maintained.

- As your baby can't provide you with choccies or scented candles quite yet, you also need to involve your family and friends in your forward planning.
- Try the following 'Praises for Persistent Parents' (Three Ps) programme, though you can call it whatever you like.
- Here are some Three P ideas you might like to sample:
  - Arrange for a friend or relative to come and put your infant to bed – or try to! – and go out on a date with your partner, friend or whoever. Of course, at this stage in the parenting lark, a date probably means popping out for a quick snack and drink at your local pub. I confidently predict you will be back within an hour, just to make sure everything's all right – I know I was! Remember to stay out long enough to *Praise* yourself and/or each other for your sterling efforts as parent over the last six to twelve months.
  - If possible, swap baby bedtime responsibilities with the other parent, using a system that you write up one week in advance. The mum or dad not on duty must ALWAYS *Praise*, *Best Guess* and give *Attends* to their partner when they succeed in their task. A square of fudge or a glass of wine wouldn't go amiss either, and a nicely prepared meal would obviously go down a bomb.
  - Make yourself a Treat Chart, where for each day you put your baby to bed you earn points towards a special outing, DVD or CD, plant, tool, or piece of clothing. Be generous towards yourself – you deserve lots of goodies for hanging on in there and loving a baby who seems to need very few hours of sleep in order to stoke up a vast store of zest for life.

I freely admit that the sleep business with my first two children was a bit of a nightmare from my perspective. I'm not sure if it's because I breastfed on demand, didn't use a pacifier, failed to establish a proper bedtime routine or didn't get the right advice. I tried leaving them to cry – heartbreak! I tried cutting out the daytime nap. I think that may have helped tire them out, though this decision on my part led to one of the only two arguments I ever had with my mother as an adult. Mostly, however, I spent hours in darkened bedrooms, soothing, pacing, pleasing and eventually grinding my teeth with frustration at my lack of success.

I saw this role as my sole responsibility, as my husband was the one working and providing for myself and our children. Thankfully, though, one generation on in my family, such responsibilities seem to be much more evenly shared. Perhaps because of a chronic absence of uninterrupted sleep over what turned out to be a six-year period, the fact that my darling daughters thrived, indeed sparkled, on less sleep than the amount I craved, was a real trial in terms of my feelings towards them on waking in the mornings. We are not talking dislike, disappointment or even desperation. It was more like resentful envy of their unquenchable buoyancy as each day began!

Luckily, no lasting harm befell our bonds with one another and my eldest daughter, now forty-five years old, gave me just yesterday the highest accolade a parent can ever realistically hope to hear. As we kissed and hugged after a successful morning at the New Year's sales, she said with a smile and a squeeze in response to my query, 'Yes, Mum, you *are* good-enough!' Praise indeed! Of course, you might be reading this and congratulating yourself on having completely avoided such stressful sleep experiences, and if so, well, good for you! You obviously have a magic touch that passed me by, though I was much more successful with my bottle-fed adopted baby son who is forty this year.

They really are tiny for such a short amount of time, aren't they? And yet we expect so much. Do we ask more of their sleep habits than we have a right to at such an early age? Let's look at a toddler scenario now and see.

Scenario Four: One-Year-Olds
You have taken the plunge and moved your now fully mobile toddler to their own bed in their own stunningly attractive bedroom, devotedly decorated by you. There are cuddly toys, books, mobiles, themed curtains and duvet cover, tiny little slippers and a cute dressing gown. You have soft music and a night light ready to

help them drop peacefully off to sleep while you flake out down-stairs during your own personal grown-up's time. But what's this? A one-year-old who will not stay in their own bed unless you are there too! What to do next?

Practical tips:
- If you are determined there will be no going back to previous sleeping arrangements there really is nothing more effective than silently, and with as little physical contact as possible, taking your toddler back to their room, tucking them up in bed, and saying something like, 'This is your bed now. I want you to stay in your bed and go to sleep. There's a good boy/girl. I love you.' A little kiss is a good idea at this point, after which you leave the room.
- Torturous though it may seem, and unquestionably exhausting enough to try the patience of even the most saintly parent, the best results are achieved by repeating this sequence each time your one-year-old gets out of bed.
- If you can summon up the energy to keep this up, although the first few nights might be extremely taxing indeed, you will be pleasantly surprised by how rapidly you can achieve success.
- If possible, sharing the burden by alternating nights on and off duty can be an absolute lifesaver, so plan ahead how you will share the responsibility and then stick to your arrangements.
- If this approach does not appeal to you, there is always the option of choosing to lie down next to your infant or sit by the bed until they go to sleep. But be warned, you too will probably drift off and then bang goes your grown-up time downstairs.

Bond building:
- Take a few minutes to review whether your timing of the 'big bedtime move' is more in line with your child's development or your own desperation for a whole night's uninterrupted sleep. Are you expecting too much too soon?
- Ask yourself, 'Were we all sleeping better before we made the change?' If the answer is yes, then you might like to consider

another month or two of the old routine before trying again. There is no real rush, is there? It is much more important for your bonding that you all sleep well. After all, most of the world's one-year-olds are still sleeping with their mummy and daddy in the same bed.

- If the answer is no, you will probably decide to press ahead with the new arrangements, so make sure you are giving your infant masses of *Praise* for time spent in their own bed.

- Remember, start to *Praise* as soon as your toddler begins to climb into their new bed, and keep going as long as they stay there – pausing for breath in between, of course!

- Whatever you do, don't smack them for 'playing up'. This just makes the whole situation a potential bond-breaking scenario instead of bond-making opportunity. Take another look at Ignoring Tantrums (page 50) to refresh your memory, and make sure you are only giving *Praise* and *Attends* to the toddler for behaviour you want to encourage.

- It's important to acknowledge that mums and dads thrive on *Praise* too, and it's important to speak out loud your admiration and support for the efforts made by your partner. What about also chatting aloud about your very own triumphs too?

I want to add a word of encouragement at this point because I know from personal experience what hard work it can be to establish a proper bedtime routine with one-year-olds. My own particular worst nightmare was when, after settling beautifully and drifting off to sleep without so much as a peep of protest, my little daughters woke up again just as I was about to eat dinner with my husband, watch a keenly anticipated TV programme or go to bed myself. Yet we all survived and the situation gradually improved, so take heart! But, what if things are still going downhill when your toddler becomes a two-year-old? We will tackle that next.

Scenario Five: Two-Year-Olds

Your two-year-old went to bed like a dream and you have had an enjoyable evening with your partner and a couple of friends. It almost felt like pre-baby times! You have snuggled down in a very happy mood and dropped off to sleep immediately, having first checked that your toddler is safely asleep. Later – it could be in the early hours of the morning – you slowly become aware that there is a third person in your bed. Yes, it's your toddler – minus nappy! What to do next?

Practical tips
- Always keep a couple of nappies right next to the bed, two each side is a good bet.
- Pop one on your toddler as quietly as possible, especially if they are asleep.
- Follow your usual routine for either returning your infant to their own bed or allowing them to spend the rest of the night with you in the big bed.
- If you are regularly going to have your baby or toddler in with you at night it is worth indulging in the purchase of a king-size bed.

Bond building
- Suppose you have got to the point where you are utterly fed-up with this particular scenario. You don't want to keep taking your two-year-old back to their bed, but on the other hand, you are tired of sleeping on three inches of mattress while your not-so-tiny toddler lays spreadeagled in the middle of your bed.
- First we need to recognise that feelings like this aren't helpful in maintaining a close, harmonious bond with an under-three.
- Next we should take into account the **Attention Rule** (see also page 283). This comes from social learning theory and tells us to:
  - Give *Attends*, *Praise* and other Baby Centred attention to your under-three *when you approve of their behaviour.*
  - IGNORE 99 per cent of the little irritating behaviours that your toddler comes up with.
  - Use TIME OUT (see chapter five for details) for the 1 per cent of dangerous or destructive behaviours occasionally shown by a child.

- If possible, talk through with your partner a plan for *Praising* and *Rewarding* your two-year-old for staying in their own bed all night, if this is your present aim. Put the Attention Rule into operation around bedtime arrangements.
- Give priority to a peaceful night's sleep for *all* the family and don't be too rigid in insisting your under-three always goes back to their own bed unless you are utterly convinced this is the best route to achieve a quiet night for everyone.

Thankfully there is now a good selection of books for parents on how to solve children's sleep problems, so if by the time your child is nearly three things still aren't going according to your plan and aims – and remember, every family is unique when it comes to solving problems like this – get a copy of one that interests you and thoroughly try their approach. I know it's very tempting to give one technique a few days' trial and then bin it if it's not bringing the results you want, but try to resist.

Few plans work out unless we are consistent in our behaviour, so don't ditch one approach for another until you have given the first one an extensive chance to work. I know of a foster family where, for around six weeks, the adults got out of bed almost hourly during the night to take the two- and three-year-olds back to their own beds. No, I don't know how they did it either! But all power to them for being consistent and persistent in that way. It worked! Since then the two little boys have always stayed in their beds and everyone gets a solid night's sleep. However, remember there are other techniques if this one doesn't suit your family, so don't give up if at first you don't succeed. After all, solutions are found, phases do pass.

How many ten-year-olds do you know who are still wrecking their family's night's sleep? Not many, unless they are poorly, in which case special allowances must be made. I myself was quite a sickly child and had to spend some months in hospital. On my return home, aged four-and-a-half, I was nursed through a long convalescence, believing myself to be queen of all I surveyed, simply because I was the sole occupant of my parents' bed. It was always a special treat for myself and my two younger siblings to spend time in our parents' bed as my mother and father were firm believers in children sleeping in their own beds. Even when my mother was breastfeeding us, and in those days that meant no solids until at least six months of age, she got up at night and sat in a little nursing chair. My own solution was much less self sacrificing and I regularly took the under-threes into the big bed during the night if they were fractious. I also noticed that I became much more relaxed about issues like this, the more babies I had! A common experience I know. Those poor little firstborns really do have a huge burden of new parent anxiety to deal with, don't they?

GOLDEN BULLETS

- **No. 1. My Baby Needs . . . Approval**
  The main subject of this chapter is making sure your baby and toddler receive all the approval they need if they are to grow up feeling loveable. Using frequent *Praise* instead of *Criticism* will make the bond between you and your baby or toddler much more secure. Give your baby, one- and two-year-olds verbal approval, not only for their behaviour – *Labelled Praise* – but also for being themselves – *Unlabelled Praise*. Use frequently.
- **No. 2. What Not To Do: Don't Criticise**
  Criticism covers those looks or comments that indicate disapproval of your under-three's actions, abilities or personality. Use as few as possible. Baby Centred to Baby Directive ratio: Aim for the optimal ratio of six praises for every one criticism and then, even if you don't quite manage it all the time, you will be giving your baby and toddler sufficient approval to make them feel loveable. The more *Praise* and fewer *Criticisms* you use, the more secure the bond between you will become.
- **No. 3. Echoes From Our Past: Feeling Smothered**
  Though you may have been parented in an over-involved or excessively emotional style, you can still make strong efforts

to allow your baby and toddler enough psychological space to protect their need to become a separate individual with their very own special contribution to your relationship bond. Giving *Praise* and trying to exclude *Criticisms* of your under-three will give you both the all important chance to learn that your approval is much more emotionally constructive when it doesn't smother independent development.

- **No. 4. Special Feature: Good-Enough Parenting**
  We are all fallible human beings toting our sack of baggage from the past and as such our aim should be good-enough parenting. Whatever the current dogma on child rearing and stages of child development, if parents provide a family environment where a strong attachment between mother and/or father and child can flourish, then all should be well – or at least well-enough.

- **No. 5. Special Feature: Baby Blues and Post-natal Depression**
  These conditions can happen to anyone and neither one has anything to do with being a bad mother or a bad dad. Share your feelings with a trusted friend or confide your concerns to a health professional and make sure you get the treatment you need. You can also help yourself. Carry on being as Baby Centred as possible and your bond will continue to grow and improve. Share your feelings: there is nothing to be ashamed of in feeling blue or depressed and the more you talk to your partner or a professional about your low mood, the easier it will be for you to go on being Baby Centred and Approving enough to your baby and toddler to enhance their sense of being truly loveable. Post-natal depression needs therapy, sometimes medication, sometimes counselling, sometimes both. Protect your bond with your under-three by seeking professional help. Do not struggle on alone. You can also help yourself by challenging your Negative Automatic Thoughts (NATs), which will help to lift your mood and make you more emotionally available to your under-three.

- **No. 6. What To Do Next: My Baby Won't Sleep!**
A sleepless baby or toddler can really tax a parent's stamina and patience, but there are practical and psychological things you can do to make sure that any negative effects on your relationship and bond with your little one are kept to an absolute minimum. What about a dummy? If you want to try your baby with one of these, start at four to six weeks old, or earlier if you are not breastfeeding, and then use it during the first twelve months of your baby's life. A dummy can keep you both calm and so improve the quality of your attachment with them. Remember, the choice is up to you.

Chapter Three

Helping Your Baby to Trust You

WHAT THIS CHAPTER IS ABOUT

This chapter provides an in-depth look at your baby's need for . . . security, the lynchpin of all relationships. In order for under-threes to feel secure in the care of their mummy and/or daddy, a parent must be willing and able to respond in similar fashion to their offspring's different yet specific needs and behaviours. As part of this process I explore *Loving Smiles*, *Positive Looks* and *Positive Touches*, three more of the Baby Centred behaviours that parents show towards their under-threes. These non-verbal Baby Centred behaviours are an essential strand in helping to build the trust that babies and toddlers need to feel towards us if they are to develop healthy relationships throughout the rest of their lives.

Also in this chapter:
- What Not To Do: Don't Smack – page 148.
- Echoes From Our Past: Inconsistent Parenting – page 158.
- Special Features: Managing Anger – page 153; Emotional Aspects of Baby and Toddler Feeding – page 169.
- What To Do Next: Feeding Challenges – page 180.
- Golden Bullets – page 192.

My Baby Needs . . . Security

If we think about our under-three's most frequent behaviours, up there at the top of the list is the way they look to us for reassurance, comfort, stimulation, information, protection, warmth, approval and a sense of being loved and loveable. Looking to a parent for all these essential aides to healthy development happens on a literal as well as emotional and psychological level. Think back to some of the most rewarding moments with your newborn and eye contact will be part of it. Look at any curious under-one-year-old who finds him- or herself in a new situation and you will notice how often they look back at their parent for reassurance. Conjure up a one-year-old trying their first attempts at walking. Searching for sight of their enthralled mummy or daddy often coincides with them collapsing on to their bottoms. Picture a two-year-old at playgroup where, even after regular attendance for several months, the most exciting and rewarding moment is when they see you waiting to collect them. There's no getting away from it, being able to see you and make eye contact is an incredibly powerful source of security for your baby and toddler.

When under-threes use their parents, grandparents and other adults they see regularly for security, we grown-ups are performing a fundamental role in their attachment development. In other words, we are their Secure Base and it is from these interactions that their bond with us begins to form. Babies and toddlers commonly look to adults for comfort when they are ill, crying, tired, hungry or thirsty, in pain, frightened or upset. This is adaptive behaviour of the highest order and probably guarantees their physical survival amidst the dangers threatening such helpless and dependent little beings from every side.

Infants need such interactions with their parent and/or carer to be predictable if the bond between us is to become *secure*. Babies and toddlers cannot use their parents as a Secure Base unless the adults behave in a manner that the children can rely on – that is, what we do does not vary too much from one occasion to another. When the baby and toddler can rely on being able to expect a particular reaction from their parents across a range of situations, then as long as the mother and father are being Baby Centred, sensitive, protective and emotionally nurturing, the child will learn to trust us to take good care of them. It is this aspect of a baby and toddler's primary bond that leads to the most secure attachments between them and their parents. This is a bond that will last a lifetime.

Viewed in this manner, security is not simply about seeing that a baby or toddler is safely fastened into their buggy or stowed out of harm's way in their playpen, walker or cot. In fact, spending too much time in any of these contraptions can undermine an under-three's emotional security because they learn that their parents don't care about them enough to be sensitive to their real needs. This, in turn, damages any sense of trust that may be blossoming as children realise their mummy and daddy cannot be relied upon to give them positive attention. A baby's need for predictable reactions from their parents is not a passing whim and they are not trying to be difficult or demanding. They are simply expressing a fundamental requirement to make a secure bond. Therefore, we must make sure we work very hard at being consistent in our behaviour towards them. We won't always succeed. There will be days when we score highly and other times when, quite frankly, it all becomes a mess. The best way to deal with the down days is to admit temporary defeat on the consistency scale, give yourself a mini-break plus a tiny treat and then start all over again!

Luckily, babies are so vulnerable that grown-ups, and particularly their parents, are strongly motivated to protect them, both physically and emotionally. Looking after our personal little creation to the very best of our abilities and beyond is a major preoccupation of all dedicated mums and dads. No wonder there is a mountain of literature, acres of shop space and hours of media attention devoted entirely to baby care. The first three years of life are of vital importance, so it's no wonder babies and toddlers are big business. I do hope though that this book is adding something new and valuable in focusing on Parent/Baby and Parent/Toddler *relationships*, because our bond-building efforts need to be the very best we can manage if our children are to emerge as individuals, secure in the knowledge they are loved and loveable. We can sum up what babies need in order to feel secure, under a few important headings. You could use these seven points as a sort of checklist to keep your eye on your achievements:

- A predictable and Baby Centred routine.
- Consistency in managing the baby's behaviour.
- Sensitivity to the infant's needs for food and sleep and being warm, clean and comfortable.
- Protection from physical, psychological and emotional harm.
- A gradual introduction to the complexities of the world.
- Gently timed acquaintance with the significant people in the baby's life.
- A parent's physical presence and emotional availability.

When we provide security in this fashion, our infants develop a deep level of trust in our ability to care for them, meet their needs and keep them safe. They will experience a blissful sense of certainty that there are at least one or two wonderful 'giants' around who make things feel very decidedly all right. Within the safety of this loving attention, our babies begin to lay down the basis of a relationship that will, because of its security and the trust it engenders, act as a positive model for all their other interactions and relationships. As a parent, we reap what we sow and when we succeed in providing sufficient emotional, psychological and physical security for our under-threes, we are much more likely to have fewer fights and more fun in the future.

ADAPTING YOUR HOME TO BE CHILD FRIENDLY

When you are making the switch to being more Baby Centred, it is helpful to remember that you are in charge of the home environment. Be adaptable. Only if you want to spend masses of time saying, 'No!', 'Stop it!', 'Get away from there!' or 'Oh my God!' should you keep your home in its pre-baby state. Being more Baby Centred means parents making changes, and that includes:

- Protecting babies and toddlers from the sharp edges of tables and worktops and glass-topped coffee tables. For example, store dangerous coffee tables in the attic until the child is much older.
- Making sure you have cupboard, washing machine and fridge locks in place.
- Securely anchoring down bookshelves, rugs and other wobbly or slippery items.
- Keeping all hot saucepan handles turned away from your baby or toddler's exploring hands.

Every newborn, infant, baby, one- and two-year-old can tell the difference between gentle and rough handling, safe and nervous nappy changing, and smooth versus jerky rocking. There are many other examples of this nature (some of which we will look at later in the chapter) simply because our interactions with our much-loved babies and toddlers are so tactile and physical. There are few other stages in our lives that feature this same degree of physical intimacy. A genuine *Smile* accompanied by a *Positive Look* can convey a level of warmth, approval and loving security that mere words cannot adequately express, especially to our tiny newborns. An under-three's grasp on their mother tongue will remain pretty fragile for several years to come. That's not an excuse for leaving out the *Attends*, *Praises* and *Best Guesses* though! Remember, one Baby Centred behaviour towards our treasured under-three is very good news for every aspect of their personality, but two or more together deliver an exquisitely intense message of love and acceptance. This is never more so than when *Positive Touches* are rolled into the Baby Centred package.

We might think we have no need to go into much detail about *Loving Smiles*, *Positive Looks* and *Positive Touches*, just because they *are* so obvious, especially when we are on the receiving end.

Yet we have all met people whose smile does not spread to their eyes, whose look could contain many different meanings, and whose touch could either be an affectionate hug or a life-extinguishing squeeze. So, although we can quite easily get the measure of extremely positive or undoubtedly negative non-verbal messages from others, there are a million gradations in between that are not that easy to read. I will focus on both giving and receiving *Loving Smiles*, *Positive Looks* and *Positive Touches* as we look at examples of their importance in strengthening the bond between infants and their very own mummies and daddies.

But what if an under-three cannot trust their mummy and/or daddy to come to their rescue when they are hurt, unhappy, confused or just plain exhausted? What happens to their bond with the most important adults in their lives? Supposing a baby is left to cry under the mistaken impression that 'it's good for their lungs'? Suppose they are not being given lots of *Attends*, *Praises*, *Best Guesses*, *Loving Smiles*, *Positive Looks* and *Positive Touches*? Suppose that, instead of being petted, a one-year-old is either smacked for being 'naughty' or virtually ignored when they are 'good'? Suppose a two-year-old's need for warmth, approval and security is put in second place to a parent's own agenda and priorities? What happens then? You can probably answer all these in a nanosecond! You would probably point out that:

- LACK OF WARMTH leads to an under-three feeling UN-WANTED
- LACK OF APPROVAL leads to an under-three feeling UN-LOVED
- LACK OF SECURITY leads to an under-three being unable to TRUST

As a result, the bond between baby or toddler and their parent/carer is fraught with conflicts, uncertainties, tension and misery.

You can see that we will have our work cut out for us if we are aiming to avoid all parental lapses, but at least if we give it a really good try we will know our children will be nurtured by good-enough mummies and daddies! Remember, aiming to get it right *half* the time and doing a good measure of Baby Centred behaviours will protect the security of your bond with your under-three and their attachment to you. And one of the best ways of making sure that happens is to stir into every possible interaction with your child plenty of *Smiles*, *Positive Looks* and *Positive Touches*.

But before we dive into examples of this new batch of Baby Centred behaviours, let's spend a moment mulling over our own experiences of giving and receiving these precious emotional commodities. Can we remember our parents' faces lighting up with pleasure when they looked at us with love? Do we have memories of affectionate cuddles and strokes from these all-powerful beings? Are we able as adults to rely on mum and dad welcoming us with open arms and big grins should we drop in on them unexpectedly? In other words, are we one of the lucky ones who, as a result of growing up on a high *Smile* diet when young, can easily dole out large spoonfuls of the same mixture when we become parents ourselves.

I am incredibly fortunate in that my mother was extremely emotionally expressive of her positive feelings towards myself, my brother and sister. Our father came from a much less demonstrative family but as he was a generally jovial type we quite often bathed in the glow of his good-humoured smiles. We were all kissed, cuddled, patted and stroked – though not if we had transgressed the family rules, however cute our behaviour. One memorable episode, frequently recounted by my mother in tones of indulgent wonder interspersed with giggles, involved my sister Liz. As she was going through a phase of 'messing about with her food', my exasperated parents said that children who behaved like little animals at meal times, had to eat like little animals – from a dish on the floor. With all due solemnity, Liz's meal was put on a plate and placed on the floor near the family dining table. What followed reduced every spectator to such a state of helpless mirth that any further attempts in this direction were hastily abandoned! Just a timely reminder that smiling and indulgent looks, if mistimed, only serve as a reward, and we all know what that means – more acting up by the object of our attentions.

On some occasions it really can be difficult to hide our smiles, even when we want to discourage a particular behaviour. I know I have to be on guard when I'm with the two-year-olds at preschool because, while their antics may not warrant praise or approval, they none the less tickle our laughter button. A recent incident involved the painting of cut-out polar bear shapes for a winter scene on the activity table. No matter that most of the bears were brightly coloured rather than white, one of the priorities is to protect the two-year-olds' clothes from too much paint damage. However, as both Ben and Hannah moved like lightning from the dressing-up corner to the paint table, their speedy triumph painting an orange bear apiece also involved orange hands, arms, faces, hair, tops and trousers. They were an absolute spectacle! As we gently wiped them down and provided clean clothes from the emergency drawer, it was almost impossible not to smile, albeit over their heads. Neither Ben nor Hannah missed those moments, as you might have guessed, and did little jigs as they smiled too. Not the message us grown-ups had intended at all! Still, no one is perfect – thank heavens!

One of the *Positive Touches* often used with children is tickling. But how welcome is it really? If we watch one- or two-year-olds, they can be seen rather clumsily trying to tickle other little ones, though whether in pursuit of pleasure or punishment is not always clear. The recipient is quite likely to protest, frown and try to swipe the offending hand away. Or sometimes they look quite frightened and may stumble in their attempts to escape. Alternatively, they might enter into the spirit of things to such an extent that they both end up writhing on the floor in a fit of over-excited laughter and choking. So, just a word to the wise on tickles – don't assume that your overtures are going to be welcome and always be gentle.

Baby massage is quite different, however, as it calms rather than excites your under-three. To watch a one-year-old being massaged by a parent talented in the use of this ancient skill is an utter delight. To be the baby or toddler involved is a visibly joyful experience. Don't miss out on the opportunity to go to a few Baby Massage classes. The sheer pleasure of being able to provide your little darling with this type of *Positive Touch* will outweigh any apprehensions you might harbour. Try it! After all, in many cultures it is an accepted part of the daily routine.

Right, now on to a selection of top tips for parents who want to make their special contribution of *Smiles*, *Positive Looks* and *Positive Touches* really count at every stage of a child's first three years.

Loving Smiles, Positive Looks and Positive Touches for Babies Under Six Months

- Be on the lookout for your newborn baby to open their eyes, then lean forward so that your own eyes can lock on to theirs as you let the joy of their safe arrival light up your smile.
- Sit quietly holding your newborn and focus your attention on the tiny miracle you have created. Let your wonder and delight flood into your eyes as you gaze at them with a Positive Look.
- Take one of your infant's tiny hands and slip one of your little fingers into their baby 'fist', as you lovingly stroke their forehead and cheeks. Think about how very precious they are to you and just how much they need your Positive Touch.
- On a *good* day, cram in as many of these moments as you possibly can. Each one weaves in even more strands of your bond with your little newborn, so don't hold back for an instant.
- On a *bad* day, make sure to go through each of these emotionally intimate moments at least four times, they take only seconds. Especially if you are exhausted, overwhelmed or feeling down, carrying out these affectionate little activities will help you to stay in touch with the plus side of your bond with your newborn baby. They can only benefit from this type of parental input, so give it a go however you are feeling.

Remember that newborns are exquisitely sensitive to touch, so always be gentle. As they also love to see a human, animated face more than anything else in the world, make your smiling and mutual eyegazing a frequent part of their daily attachment diet.

Even during these very early days your recent arrival will be experiencing your *Smiles*, *Positive Looks* and *Positive Touches* in a way that can heavily influence the degree of security and trust they feel towards you.

Loving Smiles, Positive Looks and Positive Touches for Babies Aged Six to Twelve Months

- You will be so thrilled by the speed at which your baby acquires new and astonishingly clever skills, you'll want them to be in no doubt about your approval, so it will be easy to look right into their eyes and smile your congratulations. Throw in an *Attend* and *Praise* and they will revel in your clear expression of love.

- It shouldn't be possible to give a *Smile* without a *Positive Look*, should it? However, *Positive Looks* even minus a *Smile* still carry the message that your nearly one-year-old needs to see for their sense of security. So when your infant is scooting round on all fours, or on their bottom, shower them with looks that tell them you enjoy their company.

- When you are bathing your baby, as you slowly sponge away the remains of their tea from their faces, mentally encourage your fingers and hands to express the statement that you'll always be there when they need you.

- On a *good* day, you will find numerous security and trust opportunities you will want to make use of, and it will feel easy to dish out bond-building *Smiles*, *Positive Looks* and *Positive Touches*. But don't ever feel you should ration your output of these supercharged Baby Centred behaviours. Babies can never be shown too much love.

- On a *bad* day, focus on pampering and treating yourself as soon as you can after waking up in the morning. That way you will be able to get up enough of a head of steam to give out *Smiles*, *Positive Looks* and *Positive Touches* to your almost one-year-old, because you are taking time to nurture yourself.

Loving Smiles, Positive Looks and Positive Touches for One-Year-Olds

- You will be in the thick of your one-year-old's incredible learning curve now and repetition is one of the ways in which they consolidate their latest triumph. However many times they stack, sort or scribble successfully, they will still want you to *Smile* your approval to feel really secure. If, after the hundredth time, you feel your facial muscles clenching, look back over the fantastic progress they have made in the last year or so and let your satisfaction spark some more *Smiles*.

- *Positive Looks* for one-year-olds are usually pretty easy to come by because we feel so proud of their tenacious efforts to walk and talk. Showing your pleasure in their progress will build a feeling of security for your one-year-old, whilst being there to, quite literally, pick them up, dust them down and start them off again will make their trust in you blossom.

- You'll have realised that your toddler is quite a tough little character at times, persisting in valiantly exploring their intriguing environments, come rain or shine. However, they will still need you in the background for cuddles and kisses, so don't rush them into being 'a big girl/boy' too soon. Take time to snuggle up together and savour their continuing dependence upon you.

- On a *good* day, being with your one-year-old will feel like fabulous fun, their energy and optimistic slant on life happily rubbing off on you too. It's *Smiles* and *Positive Looks* all round, even if you do have to scoot after them to sweep them up into your arms for a quick cuddle before they wriggle free and burst off in a new exciting direction. Even having *Positive Touches* on the run can give your one-year-old the unequivocal knowledge they are the apple of your eye.

- On a *bad* day, when you are feeling like death due to a heavy cold and your toddler has just thrown their specially nourishing home-cooked lunch at the cat, be forgiving of both yourself and your child. Give up the ambitious outing you had planned and instead try an afternoon snooze together, sliding in a few (albeit weak) smiles and touches on the way – they are much better than nothing! Maybe some *Best Guesses* for both you and your baby would be a good idea.

Toddlers love it when you make exaggerated facial expressions and they can bring an air of excitement to the most ordinary interactions. So, when you give your child *Smiles* and *Positive Looks*, let yourself go: open your eyes wide and make your *Smile* beam – even if you're only picking a daisy or patting a sand pie together. Your one-year-old will join in with gusto. I believe one of the most important aspects of the *Smiles*, *Positive Looks* and *Positive Touches* we dish out to our toddlers is their genuine nature. OK, so occasionally you just have to go through the motions because at times you simply don't have it to give. It's still better to try than leave your one-year-old in doubt about their security, wondering if you can be trusted. Anyway, sometimes when we make ourselves *Smile* our mood lifts, so there's nothing to lose. Each Baby Centred input we provide for our adorable one-year-old further cements the security of their bond with us.

Loving Smiles, Positive Looks and Positive Touches for Two-Year-Olds

- At two, most tiny tots can express themselves verbally, though we are not talking fluent monologues here. This provides us with a new window on their thoughts and imagination and can give us good cause to *Smile* at them. Be sure to shape your *Smiles* and words so your toddler feels approved of and not demeaned by your laughter. It can be all too easy to veer from gentle mockery to inadvertently belittling your two-year-old.
- Two-year-olds, although growing independent in some ways, are still very unsure and frequently search for the comfort of your *Positive Looks*. Though you may want them to separate from you easily, let them go at their own pace. They will need the sustenance of your all-important *Positive Looks* as they venture further and further away from you, their Secure Base.

- Lots of two-year-olds attend some sort of playgroup or nursery, and we have to deal with what can be an anxious time apart from each other. Never mind how they are faring, we can feel an unexpectedly powerful emotional wrench. The trouble is 'losing touch', even for an hour or two, can leave parents and their two-year-olds yearning to be back in each other's arms and experiencing their own brand of *Positive Touches*. This is not 'babyish' or 'silly' for either of you, just a very natural response to separation, however brief, between a trusting under-three and their rightly protective mummy or daddy. It does not show that your bond is in anyway weak or seriously under threat.

- On a *good* day, you will find much in your two-year-old's behaviour to trigger a *Loving Smile*, *Positive Look* and *Positive Touch*. You can now enjoy a chat with your toddler, which really opens up the daily opportunities for bond-building. Although they may now be pulling up their own knickers and pants, don't for a moment forget that in order to become self-confident little individuals they will continue to need lashings of these non-verbal Baby Centred behaviours from you for years – yes, years! – to come.

- On a *bad* day, when all you can see is mountains of work and no time in which to tackle it, try reminding yourself of the real priorities in your life. Does finishing the washing or writing lists and letters really beat time with your little treasure? Of course not, no question. So align your behaviour with your true priorities, leave the chores and instead have a bath with your two-year-old, plant a flower together or jump in puddles, anything to put the zing back into your *Smiles*, *Positive Looks* and *Positive Touches*. The jobs will still be there later, and you will have grasped an opportunity to strengthen your bond with your almost three-year-old.

Round-up

Let's finish this section with a quick run through of some of the pointers for ensuring that you give your baby or toddler top-quality *Loving Smiles*, *Positive Looks* and *Positive Touches*.

- Use them to show your general approval of your child, just for being themselves
- Use them as a reward for your baby and toddler's successes
- Use them to show your child that you have noticed when they have a good try at something
- Use them in an exaggerated fashion to stimulate your infant
- Use them in a way you know your baby or toddler particularly enjoys
- Use them to help your baby and toddler trust you
- Use them to build a secure bond between you and your under-three

Remember, pinning together bunches of Baby Centred behaviours significantly increases the impact they make on our under-threes. So far we have covered *Attends*, *Best Guesses*, *Praise* and we have just looked at the benefits of *Loving Smiles*, *Positive Looks* and *Positive Touches*. We are going to add three more Baby Centred behaviours over the coming two chapters: *Imitation*, *Ask to Play* and *Ignoring Minor Naughtiness*. When we manage to string several together, what lovely, warm, secure feelings of trust they provoke in our babies.

What Not To Do: Don't Smack

This is an emotive subject at the best of times and one that will get a mixed reaction – some people being pro- and others anti-smacking. I can't pretend to be a disinterested observer of the still-raging debate about parents using corporal punishment to discipline their under-threes, or over-threes for that matter. I am utterly convinced *Smacking* should be avoided at all costs if you want to nurture a secure bond between you and your baby and toddler. Let's just take a look at the likely emotional and psychological consequences of *Smacking* a tiny tot, as opposed to offering them *Positive Touches*. Notice that once more it's the difference between Baby Directive and Baby Centred behaviour.

CONSEQUENCES OF BABY CENTRED VERSUS BABY DIRECTIVE BEHAVIOUR FOR YOUR UNDER-THREE:

Baby Centred Positive Touches	Baby Directive Negative Touches
Continuity of attachment maintained	Attachment disrupted
Depth of bond increased	Depth of bond undermined
Security of attachment maintained	Security of attachment diminished
Knowledge of being loveable firmly established	Knowledge of being loveable seriously shaken
Parental approval encourages buoyant emotions	Parental disapproval encourages disturbed emotions
Positive sense of self enhanced	Erosion of positive sense of self
Growing self-confidence	Self-confidence stunted
Trust in parents expands	Fear of parents expands
Sociability develops	Anti-social behaviour develops
Emotional expressiveness flourishes	Emotional expressiveness inhibited
Balanced personality emerges	Personality balance threatened

Which developmental pathway do you want for your under-three? Is it really worth taking the risks associated with *Negative Touches*, in other words *Smacking*, just for the momentary release of venting your anger?

As a clinical psychologist working with a large number of families over the last twenty-five years, I have yet to see a parent and child's bond be in any way improved by the practice of smacking. Conversely, I persistently witness significant progress in family relationships when parents combine Baby and Child Centred *Attends*, *Best Guesses*, *Praise*, *Smiles*, *Positive Looks* and *Positive Touches* with *Ignoring Minor Naughtiness*. Yes, it's our old friend the Attention Rule again (see page 283). In family after family it has become clear that, as parents, our own childhood experiences of punishment come back to haunt us. If we were regularly smacked we are likely to have developed one of two polarised attitudes. Here they are:

1. Belief that smacking did us no harm and taught us to respect our parents
2. Belief that smacking damaged us emotionally and taught us to fear our parents

What is especially interesting is that when adults with either of these attitudes are asked not what they believe now but how being smacked as a child had felt at the time, not one claimed it had been anything other than bad news. It seems likely parents who justify smacking their own children come from the 'did us no harm' group, while those who employ alternative methods of managing their baby and toddler's behaviour and their own anger subscribe to the 'it is damaging' view. So, try asking yourselves these questions before you proclaim the 'advantages of smacking':

Was I smacked as a child?
How did I feel then?
Can I acknowledge it disturbed me?
Did I have to pretend I didn't care?
Am I anti-smacking because I see it damaged me and my bond with my parents?
Am I pro-smacking because I still deny it was harmful for me?
If I stopped being pro-smacking would it mean the quality of my bond with my parents is in question?
Am I able to sufficiently resolve my own emotional baggage about smacking, to choose to protect my baby and toddler from the fallout of my parents' and grandparents' anger management failures?

Testing questions, aren't they? If you were one of the fortunate group who were never, or very rarely, smacked then you are probably already using the Attention Rule to ensure your baby and toddler survives emotionally unscathed. If you have to answer yes to 'Was I smacked as a child?', keeping your tiny tot safe from your temper outbursts could be a much tougher number. The best I can urge you to do, if you find yourself in this unenviable position, is to put your baby or toddler *first* by making the choices listed below:

- Choose to defuse rather than display your own anger
  - By relaxing
  - By walking away
  - By *Best Guessing* yourself and your little one
- Choose to use Baby Centred instead of Baby Directive attention
  - By giving *Attends, Praise, Smiles, Positive Looks, Imitation, Ask to Play*, Ignoring Minor Naughtiness* and *Positive Touches*
  - By avoiding *Questions, Criticisms, Negative Looks, Teaching, Commands, Saying 'No'* and *Negative Touches*
  - By using the Attention Rule and the six Baby Centred to one Baby Directive ratio
- Choose to move on and leave your emotional baggage behind
  - By acknowledging the hurt from your childhood
  - By sharing your feelings with a trusted friend
  - By challenging your negative automatic thoughts

When you make these choices you are on track to give your child the most stunning present ever – a secure bond with the most important people in their lives, yes, you. *You* have nothing to lose by finding alternatives to smacking. Your tiny tot has a great deal of self-confidence to gain. And these alternatives to smacking? Well we have already covered lots of them: the Attention Rule; six to one Baby Centred to Baby Directive ratio; relaxing, and moving on from our own unresolved issues. However, there is more to come in chapters four and five, so flick forward now if you are finding it difficult to make the choices we have just discussed. Work at seeing things through your own eyes, not those of your parents. When you can separate out the two different perspectives you will truly have become your own person and therefore sufficiently free of your past to choose *not* to smack.

---

* Baby Centred 'Ask to Play' will be covered in chapter four, along with its Baby Directive opposite, Teaching.

I want to finish the smacking debate by describing for you the reactions to physical punishment shown by some of the children I have seen over the years.

Penny, aged almost three:
   frantically tried to please her parents
James, aged just two:
   flinched sharply from all adults who approached him with any
   degree of speed
Bridget, aged one-and-a-half:
   cowered silently in the corner, looking watchful
Harry, aged 10 months:
   struggled desperately to escape his parents' arms
Maria, aged five months:
   avoided eye contact with everyone

You will have noticed all these reactions are non-verbal, as would be expected of under-threes who simply can't articulate their feelings. I still find it quite difficult myself and I'm no toddler! So, when I am drawing up a developmental profile of a young child, I will always include observations on their behaviour along with anything they might be able to say to me. Some two-year-olds can be stunningly graphic in their comments about having been smacked and, of course, as they get older they have even more to say. Until, that is, they reach the stage where they are able to work out what might happen if they 'tell', fearing even more physical punishment of course. I realise that many of the families I have worked with were likely to be experiencing much more serious problems than you might be grappling with. I realise too that no one reading this book will ever want to physically or emotionally damage their own beautiful baby or terrific toddler. But it would be remiss of me not to urge you to avoid smacking, which will consequently enrich your parent/baby bond.

Your baby and toddler will feel much more secure and able to trust you when you put the emphasis on *Smiles, Positive Looks* and *Positive Touches* and give smacking the boot.

Special Feature: Managing Anger

Now I want to focus on the emotional aspects of bonding. This includes emotional expressiveness and dealing with our own difficult feelings. This book centres around increasing the positive emotional strands of our bond with our baby and toddler, so the focus here will be on how to keep the negatives under control. Anger and what to do with it seems to be a sensible place to start.

When the subject of emotional expressiveness comes up, we often hear people talking about Emotional Intelligence, Emotional Literacy and Emotional Availability. In fact, we seem to be developing a special vocabulary with which to discuss our feelings, and not before time. In my opinion, there has been far too little light shed on the subject in previous generations, with the result that millions of us were less emotionally intelligent, emotionally literate and emotionally available than is good for us. I've even heard the phrase 'emotional pygmy' used to label those unable to express their feelings, especially tender and loving ones. One of the most common complaints about men nowadays is that they are not sufficiently 'in touch with their feminine side'. Not surprisingly, these negative remarks are not usually made by other men! No, on the whole it's women who seem to long for their male counterparts to talk more easily about their internal world of feelings and emotional intimacy and be sensitive towards and perceptive about personality differences. And let's not forget the gender divide in interests and priorities that characterise so many heterosexual relationships. Given that this situation still exists, and I believe it does, I think it's particularly interesting that new dads are now allowed, even expected, to show as much emotional expressiveness as new mums towards their newborns. And they do! A situation to be celebrated, I think you'll agree.

But what does emotional expressiveness really consist of? I will try to spell it out. Quite simply, expressed emotion is what happens when we allow our feelings to show. They can be viewed as opposite pairs, such as:

Affection   and Dislike
Love   and Hate
Forgiveness and Blame
Acceptance   and Rejection
Sympathy   and Contempt
Generosity   and Greed
Serenity   and Anger

You can probably think of lots more diametrically opposed pairs of emotions, but these will do to begin with. As you can see, each positive feeling has a painful and sometimes dangerous counterpart, and in families where high levels of these negative emotions are expressed, life can be pretty tough for those on the receiving end. Strange, isn't it, that when we all long for affection, love, forgiveness, acceptance, sympathy and generosity from others and strive to achieve serenity for ourselves, so many of us spend time indulging in the decidedly less cuddly emotions?

Think back. When did you last demonstrate your affection – and dislike – towards someone? Then do the same for the other pairs of feelings. How does it work out for you? Are you mostly positively or negatively expressive? Are you a mummy or daddy? Does it make a difference? Whatever the results of your self-survey, I strongly suggest that the bond between your under-three and you will be very much more secure if you increase your expression of positive emotions and cut down on their nasty 'twins'! Your child's trust in you will also zoom up the scale, which is extremely good news for all the different kinds of relationships they will experience throughout their lives.

We have all felt angry at one time or another and we often feel fully justified in our bad tempered, critical mumblings about the railways, traffic, the weather and far too many bills. Things are rarely just how we want them, are they? In any case, grumbling and groaning seems to be something of a national pastime. But what about the other kind of anger? The one where your heart beats faster, your vision blurs, your muscles tense, your face contorts, your voice sharpens and before you know where you are, you have lashed out? I'm talking about the rage which can sweep away in an instant all your good intentions of being Baby Centred. Those occasions when you threaten the security of your bond with your under-three by losing control of your temper. Those times when you disturb the trust your baby or toddler has placed in you by shouting and smacking.

That's my view on what can happen when our emotional expressiveness has moved so far away from serene approval it has transformed into *Anger*. I believe when we 'lose it', 'see red' or 'go OTT' (over the top) with our under-threes, however provoked we may feel ourselves to have been, the emotions we express are damaging to everyone involved. As for the other negative emotions, well, how does being disliked affect you? Do you long to be hated, blamed, rejected or treated with contempt? Is being greedy a trait you admire in others or aspire to yourself? Of course not! But that leaves a gap doesn't it? A gap between how we want to feel and what really goes on when we are pushed to our limit. How best to deal with our own negative emotions when they arise in the context of parenting our under-threes? You notice I'm leaving out the momentary incandescent fury experienced between you and your co-parent in the car, for instance sparked off by taking the wrong turn and finding yourselves in the middle of nowhere! It's the 'Mummy's getting angry!' or 'Daddy's losing his temper!' times I'm talking about.

The first thing to remember is, feelings do *not* have to be acted out. Feeling angry does *not* entitle us to shout, smack, stamp about or slam doors. An angry emotional reaction does *not* justify aggression. Thank heavens! Otherwise civilisation as we know it really would cease to exist. We do sometimes experience anger though, don't we? Yet at the same time we want to protect and nurture the precious bond we have built up with our child. It really is a huge dilemma, and one that every parent grapples with on occasion. Let's look at some of the mini events that go to make up the *provocation – anger – shout – smack* sequence.

1. Our one- to three-year-old annoys us
2. Our heart rate increases

3. We tell them off in an impatient and suddenly louder voice
4. They do 'it' again
5. Our muscles tense and we narrow our eyes
6. They do 'it' again – laughing
7. We snap and shout with anger
8. They look shocked for a moment, then they do it again
9. We smack them because we have lost control of our emotions
10. We feel a few seconds' release of tension
11. They start to cry
12. We are overcome with remorse and regret
13. We apologise and try to make it better
14. They at first push us away
15. We don't enjoy their rejection and stop saying sorry
16. Everyone is unhappy with the emotional rift that has opened up

Time passes and gradually you migrate back towards each other and then make your peace – until next time. You see what's happened? Your *Anger* has driven a painful wedge between you and your child because you acted it out.

Fortunately, there are other options available and we can learn to deal with our anger, however justified, in a way that maintains the bond between you and your baby or toddler. Here are some helpful hints. Try this sequence for yourself:

- Put PHYSICAL SPACE between yourself and your child
- TENSE your whole body hard for a count of five
- Consciously RELAX your muscles
- SLOW your breathing
- SCREW UP YOUR FACE and then let it relax
- Try some gentle HUMMING
- Focus your mind on a TRANQUIL SCENE
- Now you are ready to *Best Guess*

Remember, *Best Guessing* is an effective way of acknowledging stress and other uncomfortable or even frightening feelings, while preserving a positive emotional connection. Look back to chapter one to refresh your memory about how to *Best Guess*: Mirror, Validate, Empathise and Resolve – remember? The big difference between this approach and acting out your anger is that you get to solve the problem and save your bond with your toddler all at the same time. The physical space will prevent you from smacking your child. The tensing and relaxing will give you the physical release you need. Concentrating on slowing your breathing and gentle humming to yourself will stop you from shouting, whilst putting a tranquil scene in your mind will increase your feel-good factor. You can then congratulate yourself on having maintained control in the face of a strong negative emotion and having dealt with it in a constructive fashion. Best of all, you and your toddler will still be in touch emotionally, your bond perhaps even more secure as a result of weathering the storm.

Of course, our infants also experience rage, which can be pretty scary for a child – especially when they're not even sure where they end and the world begins, and especially if they have no means of controlling the frightening sensations they are experiencing. Here is where we parents have a really important role to play because we are their main hope of helping them to learn how to soothe themselves. The sequence set out above is really a method of calming and soothing adult rage. Naturally, babies and toddlers cannot manage anything like that on their own. They desperately need our input.

So what should we do when our infants are in an enraged state? The solutions vary enormously from age to age, so what is suitable from a newborn's to a one-year-old's perspective could be entirely inappropriate for an almost three-year-old. In general terms, babies need to be held and physically rocked and comforted, while older toddlers may have to be left to themselves until they have gently hiccuped themselves into silence. There is quite a fine line between ignoring a one- to two-year-old's tantrum and knowing when they have worked themselves up into such a state that we should step in and hold them until they calm down. I will be going into all of that on page 289, when I discuss how to deal with disobedience. That leaves babies from newborns to those turning one.

It is in these early months that we have an incredibly important opportunity to enable our babies to learn a life skill that will mean they can avoid acting out their anger and instead calm themselves and *Best Guess* their way out of bond-threatening situations. It seems extraordinary, doesn't it, but the neural pathways enhanced in babyhood by parental lessons in soothing can literally last a lifetime. So, how best to go about it? It seems that only in a few cultures are babies ever left to cry untended, while across most of the world the aim is to meet their every need almost before it is signalled. Certainly the under-one-year-olds are comforted and soothed well in advance of their becoming distraught. But, I hear you protest, if they never get enraged how are they going to learn to calm themselves? The answer seems to be nipping any potential baby anger in the bud by soothing them before they get too distressed. Of course, this may go right against the grain of how you had intended to manage things when your baby is still very young. In that case you will obviously make your own decisions on the matter. Even so, I would strongly suggest that you reconsider, especially in light of your privileged position as comforter-in-chief for your new addition. Soothing babies strengthens bonds, while leaving them to cope alone with terrifying waves of anger can mean the security of their attachment and trust in you is undermined.

Echoes From Our Past: Inconsistent Parenting

Here I want to tell you about – amongst other things – my own experiences of *Smiles, Positive Looks* and *Positive Touches*. I'll also be mentioning anger. Yes, I too have felt the red mist rising – you are not alone! However, most of the echoes in this chapter will be about inconsistent parenting. You know, the 'I know I said yesterday it was fine to play with bubbles in the bath but today it's driving me mad!' style of interacting with an under-three. In other words, the under-three behaviours that provoked *Smiles, Positive*

Looks and *Positive Touches* one day and gritted teeth and scowling the next.

My own parents were, much to my good fortune, pretty consistent during their efforts to bring up their three offspring. My mother was a great believer in routine, which is important for babies and toddlers if they are to benefit from the security that predictable parenting conveys. Mind you, being breastfed by the clock and potty-trained at three months probably wouldn't be recommended nowadays, because we know much more about infant development than my mum's generation. There were no baby and parenting TV programmes – in fact, there were no TVs. I'm talking Second World War here; history, as my grandchildren call it!

But what about my share of *Smiles, Positive Looks* and *Positive Touches*? Luckily, my parents were so besotted with their firstborn that, whatever the books of the day said about babies not being carried and cuddled too much, they went ahead and gave me masses of both – or so I'm told. Naturally, I can't remember a great deal from that far back, though the impact of all their affectionate attention naturally left an indelible imprint on my mind. I still adore being the object of demonstrative affection as well as snuggling up to my nearest and dearest. Despite the undoubted upside, I'm probably still trying to make good the absence of my father's hugs and kisses, who was called up into the Navy when I was only just three! You could say that because of world events, my father's style of parenting was 'inconsistent', but this isn't the sort of thing I mean by the term – as you will see in a minute when we go into more detail on this style of parenting.

And the loving *Smiles, Positive Looks* and *Positive Touches*? Special memories of times when I was the recipient of this fabulously rewarding triple strength input include:

- Being dressed up as Rule Britannia for a toddler fancy-dress competition. (My sister Liz won the Beautiful Baby prize. Was I jealous? I honestly don't know, it was such a very long time ago!)

- Being a buttercup in a school fête day
- Being kissed goodnight, good morning, hello and goodbye (this went on all through my life while my parents were still both alive)
- Being held by the hand
- Being in bed cuddled up to my mummy
- Being carried on my daddy's shoulders
- Being smiled at by my mother as she awarded me a prize for my mud pies
- Being hugged and kissed by my father on his return from the war in North Africa

Lucky me, because after all I was no more deserving of such parental largesse than any other baby, toddler or schoolchild. None of us gets the chance to choose our parents, do we? It really is the luck of the draw.

So, what happens when this same lucky – or unlucky for some – draw provides us with a mum and dad who are inconsistent parents? What might have happened to the security of our attachment to them, or our ability to trust them – especially when we felt afraid or unsafe? It really can be a confusing experience, can't it? Do you remember being unable to predict whether your mother or father would be warm or rejecting on any given occasion? Were you anxious because sometimes your parents were readily available and at other times they were nowhere to be found? Did it worry you when you received approval for a particular behaviour one day and criticised the next? Could you work out when your parents would be comfortingly in charge as opposed to frighteningly overwhelmed by their responsibilities? I realise that, like myself, you probably can't recall a great deal from your first three years. But I want you to cast your mind back as far as you can to see if you recall lacking self-confidence during childhood. Do you have memories of feeling insecure and finding it difficult to trust other people? You may still experience some of these painful emotions. The reason could be that despite doing their very best your parents were not able to give you the stability we all need so much when we are little.

Perhaps there were times when promises were not kept, when your very best efforts produced *Smiles*, *Positive Looks* and *Positive Touches* one minute and *Criticism* the next. If our own parents were inconsistent, it's likely we still can't tell whether they will be there for us or not. We may have felt afraid because sometimes *we* seemed to be the ones running the show as they didn't always know how to take charge. It can be very scary indeed for babies and toddlers when their mummy and daddy, who must surely know *everything*, don't manage to make them feel safe at crisis points. Of course, a crisis for an under-three might not look that threatening to a grown-up. Your under-six-month-old may have inadvertently stabbed themselves in the eye with one little finger. Your under-one-year-old could have accidentally drenched themselves with a nice cold drink. Your one-year-old may have decided that a mouthful of gritty sand does not taste nearly as good as it looks, while at two your toddler suddenly freezes at the top of what is, after all, an extremely small slide. It's at these crisis points that our under-threes desperately need to be able to predict with certainty that we *will* rescue them, keep them safe and comfort them until the scary time has passed and they are ready to face their world once more.

We can all see how crucially important it is that our infants feel secure in our love and can trust us to take good care of them. But what happens when there is no way for babies and toddlers to predict exactly what mummy or daddy will do next, as their responses don't seem to have much to do with the little one's actual behaviour? These are some of the signs of an insecure child:

- Poor self-confidence
- Anxiety
- Emotional problems
- Behavioural difficulties
- General unhappiness
- Experiencing issues of trust

Understandably, we do not want our under-threes to suffer these painful feelings, particularly if we were treated inconsistently by our own parents. Looking ahead, you may have taken that all-important first step towards being more predictable by acknowledging you have been at least a tad too inconsistent in the past. If you can also link in some awareness of unresolved issues of trust from your own childhood – and we *all* have them to one degree or another – you will have made a good start towards making positive change.

If you notice you are behaving in the following ways – with the emphasis on the *and* . . .

- in control *and* sometimes overwhelmed
- warm *and* sometimes rejecting
- reliable *and* sometimes unpredictable
- emotionally available *and* sometimes remote
- close by *and* sometimes nowhere around
- approving *and* sometimes critical

. . . then there are things you can do to ensure that in future you come up with a much more consistent, bond-building, secure and trust-making style of caring for your baby and toddlers that leaves them in no doubt as to your warmth, approval and whole-hearted love.

Before going into details about moving on from being inconsistent, I just want to tell you about two of the many, many families I have worked with where inconsistent parenting was leaving young children feeling all at sea, as opposed to safe on home ground.

Case Study One

When I first met them, Nadine and Bill were in their early thirties and had two-year-old twin boys – quite a handful for anyone, you'll agree. Both parents were working long hours, and although Bill's business allowed him to work from home, Nadine was regularly away for two or three nights consecutively. This left Bill with the lion's share of bedtime responsibilities and in order to cope he had successfully pioneered a gentle wind-down at the end of the day. At 8.30 p.m. all three of Nadine's boys were often snuggled up and asleep on the couple's giant-size family bed. Nadine and Bill had arranged for their two little boys to attend nursery every morning, which gave Bill time for his work. An afternoon nap of one to two hours for the twins provided even more grown-up's time for Bill. So what was the problem? Let's unpick their situation and take a look.

On closer examination it became clear that difficulties in the twins' sleep time behaviours only seemed to occur when Nadine was around. This was causing conflict between the couple as Bill blamed his wife for messing up his successful routines, while Nadine maintained that because she was the twins' mother, when she was at home her boys would do things *her* way. Nadine herself had grown up in a large family where strict ground rules operated vis-à-vis bedtime and she expected her tiny sons Sebastian and Edward to toe a similar line. Bill on the other hand was an only child and had always longed for siblings. He strongly felt Sebastian and Edward should have lots of time together. Bill, who strongly wanted to be a participant in the two boys' close moments, especially treasured their bedtime cuddles and resented Nadine's insistence on her routine being the 'winner' in this increasingly acrimonious dispute.

As you might imagine, soon both Sebastian and Edward did not know what to expect at bedtime, apart from the shouting matches between their mummy and daddy! Seb started to be clingy and upset when being left at nursery, whilst Teddy seemed to be turning into a tiny thug, kicking, biting and generally terrorising other children. Clearly their parents' widely differing views on what constituted an acceptable bedtime routine was unsettling the twins and making them feel anxious and insecure. I orchestrated initial negotiations between Nadine and Bill, asking each to explain to the other about the childhood experiences which had led to their current positions. Once the couple were able to discuss their different views, it was not long before they came up with a compromise that meant the twins had the same bedtime routine whether mummy or daddy was in charge.

Seb and Teddy seemed to flourish once they could rely on being able to predict that, each and every night, they would first have a fun bath time, then downstairs for a special cuddle on the sofa with daddy – and mummy, if she was at home – then upstairs at a time agreed by the grown-ups for teeth brushing and into bed for a story, a kiss and 'night, night'. I think what Seb and Teddy showed us very clearly is that even otherwise identical little beings can react in quite different ways to the same source of stress, in this case their parents' inconsistent approach to bedtime. Though both boys were distressed at being unable to safely predict their bedtime routine, Seb's reaction was more emotional whilst Teddy acted out. Happily, once Nadine and Bill successfully addressed the issue of their inconsistent parenting, their two-year-old sons benefited very rapidly and family harmony was restored.

Case Study Two

Although inconsistency between parents is undoubtedly a factor that many families find taxing, equally common is the situation where one parent's behaviour varies a great deal in a way that seems to indicate they find it difficult to maintain a predictable child-centred style of attention. Every time we vacillate from one extreme to another, we are in fact breaking the Attention Rule. You know, the one about responding to our infant's behaviour contingently and consistently, with *Praises* for good behaviour and *Ignoring* the bad, whilst being prepared to spring into action for any dangerous moments. All much more easily said than done I'm sad to say – especially if we are feeling stressed ourselves, for some reason.

Taking that sort of consistent stand seemed out of the question for Verity, a newly single mother of four children whose ages ranged from eight months to five years. Verity had been left to cope alone after the tragic death in a road accident of her partner Rick, just before she discovered she was pregnant with their fourth child Bryony. Verity's parents and sister had been a tower of strength for many, many months as she and the children struggled to come to terms with their shocking loss. Finally, Verity believed she could manage without her family's pretty constant input, and arranged for Mondays and Thursdays to be their only practical support times. She was sure she could cope alone for the rest of the time. But she found she couldn't. Her mood was positive one day and distinctly low the next. Verity seemed to be losing her temper with her children one second and smothering them with penitent kisses the next. She was particularly worried about the impact her inconsistent behaviour might be having on Bryony, as the older three: Rufus, five; Dominic, four; and Prudence, three, had all had a much steadier first few years than their baby sister. Verity and her family contacted me to ask for help in being able to achieve a more emotionally stable atmosphere between the children and their mummy.

A first step was to make sure Verity participated in grief counselling sessions so her attempts to deal with her own sadness and anger at the loss of Rick could be distanced from her relationship with her four offspring. Secondly, Verity's parents and sister were drafted back in to help five days a week. Verity had expected far too much of herself far too soon. Finally we worked together on reducing the inconsistencies in how she was handling particular trouble spots involving Bryony. Verity's progress was fairly slow at first, but after two months she was beginning to see significant changes for the better and felt reassured that baby Bryony's bond with her mummy was being strengthened to the point where the infant trusted Verity and felt emotionally secure in their relationship. Three years later, Verity wrote to tell me she was getting married to Alan, who already had two children of his own. What a houseful! Some of the things Verity and I covered together could be relevant to anyone who fears their inconsistent style of parenting is damaging the attachment between them and their baby or toddler.

If you have identified yourself as someone who is a rather inconsistent parent, and realised you may have unresolved issues of trust, probably linked to your own childhood, then try some of these ideas for helping yourself psychologically. Say to yourself or out loud:

- 'I do have the skills to be a balanced parent.'
- 'There is a lot to be gained by lovingly taking control.'
- 'My baby and toddler need me to be more consistent so they can learn to trust.'
- 'When I am in control as a parent I will be more in charge of my own life.'
- 'I can learn to trust myself.'

It truly is *never* too late to start moving on from the emotional baggage we all tote around with us. Although we are always left with some strong reminders from our childhood experiences, we can noticeably lighten the burden by chucking out those that limit our potential as grown-ups and parents. Don't let yourself be defined by other people's ideas of who you are. *You* can choose.

There are other steps you can take to help you on your journey to becoming a more consistent, balanced parent. Give some or all of these a try and you will find that exchanging confidences with a sympathetic friend, relative or an approachable professional can really fire you up to make changes. So . . .

- Talk to someone you trust about your plans to become less inconsistent.
- Tell them something about your own childhood – as much as you are comfortable with – and then listen in turn to what they choose to confide in you.
- When you feel the moment is right, discuss with them the links you have seen between your early experiences and your intentions to be a more balanced parent.

Remember to include your baby's other parent. Share your ideas, hopes and fears so that you can present a united front to your offspring when tackling those family hot spots that can have us all abandoning even our own ground rules! Hold on to the certain knowledge that you *don't* have to be perfectly consistent, simply good-enough.

I am going to run some practical suggestions past you now. When you put them into practice with your under-three, it will immediately bump up your consistency rating. Here we go:

- Give balanced attention – praise your children for good behaviour and ignore all the minor irritating things they do.
- Save any 'punishments' for dangerous and destructive behaviour.
- Give your toddlers clear commands and praise them straight-away if they start to do as they've been told.
- Write out a plan of campaign for yourself and fix it to the fridge door.
- Reward yourself, and/or your co-parent, with treats of all sizes for making moves towards being more consistent.

Remember that infants under one really have *very* little ability to be naughty because they simply are not up to thinking things through at that level. They don't intend to be irritating. In fact, they don't intend anything much at all, because they can't. So I'm talking about the ones and twos here, though the same general principles apply to all our interactions with our infants. It's that old Attention Rule again! Without it, our relationships with our children would veer ever closer to chaos because we wouldn't have effective guidelines for behaving more consistently towards them.

However, despite all our best resolutions, chaos can threaten at times. You know, those moments when several things go wrong all at once and our stress levels rocket . . . the cat is sick on the carpet just as the toddler gets jammed under the kitchen table and, at the same time, the phone rings, the washing machine leaks all over the floor and you realise you forgot to get vital supplies when rushing round the shops yesterday! It would certainly tax the patience of a saint, wouldn't it? Yes, yes, and yes again! It's at these moments of crisis that good intentions slip from our grasp. Our best best bet is to use an emergency desperation mantra. You may have your own already, but if not, see if this one suits:

BE CARING – BE CALM – BE CONSISTENT

Like all mantras, it needs to be repeated over and over again. I know self-instruction can seem a bit feeble when put up against domestic calamities, but it can be surprisingly effective. If you add 'I CAN' before each 'BE', you are sending powerful and positive coping messages to the brain. Messages that will improve your ability to rescue your toddler, prompt you to switch off the leaking washing machine, put the cat outside, cover the mess with a kitchen towel, ignore the phone, and decide that the forgotten supplies are not that vital. All at the same time! Or not – remember no one is a perfect parent, we just do our best from moment to moment.

A useful tip is that when we manage to be cool and calm about catching ourselves being inconsistent, we really are winning in the struggle to ensure our bonding skills are giving our under-threes the confidence to trust we can keep them secure, even on a bad day. It's this confidence that will enable them to grapple with life's challenges instead of being overwhelmed. By becoming more balanced and less inconsistent towards your child, you are boosting the size of the self-confidence bubble which will keep them afloat for the rest of their lives.

Meanwhile, let's see what extra help you might need when you are tackling all those issues to do with feeding your under-threes including, of course, the two Scary Lists on the topic. Making sure they get the right amount of the right stuff is a huge responsibility, isn't it? It is, after all, about keeping your baby or toddler alive and it doesn't get more scary than that!

Special Feature: Emotional Aspects of Baby and Toddler Feeding

This feature will focus on the emotional aspects of feeding, particularly hard-to-handle scenarios and Scary List items. The weight of responsibility associated with being in sole charge of making sure our children are getting enough sustenance to keep them ticking over and fighting fit can be pretty crushing. So, let's move on to the topic of how we cope emotionally – or at least try to – with the whole business of feeding our little ones. There seems to me to be several distinct phases involved. See if you agree: Ideas come first, followed by Plans which inevitably evolve into Reality. What's your perspective? I think that along with the Ideas phase come the Dreams, with the Plans go Hopes and by the time Reality hits we are facing our Fears. And don't forget, we each bring to every stage of the process our own attachment histories with all their pluses and minuses.

Ideas and Dreams
Some of us, even before we become pregnant, and I include couples here, already have decided ideas on breast- and bottle (or formula) feeding. We may believe a variety of things about infant nutrition. Ideas like:

- Breastfeeding is best because it's what nature intended
- Breastfed babies are closer to their mummies
- Breastfeeding helps a new mum get back her flat stomach faster
- Breastfeeding is much cheaper
- Breastfed babies are immune to lots of illnesses

Or:

- Breastfeeding makes a woman's breasts sag
- Breastfed babies don't sleep through the night for a long time
- Breastfeeding makes you anxious because you can't see how much the baby is drinking

- Breastfeeding is impossible if you have small breasts
- Breastfeeding totally exhausts the mum

Or:

- Bottle feeding lets dads take their turn with feeds
- Bottle feeding is the modern approach
- Bottle feeding gives parents more time together
- Bottle-fed babies sleep through the night from quite a young age
- Bottle feeding is easier to do

Or:

- Bottle feeding doesn't give a baby enough sucking time
- Bottle feeding makes babies bring back their milk all the time
- Bottle-fed babies get too fat
- Bottle-fed babies are more prone to illnesses

Clearly, this list could go on page after page! But let me try to confine myself to a few more items about individual attitudes to the two types of infant feeding:

- It is a woman's duty to breastfeed her baby
- I'm not going to do it all myself, so it will be the bottle
- It's the woman's decision, really
- My mum did it so why can't I/you?
- I'd be too embarrassed to breastfeed
- We'd never get a moment alone unless we used the bottle
- The thought of breastfeeding puts me right off
- I'm determined to breastfeed
- I'd feel like a failure if I didn't manage to breastfeed
- I believe in breastfeeding so I'm going to support my wife/ partner all the way
- I'm not going to bother with all that breast business, it's too messy

I dare say you can think of lots more, but let's move on to ask what matters most: accurate facts or actual feelings? Should we be struggling to breastfeed, because we have become convinced it's best for our baby, when even contemplating the venture makes us shudder inside? Or should we gracefully acknowledge that it's not for us and confidently go ahead with formula in a bottle? In order to help resolve the dilemma I suggest you conjure up your dream image of feeding your baby at the same time as focusing on the feelings and thoughts that pop up alongside your rosy and worrying pictures. Dream scenarios come in many varieties, so look at these examples and see which one feels most like you:

Blissful breastfeeding: Your baby is laying in its mummy's arms, perfectly latched on and sucking enthusiastically and gazing up at you adoringly. Nearby an entranced new daddy looks on with supportive satisfaction.

Anxious breastfeeding: Your baby does not seem to latch on properly and you feel embarrassed about having your breasts exposed. The baby is fretful, screwing up their face and eyes. Nearby, the new daddy hovers, looking concerned and exhausted – just how you feel too. Perhaps a bottle should be tried instead.

Blissful bottle feeding: Your baby is lying in its mummy's or daddy's arms, sucking their bottle enthusiastically, gazing up at its mummy or daddy adoringly. Nearby the other entranced new parent looks on with supportive satisfaction.

Anxious bottle feeding: Your baby doesn't seem to like the bottle teat and you worry the formula might be going through too fast or too slow. You both feel guilty about not having persevered with breastfeeding and wonder if that might mean you are already failing as a parent.

OK, now ask yourself two questions:

- Would I rather be blissful or anxious when feeding my baby?
- What would my baby choose, a blissful or an anxious parent?

Not too difficult to answer are they? We would all go for blissful, surely! So the problem to solve then becomes working out how best to bump up the bliss quota and avoid the anxiety.

I want you to know about my own involvement with breastfeeding – both personal and professional – so you can begin to understand how I have arrived at my present position on this emotive issue. My first active memories are of my mother successfully breastfeeding my baby brother, who is eleven years my junior. She used a small pale green wooden chair and used to sit near the range cooker – this is before they became a status symbol – looking down at her baby and occasionally glancing out of the window at the garden.

Next comes my own experience, aged twenty, of breastfeeding my first baby and the excruciating pain of not only cracked nipples but an abscess in my left breast. Despite the pain I decided to carry on because I believed breast milk to be better than formula and also because, when it didn't hurt, I loved the whole activity. Feeding my second baby, born twenty-two months after the first, went swimmingly. My friends breastfed, my relatives breastfed, my sister breastfed, too. I felt compassion for women who had tried to breastfeed and then given up, whilst I felt that those who had not even tried breastfeeding were either ignorant, foolish or both. How judgemental and patronising of me! I'm ashamed now at my lack of sympathy. My only excuse for my attitudes back then were my youth and ignorance.

I remained fascinated by the whole topic, though, and chose it for my Master of Philosophy thesis. I carried out an intervention study where I offered information, support and advice on breast-feeding to women who had never heard of the National Childbirth Trust. My input plus their own motivation and their husbands' or partners' active support enabled the vast majority of these women to succeed in using breast milk alone for a minimum of four months.

I then gathered data for a Doctor of Philosophy degree with similar results, though I have never finished writing up this study. Actually, it was all so long ago that many of those babies must now be parents themselves! But, and it's a BIG but, all the eighty or so women involved were keen to breastfeed anyway. I did not and do not see that there is anything to be gained by leaning on a new mum to breastfeed if she herself does not want to. Some of the women I went to meet and invite into my little study were, to say the least, surprised to see me. Why? Because right from the start they had never intended to breastfeed, though somehow this had not been accurately recorded in their antenatal notes.

There is a clear line to be drawn between giving couples accurate information on breastfeeding and sowing seeds of guilt if they should fail, or not even want to try. People who actively crusade about breast milk being every infant's birthright would, in my opinion, do well to remember that babies do not become attached to their parents on the basis of the type of milk they are given. As we have already discussed, it is the social and emotional context of their feeds that are paramount in terms of their experiencing the warmth, approval and security they need in order to develop into self-confident and caring individuals. And the source of that emotional and social context? You've got it in one – it's you! There is no doubt in my mind that a baby's relationship with their parents will thrive when the method of feeding chosen is the one which more nearly approaches the blissful dream scenario, be it breast or bottle. So, listen to your dreams as well as your ideas and then join them up with a good look at your feelings on the topic.

But, what if you are still undecided? Torn between wanting to give your little treasure designer breast milk and dreading exhaustion or failure, whichever hits first. How can you plan ahead and build on your hopes rather than your fears? Let's see:

Plans and Hopes

When we approach plans for filling our baby's tiny tum from an 'attachment rules' angle, then hope can really spring eternal because we won't be focusing on a success versus failure model of infant nutrition. So, putting emotional bonds first, we could have plans like this:

- I plan to breastfeed, but if it doesn't work out for us, I'll swap to bottle feeding
- I plan to breastfeed and bottle feed together, then we can have the best of both worlds
- We plan to bottle feed whatever anyone says, because we know it's going to suit us best
- We plan to wait and see how we feel after our baby is born

You'll notice that each of these plans feature 'us' or 'we'. That's because planning for that all-important activity of feeding and making sure your baby thrives really is a family affair. As women still do the majority of baby and toddler care, it can be all too easily assumed the decision of breast, bottle or both is their domain alone. Unfortunately, this can set new parents up to experience couple trouble at just those moments when their precious baby needs them to function as a team, in particular, at feeding times. It's much more constructive to make plans together and talk about your feelings on the issue, putting aside the facts of the matter. Obviously, if one of you is devotedly pro-breast and the other convinced the bottle has it beaten into a tight corner, you will need to negotiate a compromise. Most importantly, your newborn baby will undoubtedly benefit the more mutually supportive their mummy and daddy can be.

And your hopes? I know it's often difficult to see beyond the birth of your own baby, but images of our little darling growing bigger and stronger with every passing day are likely to become more frequent the nearer the estimated date of delivery becomes. Hopes like:

- 'We hope everything will go well with the breastfeeding.'
- 'We hope our newborn will go straight on to the breast.'
- 'We hope we can combine breastfeeding with both of us going back to work.'
- 'We hope our baby will be able to breastfeed for at least two years.'
- 'We are hoping bottle feeding means we can both go back to work quite soon.'
- 'We hope our baby will be completely off its bottle by twelve months.'
- 'We hope we will be able to find just the right formula for our baby.'
- 'We are hoping the baby goes straight on to the bottle with no fuss.'

Our plans and hopes loom pretty large during the latter months of pregnancy, as they should. It's only the biggest life event ever we are expecting! And providing the pregnancy is going smoothly, planning and hoping can prove to be a most delightful way of rehearsing for your future as a new family or one that is upping the number of offspring leaping about.

If you already have a child then you will be blindingly aware of how becoming a parent changes everything for ever. If you have yet to attain the dizzy heights conferred on those of mummy and/or daddy status, plan and hope optimistically but be prepared for the fact that the whole business is truly earthshaking in ways that simply cannot be grasped until after childbirth. This is not to say it's all bad news, just that as quantum leaps go, making babies is right up there at the top of the cosmic events scale. This is also the point when Reality kicks in, along with our Fears about whether we are up to the job of feeding our precious bundle properly. First, Reality, then the Fears, including the Scary Lists.

Reality and Fears

After our baby has been born, we are immediately faced with the reality of their urgent, and frequent, need for their food of choice: milk. It's probably wise to anticipate we might well experience some of the baby behaviours on this list:

- Our baby is very hungry
- Our baby keeps falling asleep at feed times
- Our baby never seems satisfied
- Our baby wants to feed every one-and-a-half hours
- Our baby doesn't seem to like the formula we have chosen
- Our baby could be allergic to cows' milk
- Our baby is getting masses of breast milk
- Our baby just guzzles up every bottle
- Our baby seems to be fine – they are filling out nicely
- Our baby suffers from wind
- Our baby might have colic
- Our baby never fusses over a feed
- Our baby cries so much for their feed, they get hiccups

What we are doing as we grapple with the reality of feeding our baby is a kind of constant sequence of checking our observations to see if our methods are working and, if not, altering our behaviour. All parents, even those with lots of experience of feeding their infants, are to some extent anxious about whether they are getting it right. And that's how it should be, because a degree of apprehension on the topic actually sharpens our level of attention and therefore acts as a protective mechanism. Increasing the chances that our observations are spot on and our responses sensitive to our baby's particular food requirements has to be helpful, doesn't it? Of course it does. So some anxiety about what, how and when to feed our baby is actually beneficial. Go ahead and observe minutely every look-around, suck, breath, wriggle, snooze, and burp your baby comes up with – it's an important, very important part of your job.

I recently watched a young mum bottle feeding her four-week-old baby boy. He had a really nasty cough and a blocked-up nose.

As you can imagine it was a pretty anxious business because her newborn could not suck and breathe at the same time and then choked a little, ending up with a racking cough every few sucks. The new mother – let's call her Melanie – was obviously very concerned about her baby, yet despite or even because of her anxiety, she handled the whole procedure quite beautifully. Melanie kept up a constant flow of *Attends*, *Best Guesses*, *Praise*, *Smiles*, *Positive Looks* and *Positive Touches*, which reassured little Robin that his mummy was just loving him to bits during this taxing time. Melanie, meanwhile, was making successful efforts to help Robin breathe by gently removing the teat from his tiny mouth after every three or four sucks. She also made sure to wind him several times and keep him in a more upright feeding position than usual. Melanie's remarks to Robin as she managed this distressing feed were a lesson in warmth, approval and security for her baby son, as you can see:

- 'Oh darling, you're being such a brave boy.'
- 'I know you can't suck properly today but you're still my best boy.'
- 'What a good little man you are to bring up your wind.'
- 'There, that's better for you, when I help you breathe you can suck better.'
- 'My poor little darling. Don't worry, Robbie, Mummy's here. I've got you.'

Though Melanie told me afterwards she had been feeling quite upset and anxious throughout the feed, she had clearly been able to put baby Robin's need for emotional reassurance and practical help before her own feelings. She had shielded him very successfully from her own apprehensions in a mature and Baby Centred fashion, despite the distress she herself was experiencing. That does not mean to say Melanie had avoided having a Scary List, or even two! I expect her Fears were little different to the ones that plague lots of parents, mums and dads alike. Cast your eye down the page and see if any of the items on the Official Scary List ring a bell. If they do, relax, you are absolutely normal! We have all felt like this at times.

Feeding your Baby
OFFICIAL SCARY LIST

Mum	Dad
I might not have enough breast milk	I wonder if there's enough breast milk.
Suppose my baby doesn't gain weight?	I'm worried my baby won't grow fast enough.
I won't be able to cope with the night feeds	The night feeds will be a complete nightmare.
Feeding will take all my time, I won't be able to get anything else done	Feeding could leave me out of the picture.
I might not be able to keep going	Feeding our baby is utterly exhausting, it never ends

We are not alone in our fears and, as all parents know, the responsibility for ensuring your baby plumps up nicely – whether on breast, bottle or both – can feel overwhelming at times. This is especially true when we are on our knees with sleep deprivation and fatigue, or feeling under par in terms of health, or in the midst of Baby Blues or post-natal depression. It's during these stressful periods that Unofficial Scary Lists can show up – just when we don't need them! The answer to both Scary Lists centres around relaxation as a first step, backed up by the specific advice already given in previous chapters. So, if relaxation alone isn't reducing your anxiety levels about successfully feeding your baby:

- Look back at pages 53 and 60 if your major vulnerability is the shock of the birth or fatigue.
- Look back at pages 106–7 when you are vulnerable due to Baby Blues or post-natal depression.

Then put into practice whichever of my suggestions for coping you see as most relevant to your fears about feeding. Don't be embarrassed to seek outside help if the Unofficial Scary List starts interfering with your ability to put aside your own anxieties when feeding your little one – as with Melanie. Check out the lists instead, and then take appropriate action.

Feeding your Baby
UNOFFICIAL SCARY LIST

Mum	Dad
I'm starving my baby	My baby's not growing properly
My baby's brain won't develop properly because they're not getting enough food	My baby won't develop properly
My baby will die and it's all my fault	My baby could lose weight
I'm a terrible mother	I don't seem to be a very good father.

I expect you notice that, generally speaking, Scary Lists for dads are a tad less intense than those for mums. Well, no wonder! Fathers do not directly experience being pregnant. Fathers are not directly involved in giving birth. Fathers' hormones aren't careering around all over the place and fathers' breasts do not swell up with milk to sometimes alarming proportions. The plus side for new mums is that fathers are usually less tired, less fraught, less stressed and less likely to have a low mood, which leaves dads in prime position to be Mr Supportive as well as Mr Practical.

Of course, you may be one of the fortunate parents whose newborn suckles strongly, whose infant gains weight admirably and whose baby and toddler moves without hesitation through weaning to solids. I really hope that feeding your little treasure turns out to be an absolute cinch. If it doesn't, remember that *Smiles*, *Positive Looks* and *Positive Touches* for your baby can help you relax and at the same time make sure they are in no doubt that they can trust you, because you are the reliable, predictable, source of their security. Feeding problems may come and go, but secure attachments can last for ever. Right, moving on: What To Do Next.

What To Do Next: Feeding Challenges

In this section, I am going to cover the sorts of baby- and toddler-feeding challenges that might occur at the differing phases of development over the first three years in your baby and toddler's life, as well as the emotional impact for parents. How to preserve your bond with your child will also be covered along with some practical tips. Your emotional reactions to each scenario will also be discussed.

Scenario One: Babies Under Six Months Old

In the first three or so months you could find your baby has an absolutely ravenous appetite. However much breast milk you try to give them, sometimes feeding almost hourly, they are awake and crying for more after a maximum of a couple of hours. If they are on formula, you seem to be forever adding another ounce of their feed because the recommended amount really does not satisfy them.

Think of the scene. You have always wanted to breastfeed. Several relatives and friends have successfully provided ample amounts of tailor-made milk for their various infants and toddlers. With such wonderful examples all around you, how could you fail to make good? Well, for a start, we know high expectations can be a mixed blessing, bringing with them both support and pressure. Anyway there you sit. It's 11.30 a.m. and you are still in your deeply functional bathrobe and slippers, unwashed and having the ultimate bad hair day. To cap it all, your baby seems to have been suckling non-stop since around 4.30 a.m. Don't they know the difference between night and day? No! They don't, not at first. As in so much else, we have to help them adapt to a regular diurnal pattern, hopefully one much more in tandem with your own! You are, quite naturally, exhausted almost to the point of collapse, and still your newborn wants more. I can remember quite clearly a very similar situation with my first baby. I came from a family where generations of women had breastfed and fully expected to sail through the whole experience without any bother at all. I imagine from the outside that is probably how it looked. What a different story it was on the inside though, where doubt and apprehension abounded. When I look back I realise I was labouring under completely unnecessary stress simply because I didn't know how to interpret my daughter's insatiable appetite. So, instead of translating her need for frequent food as a clear sign she was efficiently absorbing my breast milk I chose the frightening empty tummy option. My Official Scary List option had items like this:

> I don't have enough breast milk to satisfy my baby
> My breast milk is too thin to satisfy my baby
> My breast milk doesn't suit my baby and has left them
>   unsatisfied
> I am a breastfeeding failure!

Never mind going on to breastfeed my baby through their first year or so, I wasn't likely to make it to the end of the first few months!

What about the same scenario with a bottle-fed baby? Picture this. You have made up the required number of bottles of formula for your newborn and are feeling pretty satisfied with your organisational skills; it is 10 a.m. and all is well. Your baby has been blissfully asleep for just over an hour and you expect them to stay that way for at least another sixty minutes. You plan a quick shower with thirty minutes' coffee break immediately afterwards. But it is not meant to be! Baby begins crying with great dedication and will not be soothed by rocking, singing, winding, or changing. In fact, even though they have only just knocked back a good 3 ounces, they seem to want more! I can relate to this situation too because I used formula when we adopted our third child as a nine-week-old baby. After breastfeeding the first two, I wasn't at all sure exactly how much to offer him, or indeed when to give him his bottle in the first place. Breastfeeding on demand undoubtedly has its challenges, but at least you don't get to count the exact ounces drunk per day or worry about giving your recent arrival too little or even too much! Perhaps we are primed to be anxious about our newborn's intake of food, whatever the method of delivery, because it's all about survival.

So, your emotional reactions probably consist mainly of anxieties, though there could be some frustration and irritation too. These anxieties would cover the sorts of fears expressed on your Scary Lists, with the worst one being that your baby's hunger shows you are failing to meet the challenge of giving your little treasure sufficient milk. At your most terrified? Well, it's obvious! You are starving them to death! These irrational fears spring from the great sense of responsibility we feel for our baby's welfare and in no way reflects the reality of the situation. A sensible part of us knows newborns have to be hungry in order to grow into the bouncing babies we are so proud to display to the world.

But what to do about our anxieties if accurate information alone does not dispel them? What I suggest is a three-pronged attack, aimed not only at reducing your fears but also protecting the quality of the bond you have with your baby. This approach would apply to any and all of the anxieties about feeding you might experience in the early days of parenthood.

First: Relax

Put on some soothing music

Sit with your eyes closed and breathe gently in and out

Slide into your mind your Blissful Feeding image

Say to yourself, 'Hungry babies are healthy babies.'

Repeat this several times as you allow every part of your body to warm, soften and relax

Second: Make Contact

Ring another new parent you have met

Ask how they are coping

Listen to their response
Tell them what you have been worrying about
Say you're trying to be relaxed about it but that it's not always
   easy
Promise to meet, phone and keep in touch – and mean it

Third: Check the Facts
Look at your baby closely and acknowledge they are filling out
Notice if their Babygro is getting a little tight
Compare their birth photo with a recent snap
Consult their weight chart and check they are staying on or
   above their birth centile

Remember to give your under-three-month-old lashings of *Smiles*, millions of *Positive Looks* and a pretty constant supply of *Positive Touches* while you are working at calming your fears. This, along with the *Attends*, *Best Guesses* and *Praises* that will become second nature to you, protects the bond with your baby from any negative fallout from your anxieties. You could also take some practical steps like:

- Contact your health visitor for a special visit to discuss your fears.
- Ask your health visitor about different feeding regimes you might try.
- Check with your health visitor whether they are happy with your baby's weight gain.

Perhaps the most helpful arrangement of all would be to employ a doula! I don't know where the word itself comes from but the fact of the matter is, in many societies, doulas are considered an essential support for parents of newborn babies. When I was researching for my studies of breastfeeding and first came upon the practice, I was immediately envious! Fancy having an experienced woman in your home to calm your fears, take over while you have a nap and, best of all, understand just how scary and tiring those first few months can be. Would I have liked a doula? You bet! These precious individuals can now be found, for a price of course, in western industrialised society via relevant websites. If you believe that you and your baby would benefit from their invaluable services, get out and find one! I wish I had had the chance!

I should mention at this point the business of when to stop breastfeeding. It has to be up to each individual family surely, even though the sight of three-, four- and five-year-olds casually latching on for a quick guzzle might give some pause for thought! Interestingly, when I was with a small group of specially trained breastfeeding counsellors recently, there were very mixed reactions to a television programme covering the topic of extended breastfeeding. Each counsellor was quite passionately in favour of breast is best and yet some were decidedly uneasy about these older children continuing to nurse. My own view? Families must be free to make their own decisions on extended breastfeeding, though they should expect to encounter some degree of disapproval from the general public as others may not see things from their rather unusual perspective.

Scenario Two: Babies Aged Six to Twelve Months

In the second half of the first year of your baby's life, feeding challenges, like everything else, can move on to another phase. One of the things parents often complain about is their six- to twelve-month-old's fascination with their food. That's not fascination as in 'Mmm, I wonder if I'll be having apricot dessert today?' No. It's fascination as in poking, smearing, squeezing, swiping, patting, splashing, licking, spitting, snuffling, and generally playing about with the food they are offered. Someone asked me recently whether babies did this on purpose to wind their mummy and daddy up. The answer is no, of course. Six- to twelve-month-olds simply don't have the intellectual equipment to plan a campaign of food demolition in order to get under our skin. They do it because it feels nice!

In the second half of their first year our little darlings are dedicated to exploring their immediate environment. One of the ways in which they learn that they can act upon their surroundings is to make a connection between doing something and seeing what happens next. And in fact, this is immensely exciting for them. The bread sticks have become a pulpy mass since your infant swished them round with their juice. The apricot dessert is glistening in their hair. The delectable pasta-and-cheese concoction you made with ultra fresh, healthy ingredients has, handful by delighted handful, been thrown around the kitchen. It's the final insult, and you feel a swift surge of irritation towards the angelically smiling baby grinning up at you through a face glazed with baby yoghurt. Actually, you're more than irritated, you are very irritated! Your heart sinks as you survey the debris that was to have been a cosy meal-à-deux.

We don't really expect to be feeling irritated, all right *very* irritated, with our babies at meal time. So it doesn't fit in with our Blissful Image of feeding at all. Clearly, something has to change, but what? Your baby? You? Mealtimes? Well, let's get something straight – it won't be your baby's creative food treatments. Why? Because they all need to experience as many tactile textual messing-about opportunities as possible during their early years, and food makes for an interesting beginning. In other words, from your baby's perspective, mealtimes are play times. So how to avoid limiting their obviously satisfying – to them! – poking, smearing and squeezing, whilst ensuring they actually get some nourishment, all the while keeping your irritation levels on a very low flame?

Reducing irritation

Plan ahead for messy eating and messy playing with food
  • Try spreading an old sheet on the floor
Accept that clothes will get mucky
  • Remember, babies can happily eat in just their nappies
Tell yourself your baby needs to poke, smear and so on
  • Give them different, interesting textures and tastes to try while you feed them

Remind yourself most babies choose a fairly balanced diet when given the opportunity
- Make sure your baby's milk intake is on target, then you will have nothing to worry about

A snack and a drink relaxes everyone, parents included
- Eat and drink with your baby

See mealtimes as an opportunity for modelling sociable eating habits
- Eat and drink in an exaggeratedly 'polite' fashion

Use self-instruction to help you keep calm
- Say to yourself 'Mess doesn't matter, bonding does.'

The more you reduce or pre-empt your irritation, the more you are protecting the positive aspects of the bond between you and your six- to twelve-month-old. Put your energy into challenging the Negative Automatic Thoughts which pop up. Remember NATs? When you hear yourself thinking, or even muttering, 'It's all ruined!', or 'I'll never get this cleared up!', and 'Oh no! Not again! It always happens to me!', catch hold of that NAT. Then pin it down and identify the thinking error involved. Then look at the facts, especially the evidence *against* your NAT. If this talk of NATs rings no bells, you need to go back to pages 116–18 where all will be revealed. Just as an added mini rehearsal, you would work on the first example above like this:

'It's all ruined' = NAT
Thinking error: Over-generalisation.
Evidence and challenge to NAT: One new baby outfit stained with greenish gunge is *not* 'all' and *not* 'ruined.'
Evidence and challenge to NAT: The baby outfit can be washed.
FACT: Your baby has six other new outfits.

Try the other two examples yourself. Just to help you along, the second NAT is catastrophic thinking, and the third over-personalisation. Then try *Smiles, Positive Looks* and *Positive Touches*, starting with unclenching your teeth, if they happen to have locked together with the irritation you are trying so hard to reduce. Smiling boosts *our* feel-good factor, as well as bumping up our baby's trust in us, so there's absolutely nothing to lose and lots to gain by lightening up.

Scenario Three: One-Year-Olds

Moving swiftly on – after all, life with a baby and toddler is one long sequence of changing phases – let's focus on the one-year-olds for a minute. You may find the major feeding challenge posed by your one-year-old is their unwillingness to try any new foods you try to introduce. This can leave those of us involved in putting food on the table feeling pretty rejected.

You recognise this scene, don't you? It's lunch time and you are all at the restaurant in a large department store. Finally, you emerge from the long queue for hot meals and, having paid up, you head for an empty table you spy through the throng of shoppers. Eventually you are seated, your one-year-old in a high chair, swinging both legs vigorously and enthusiastically thumping the tray with a podgy little hand. You and your partner have chosen smoked salmon bagels, a sizeable wedge of gooey gateaux and a modest glass of spring water each. For your darling you have selected a child-size portion of carbonara pasta, some dinky broccoli florets and a pretty fruit jelly plus juice in a carton. The cost of your treat – you don't get the chance to eat out these days – is exorbitant. Never mind, the bagels look bewitching and the pasta is sure to be OK because you often have it at home. The same goes for the broccoli.

Your one-year-old is beginning to use a spoon now so they hold one while you use another to pop their 'yummy dindins' into their cute little mouth. They spit it out. You try again. They spit it out and start to cry, banging their own spoon hard into the pasta, pieces of which flick on to your carefully chosen clothes. You aren't cross, but as your one-year-old opens their mouth wide and starts to yell, you begin to feel rejected. This sensation intensifies as with one well-timed sweep of their chubby left arm they send the whole dish spinning to the floor. It's the same performance with the broccoli, and the jelly might just as well have been poisoned for the disgust it produces. As you courageously battle through your bagels and make inroads on your gateaux, you're feeling crushed. It's as if everything you have offered your toddler has been thrown back in your face. In this case, probably literally!

Rejection is almost never a welcome emotion, and when the person doing the rejecting is a beloved one-year-old it can be exquisitely painful. After all, you do *everything* for them but they won't even eat a tiny bit of posh pasta for you! Sounds childish! You're right, rejection stirs up a lot of pretty primitive reactions. It's almost as if the feelings that drove us as young children to pout, turn away, kick sulkily at the nearest object, then burst into tears and run away have all suddenly risen up inside our now grown-up body. We feel affronted, let down, hurt. It's even worse if you have yourself lovingly prepared a special new dish for your toddler, only to have them push it away without even tasting the offering. Grown-ups have no right to be so rude. But at one year of age? Is our feeling of rejection to our under-three ever going to be justified? The short answer is no, because it is not *us* our toddler is turning down – it simply feels that way! But giving or preparing food is a way of offering love, which is why it hurts when it is rejected.

Let's go back to the lunchtime fiasco. You have calmed your one-year-old with a drink of milk and as they gently fall asleep in your arms, you realise you no longer feel pouty with rejection. Where have those painful feelings gone? I guess the sequence of emotional and psychological events might have gone something like this:

1. Rejection sweeps through you – it hurts
2. You feel unloved and unvalued – it hurts
3. You squash your feelings down – it's difficult
4. You gird your loins and cope with the practicalities of the situation – not so difficult
5. You think, 'It's not their fault, they're only one' – pleasantly forgiving
6. You give them a kiss, cuddle and quick wipe – it's easy

7. You snuggle them up and offer comfort and love – it's great
8. You have given them their milk – it's relaxing
9. You hold them as they sleep – lovely
10. You look down and smile – no hurts left

We all go through these painful emotional mini storms, justified or not, when we feel rejected. The important thing to do is to race through stages 1–3, act on 4 and speed on to 5. It's the *thinking* about how our feelings are illogical that lets us move on from 6 towards resolution by 10. Thinking about our toddler, and how very young they are, alters our expectations so that empathy towards them and insight into ourselves can flourish. The result? A stronger bond exists between you and your toddler, one tested in the fire of eating out. Your ability to manage your rejection constructively has forged new attachment links with your one-year-old. You have used your superior intelligence, along with *Smiles*, *Positive Looks* and *Positive Touches*, to rescue what could have become an alienating experience. And anyway, not *everybody* likes carbonara, broccoli or jelly! So better luck next time!

Scenario Four: Two-Year-Olds

When we move on to the feeding challenges typical of our much more sophisticated two-year-olds, one of the most frequent scenarios could go something like this. It's late on a summer afternoon and you have just returned from a fun time in the giant sandpit at your local park. As it's still warm, you decide to allow your toddler ten more minutes open-air activity in your own – albeit much smaller – sand box, while you prepare tea. You keep your eye on your two-year-old intrepid adventurer while you prepare the latest craze in shaped fish fingers as a brain-nourishing meal. 'Teatime', you carol enthusiastically, but with no sign of a response from your toddler. 'Time for tea', you try again, with much the same result. Your cheeky two-year-old is finally captured by dint of chasing them as they scamper away with shrieks of delight. You carry your prize into the room where you have set out a mini chair and table in front of the TV which has been loaded with your toddler's favourite video or DVD. 'Mmm!' you simulate enormous enthusiasm for the food put out to entice what can be a fickle appetite. Your toddler picks up their spoon, shovels in two large mouthfuls and then makes a determined break for the garden. As they can somehow move at the speed of light, you once more find yourself back in the position of chasing them. By the fourth repeat of this domestic carnival everyone is breathless and dinner has congealed into an unappetising blob. In various guises, this little scenario is being repeated across the land in homes with active two-year-olds. And it can leave us adults desperate to control the situation and take the reins into our own usually capable hands. We are also very likely to be in a pretty bad mood – in fact, we're furious!

Being angry, of course, actually robs us of those very powers we need to exercise if we are to be the one in charge of things. Now, while we *know* this, all we can *feel* is our body becoming incandescent with frustration and rage. When we reach boiling point we often feel much better once we have 'exploded' in some way. It's a discharge of tension, a release of built-up emotions and, once over, can leave us in a much more reasonable state of mind. Though isn't there a clash here? You need to 'explode', whereas your little one needs not only their fish fingers, but some loving yet firm control. How to solve these apparently mutually exclusive desires simultaneously? Read my suggestions and see what you think.

Step 1:   Give up on the dinner. You will then feel much less harassed, especially if you scrape it into the bin energetically, thereby discharging muscle tension harmlessly

Step 2:   Make yourself your favourite drink and offer something suitable to your two-year-old. Take the drinks out to the back garden and settle yourselves near – or even in – the sand tray; you are now distracted and your emotions have been defused

Step 3:   Look up at the sky, breathe deeply three times, but make sure you breathe out gently. This will relax you mentally and physically

Step 4:   Acknowledge there may be changes you should make: establishing and sticking by child-centred daily routines, focusing on a healthy snack rather than big meals and tweaking your expectations of your small desperado until they are more realistic. Perhaps involve other children and make all snacks 'mealtimes' by always sitting at the table. You now know to plan ahead to avoid a repeat performance

You can use this sequence of responses in other situations too, the main route to success being NOT to scrimp on Step 1, the 'Discharge Muscle Tension Harmlessly' phase. Here are some other ideas on how you might guarantee success in managing your 'explosion' and your toddler simultaneously. They may even want to join in!

Punch a few cushions – viciously
Sing a favourite song – dramatically
Throw a wet flannel at the wall – forcefully
Chuck out the rubbish – fiercely

Right – having defused the danger of fallout from a temper tantrum of our own and simmered down sufficiently to make it through Steps 2, 3 and 4, it's time to remember that from your two-year-old toddler's perspective, the whole episode has been a continuation of the fun you had in the park. Remember, they see the world very differently from us and, at two, fun takes precedence over food. Relax, too, as it is most unlikely your tiny tearaway will fade away because of a missed dinner. At this point, in my opinion, you should also be patting yourself on the back for your success in avoiding recourse to smacking as a way of relieving your frustration and anger.

GOLDEN BULLETS

- **No. 1. My Baby Needs . . . Security**
  Your baby needs to know you will always 'be there' for them. This doesn't just mean catering for their physical needs but their emotional needs, too, by behaving in a consistent way towards them and showering them in positive expressions of your love. Using frequent *Loving Smiles*, *Positive Looks* and *Positive Touches* instead of *Negative Looks* and *Negative Touches*, including *Smacking*, will make the bond between you and your baby or toddler strong and rewarding. Give your under-three warm-hearted, non-verbal approval contingent on them being gorgeous, behaving well and doing their best. Use often. Look at your baby and toddler with visible love and approval. Use often. Give cuddles, kisses and strokes you can see your under-three really enjoys. Use often.

- **No. 2. What Not To Do: Don't Smack**
  Never, ever tap, slap, jerk, push, pull, shake or smack a baby, even at your most stressed. Instead, when you feel pushed to the limit, put your baby down somewhere safe and walk away to cool off. Each time we tap, slap, jerk, push, pull, shake and smack our toddler, our bond with them is threatened. Too many negative touches destroy attachments. This goes for *Negative Looks* too – that is, any facial expression indicative of dislike, disapproval, criticism or rejection towards your baby or toddler's actions, abilities or personality. Use as little as possible. It is *Attends*, *Best Guesses*, *Praise*, *Loving Smiles*, *Positive Looks* and *Positive Touches* that build strong bonds. Aim to deliver six *Smiles* and *Positive Looks* for every *Negative Look*, although, even a four to one ratio would do very nicely. Try your hardest to give only *Positive Touches*. Avoid *Negative Touches* and *Smacking* at all costs and your attachment with your baby will flourish.

- **No. 3. Special Feature: Managing Anger**
  Expressing positive emotions towards our babies and toddlers gives them a firm foundation of love. Parents must learn to manage their anger in order to protect the bond between them and their under-threes.

- **No. 4. Special Feature: Emotional Aspects of Baby and Toddler Feeding**
  Feeding your baby and toddler can sometimes be challenging and anxiety provoking. Parents can feel overwhelmed and sometimes guilty about not doing things right. Many parents have these emotions but this most definitely does not make you a bad mum or dad. Ideas and dreams, plans and hopes, reality and fears about whether breast, bottle or both are best for our baby should be acknowledged and discussed. Remember, the choice is yours. Your baby needs your *Loving Smiles*, *Positive Looks* and *Positive Touches* at feeding time just as much as the milk or food. Baby Centred behaviour at feeding time builds up a trusting bond between parents and their under-threes.

- **No. 5. Echoes From Our Past: Inconsistent Parenting**
  Even though your parents may have been inconsistent towards you, it is still entirely possible for you to move on and be calm, caring and consistent enough so that your baby and toddler can rely on being able to predict your reactions to their behaviour. Nurture your relationship by giving lots of Baby Centred *Loving Smiles*, *Positive Looks* and *Positive Touches* and exclude their Baby Directive opposites so you and your under-three can feel secure and have fun together.

- **No. 6. What To Do Next: Feeding Challenges**
  A very hungry newborn, playful baby, fussy one- and busy two-year-old can make parents feel anxious, irritated, rejected, controlling and sometimes angry. Don't worry, there are many psychological and practical things you can do to reduce any negative impact on the relationship between you and your baby or toddler.

Chapter Four

Giving Your Baby Confidence

WHAT THIS CHAPTER IS ABOUT

In this chapter, the main topic is your baby's need for . . . Stimulation and how you can give your baby the Confidence to explore their amazing world. Why is stimulation so important? How come it's up there with Warmth, Approval and Security? What does it actually do? The answer to these questions can be summed up in one word – 'novelty'. Novel experiences are what help those all-important neural connections develop in the brain and so trigger the fantastic developmental progress seen in babies and toddlers. To aid this process we look at two more Baby Centred behaviours – *Ask to Play* and *Imitation.*

Also in this chapter

My Baby Needs . . . Stimulation

Human beings depend upon a pretty constant source of novelty in order to keep their brains active and alert. Babies and toddlers would not be able to make such incredibly rapid progress in their development were it not for the powerful impact of novel stimulation. School-age children would not be able to move on to the complexities of literacy and numeracy were it not for the cumulative effect of past and present stimulation with new events, experiences, ideas and feelings.

And so on throughout each individual's life cycle, leading hopefully to an equivalent to my own enviable situation at the moment where I can more or less pick and choose which direction to explore next. This year it's making jewellery. Last year it was gardening. Next year it will be narrowboat cruising. But then I'm in a position of some control over my life, whereas under-threes have to rely on their mums and/or dads to provide the novelty, to vary the stimulation and help their child develop the confidence to explore each new sensation as it occurs. Luckily for us and our babies and toddlers, an under-three's response to our stimulating input is extremely rewarding for the adult involved. All parents find themselves pulling a ridiculous face for their tiny tot time and again, simply for the thrill of seeing a gummy or toothy grin and hearing their delicious little chuckle.

I suppose much of what comes under the heading of 'stimulation' could as easily be called 'infant education', although I believe this is too narrow a term. Just as there are many different types of rewards, so there are many different types of stimulation. For example:

- **The five senses:** Touch, taste, sound, vision and smell. A baby or toddler's five senses provide an immense range of stimulating input day in and day out, starting during pregnancy.
- **Interpersonal interactions:** These include talking, laughing, smiling, cuddling and Baby Centred behaviour by parents. Interacting with their mummy and daddy gives under-threes a constant stream of emotional and psychological stimulation.

- **Playtime activities:** These could be clapping hands and peek-a-boo, banging pegs and splashing water, handprints and gluing, princesses and superheroes. Playtime for babies and toddlers is a wonderful source of stimulation.
- **Exploration:** Kicking, licking, sniffing, looking, touching, tasting, reaching, grasping, manipulating, dropping, throwing, crawling, cruising and, finally, walking. Under-threes are relentless in their attempts to explore their own bodies and the environment in which they find themselves.
- **Language:** Speaking, listening, understanding, explaining, commanding, reassuring. Parents are a vital source of stimulation in that most complex of human skills: verbal communication.

But what happens if our under-three is deprived of the opportunity to use their senses, interact socially and emotionally with others, enjoy playtimes and explore their environment? Depending on the degree and duration of under-stimulation, the consequences can range from a passive, undemanding personality, through to poor self-confidence, language delay and immature brain development. When babies receive too little in the way of opportunities to play with age-appropriate toys, they do not learn how to interact successfully with their physical environment. They do not gain confidence. They are not benefiting from the novelty of squeezing a squeaky elephant or lunging at the fascinating objects dangling from their baby gym.

Toddlers who have been deprived of stimulation do not learn how to play, much to the detriment of every area of their development. Babies need a whole variety of play materials so they can be lured into reaching out, grasping, licking, sucking, chewing and even just observing, in order to encourage their sensory and motor progress. Toddlers need opportunities to become mobile and therefore bring within their reach even more interesting new sources of stimulation. By the time we are talking about one- and two-year-olds, their voracious appetite for novelty is impossible to ignore. If we are not careful we can find ourselves totally exhausted as we vainly attempt to keep up with their punishing pace. Our under-three's efforts may look a trifle primitive, but we must remember that these activities are the foundations upon which their later abilities to master all sorts of skills are based.

It is quite clear, at every phase of your baby's first three years, they learn best and enjoy themselves most when you are part of the process. Even infants delight in social interactions, especially with mummy and daddy. For every contact between you, they are inevitably building up their person-to-person skills, which form the core of their later communication abilities. Face-to-face fun and games are a big favourite for all the family and also provide a wonderful context in which intellectual, language, psychological, social, emotional and, last but not least, attachment development can flourish.

If you truly want your under-three to grow up to be inquisitive and assertive in their dealings with the world and the people in it, please do not stint on either play or social stimulation. As parents we are in an enormously privileged position because we have the joy, and responsibility too, of opening the gateway to the wonders of the world for our children.

So we must tackle the task seriously, even if we do often end up having as much fun as them! *Ask to Play* and *Imitation* are two really helpful Baby Centred behaviours to use when we are responding to our baby and toddler's need for stimulation in a way that will also give them a large dose of confidence in exploring everything and anything if given even half a chance. Mums and/or dads obviously have central roles to play in this adventure, as you can see from these pointers on giving your under-threes a wide range of stimulation:

- Offering a variety of colours, textures, sounds, shapes, tastes and smells
- Giving access to age-appropriate play materials
- Giving time, energy and imagination to playing together
- Giving warmth, approval, security and Baby Centred input
- Providing opportunities for gradually meeting new people and going to new places

When we give our baby and toddler an *Ask to Play* we are inviting them to take the lead on what we should do next, which is not nearly as scary as it sounds! Trust me! This is a big confidence booster because it gives our infants a taste of feeling in control of their surroundings, of which you are, of course, the major feature. *Imitation* of our under-threes' actions, noises, words and emotions is another powerful message to them that we have not only noticed their activity, but also admire it so much we demand an immediate encore. It's all about the stimulation of doing things together, yet with time and space for your baby and toddler to safely test out their own little 'experiments'. And not really so little when you stop to think that, from day one, or even before, they are testing out the laws of our universe. They may seem to be focused on satisfying their need for warmth, approval and security, but don't be fooled – they are really reaching for the stars! They want to learn about the world and they need you to give them the confidence to complete this most enthralling journey.

Ask to Play – sounds rather odd, doesn't it? We usually associate asking someone to play as an activity used by children when they want to be involved in an activity with another little one. Alternatively, it can lead to exclusion from the group, as in 'Can I play with you?' with the answer, 'No!' Although you could use the question outright with a child aged eighteen months to three years, you have to be prepared for a similar response because, as you remember from page 36, any question can lead to either a 'Yes' or 'No' reply. But when we look at the Baby Centred version of *Ask to Play*, the most thrilling part for your under-three is when you enquire, 'What do you want me to do now?' When I first suggest this to parents of babies and toddlers, there is often an initial ripple of alarm. It's almost as though a 'Whatever next?' reaction has occurred. However, I remain utterly convinced of the great benefits our precious treasures receive when we give them the power to tell *us* what to do for a change. More on the stimulating and confidence enhancing aspects of *Ask to Play* on page 201.

Imitation can be a much derided behaviour, especially amongst school-age children. We have all heard taunts of 'copy cat' being bandied around the playground, park, garden, beach or Kidz Zone. Let's remember, though, that these are children whose intellectual, social, language and emotional development have a very long way to go before catching up with our level of sophistication. The type of *Imitation* that is Baby Centred involves an entirely benign copying by parents of their children's behaviour and language. This gives our under-threes a surge of self-worth. Stirring in lots of *Ask to Plays* and *Imitations* along the way means your infants will get the supercharged version of stimulation guaranteed to launch them as truly confident explorers. Once more mummy or daddy are in pole position to provide their own very special contribution.

In this section, I will be going through examples of *Ask to Play* and *Imitation* for newborns, babies, and one- and two-year-olds. But first let's dip a toe into the sometimes murky waters of our own childhood memories. Can you recall either of your parents seriously enquiring what you would like them to do next? What about a different type of choice, one where you were given an either/or option? Perhaps you have memories of both, but only within the context of put-downs. Or were your mother and father's questions rhetorical? You know the sort of thing: 'Well, what do you expect me to do now? Stop what I'm doing so I can see to you?' All said with an exasperated irritation bound to convey a strong message of parental disapproval.

We knew the answer to their question though, didn't we? They were *not* about to immediately curtail their activities in order to give us time or attention. Those types of interactions all too often lead to bad feelings, disappointment, confusion, anger, frustration or helplessness. Sometimes desperation. And that's just the babies and toddlers! The upshot of these pseudo questions is always the same, because the security of the bond between parent and child is undermined instead of nurtured. Can you recall urgently wanting your mother or father to join in a game or activity, only to have them swat you away with that perennial parental rejection, 'Not *now*! I'm busy'? What about, 'Don't be such a nuisance'? Any bells ringing? Because if, as children, we were fed a diet rich in put-downs like these, then we may have to work extra hard to make sure we don't perpetuate the same fault with our own children. I'm afraid there really is no way of escaping the powerful influence of our own mum and dad's parenting style. It's just the luck of the draw whether they came up with genuine *Ask to Plays* as opposed to the mock variety. It doesn't have to stay that way though, does it? You have a wonderful chance to rewrite history now you are in the driving seat. Make a start by using lots of *Ask to Plays* with your under-three, so they get a strong dose of stimulation and confidence building all wrapped up in one irresistible parcel.

A genuine, open invitation for suggestions from our under-threes on what we could be doing to please them often results in an easily fulfilled request that leaves everyone satisfied with how things have turned out. My own experiences as a mother, grand-mother and professional have taught me in no uncertain terms that children can sniff out insincerity quite quickly, though of course they often don't know how to handle it when an adult gives them a message with a double meaning. So when I think back to my childhood, I am aware of my great good fortune in having a mother who gave genuine choices to her offspring. 'Do you want egg or cheese?' 'Hot or cold drinks?' 'Washing up with me or a story with Daddy?'

My siblings and I were also often asked, 'What would you like to do now?', but though this undoubtedly opened up vistas of untold pleasures, it does not have the same psychological impact of an *Ask to Play*. Of course, when we look at *Ask to Play* ideas for new-borns, they won't be saying much! Not that this seems to prevent us asking for their views on any given situation, the only difference being that we also supply all the answers when they are at that stage. You'll be surprised, however, at how rapidly your baby manages to get across to you their likes and dislikes. They certainly don't need to be able to talk to make their wishes clear, do they? Even if their efforts do involve a rather primitive approach. Things like spitting out milk, tipping out cereal, mashing-up fruit or simply sideswiping their entire meal on to whomever happens to be passing at the critical moment.

Turning to *Imitation*, I am reminded of all the under-threes' delectable attempts to mimic their parents' example. The joy when your baby first claps their hands as you demonstrate applause. The undeniable thrill when your toddler attempts to manoeuvre a spoonful of apricot sponge into their mouth. The rush of pride when your under-three brings home their first artwork from nursery, not to mention the huge lump in your throat when they sing in front of others the sweet little song you have so painstakingly taught them (with accompanying gestures, of course!). Their opportunities to copy us adults are pretty constantly on tap. But what about the other way round? How many times in the last week, for instance, have you purposely waved your arms in imitation of your newborn? How many times have you played back to them their vocalisations? How many times have you responded to their statement, 'Biccit!' with a repetition of their delicate request?

Imitation is a bit like *Attends* in that they both seem to peter out rather as infants begin to learn to speak. By the time they are rising three and coming out with remarks along the lines of, 'I'm going to make a snowflake', all too often our response is a rather unsatisfactory 'Ummm'. Not a huge amount of stimulation or confidence-boosting going on in such a reply is there?

Mind you, we have all done it. Parents have rights too, don't forget, and cannot always be supersensitively tuned into their under-three's behaviour twenty-four hours a day, seven days a week, four weeks a month . . . you get the picture! That's why we must make sure to get the ratio on *Imitations* right. For every *Teach*, we should give our precious baby and toddler six *Imitations*. Just as for every *Command*, our under-threes need six *Ask to Plays*. *Imitation* really is the sweetest form of flattery, so when we copy our little child's behaviour, words or funny faces in an enthusiastic and admiring fashion, it buoys them up. They then often go on to experiment with novel behaviours and skills. In other words, our *Imitations* inspire them not only to repeat a behaviour, but also to elaborate on it. This way lies self confident exploration and even more stimulating experiences.

Ask to Play for Babies Under Three Months

- 'What is it you want, sweetheart? Do you want daddy to bring up your wind?'
- 'You need me to give you a quick top-up with milk, don't you, darling?'
- 'What can I do? You seem to be crying a lot today. Would you like me to dance you round the room? Yes! Off we go then.'
- 'Aah! You like me stroking you! Shall I do some more, precious?'
- 'I'm going to lay you down on your side. You want me to do it that way I know. Have I got it right or would you rather I changed things around a bit for you?'

On good days
You will really enjoy these little interactions with your baby, with lots of *Ask to Plays* tripping effortlessly off your tongue. Enjoy!

On a bad day
You may hear yourself sounding much more complaining than genuinely enquiring when you try to do *Ask to Plays*. Best to soldier on and soon you will be back on the right track. When you persevere with *Ask to Plays*, and all the other Baby Centred behaviours too, of course, there is always a positive emotional pay off, so don't give up.

Your very recent arrival depends utterly on you for the stimulation they need in order to venture out into the world without being crippled with anxiety. So be lavish with those *Ask to Plays*, even though at first your tiny bundle doesn't seem to visibly respond to your efforts.

Imitation for Babies Under Three Months

- When your newborn yawns, do the same. Not difficult I bet!
- When your under-three-month-old stretches, copy their actions
- When your recent arrival widens their eyes at you, mimic their gaze
- When your infant makes little mouth movements, imitate their actions
- When your newborn peacefully drifts off to sleep, take the hint and doze too!

On good days

You will find yourself so marvellously in tune with your baby that separating out your own responses from theirs could feel difficult. Allow yourself to savour these precious sensations as they are really bonding-friendly.

On a bad day

It is not easy, on days when we are exhausted, down or poorly, to stay attuned to our recent arrival's every little move, but don't let that stop you from coming up with a few *Imitations* when the spirit moves you. For each Baby Centred *Imitation* you provide, even if they are hours apart, yet another strand of your bond with your newborn will be strengthened.

Remember, the under-three-month-old's brain is developing rapidly, and your input is prompting zillions of new neural connections. You can help make sure they are positively adaptive by plugging in lots of *Imitations* and *Ask to Plays*.

Ask to Play for Babies Aged Three to Six Months

- 'Do you want me to get you a drink now, or later? Now! OK, here we are. You're a thirsty little star!'
- 'You're telling me you're sleepy. Would you like me to cuddle you up for a snooze? You would? Snuggle up then, precious.'

- 'Oh! I can see you want me to pick your "fluffy" up. Right, here you are, sweetheart.'
- 'What's that? You're bored? Well what can we do about that? I know, you'd love me to fix up a playtime under your baby gym, wouldn't you, angel?'
- 'Darling! Oh, sweetie, you've got your little hand stuck in your top. You want me to sort it out for you right now! There you are. Better?'

Remember, from three to six months old your baby still needs you to be doing lots of inspired guesswork when using *Ask to Plays*. You might not always get it right, but we must keep in mind how much they rely on us to carry on trying until we hit the nail on the head.

On good days
Things will zoom along in a haze of harmony between you and your baby. When the going is this good make it a priority to bask in the glow of your own success as a parent. Go on, go ahead and give yourself a little treat.

On a bad day
All your best attempts to work out what your baby wants you to do for them seem doomed to failure. You try them with some milk, they swat it away. You carry them round, they wriggle all the more. You are beginning to feel like a failure as a parent. Take some time out before you start to feel irritated as well as frustrated. Put your baby safely in their baby chair, play your favourite music, make a drink and ring a friend. After this little break, you will probably find your sure touch as a parent has returned.

Imitation for Babies Aged Three to Six Months
- When your baby smiles, smile back and add an *Attend* and a *Praise* for good measure
- When your three- to six-month-old pats things, you pat them too

- When they make noises, blow bubbles, squeal and giggle, make sure to follow suit
- When your three- to six-month-old nuzzles up to you, return the favour

Only *Imitate* the behaviours you would be happy to see your baby come up with again. Even at this incredibly young age our tiny tots have embarked on the life-long journey of socialisation, so they desperately need us to start guiding them along the right path, almost from the word go. *Imitations* are a definite bond builder, so keep on keeping on.

On good days
You and your three- to six-month-old will find yourselves involved in a whole rolling series of *Imitations*, back and forth between you. Relax and enjoy these carefree moments, as little games like this increase your attachment to your baby and signal to them that you think they are very special indeed.

On a bad day
You just don't feel like playing games. You feel more like getting back into bed and pulling the duvet up over your head! What to do? Well, how about giving yourself permission to produce only three *Imitations* all day? Write it down if you want to. You'll be surprised how soon afterwards you will find yourself, smiling, patting and snuggling along with your baby.

Ask to Play for Babies Aged Six to Twelve Months
- 'Where do you want Mummy to take you? Oh! Over by the window. You want to look for the cat! What a clever boy/girl!'
- 'You're looking for your book. Shall I get it for you, precious? Yes? OK, here you are, Daddy's found your book.'
- 'Do you want me to reach down that tin? You do! Fine, I'll do just what you want, darling – here comes the tin.'
- 'You are positively scooting across the room, treasure! And now you're trying to stand up and cruise around. You'd like me to move the chair nearer, wouldn't you?'

- 'What is it you're giving me? Oh! A lovely brick. Brilliant. Ah, I see, now you want me to give it back to you! Here you are, sweetie, well done.'

Remember, though it can still feel a bit like a guessing game, using *Ask to Plays* with your six- to twelve-month-old gives them countless opportunities to make adaptive connections between how they feel, what they do and exactly where you come in on the act. In other words, you are stimulating their development in just about every important area.

On good days
Go with the flow and enjoy the opportunity to build up a cushion of Baby Centred behaviours in the bonding bank. What I mean by that last term is the process by which every single Baby Centred input you provide adds to the sum total of goodwill between you and your child. And that's definitely good news for your relationship with your six- to twelve-month-old.

On a bad day
Own up as soon as possible that getting from breakfast to bedtime today is going to be something of a struggle. If at all feasible, fix up a substitute mother or father to take over for at least a couple of hours. This will give you the opportunity to recharge your batteries so you can re-enter the fray feeling stronger. You will probably be able to manage a few *Ask to Plays* by then. Forgive yourself for not being perfect!

Imitations for Babies Aged Six to Twelve Months
- Crawl around with your six- to twelve-month-old as they explore their environment
- When your baby slots rings on to a stick, have a go too
- Echo what your six- to twelve-month-old says, even if it sounds like gibberish
- When your baby 'sings', sing along as well
- Copy your six- to twelve-month-old as he or she splashes in the bath

Remember, much of this won't necessarily be your idea of fabulous fun. However, do give it a try because during the last half of our under-threes' first year, they are very busy sorting out friend from foe. From their perspective, by copying what they are up to, you will be sending out a powerful message to the effect that you are very definitely on their side. That has to be a big plus in the bonding business, doesn't it?

On good days

You will probably be so much into 'follow my leader', you won't even realise you are *Imitating* like crazy. It is truly amazing how many new and different things your six- to twelve-month-old will be able to accomplish. Lots of opportunities for *Imitation*!

On a bad day

Don't push yourself too hard on the *Imitation* score. Remember that if you can't get up the steam for lots of modelling, as long as you avoid *Teaches* (see page 212), the 'bad twin' opposite of *Imitation*, you will be doing well. Tell yourself tomorrow perhaps things will look up – which they often do!

Ask to Play for One-Year-Olds

- 'What would you like me to do now? Sit on the toy rabbit and steal its carrot? Are you sure? OK, here I go, I've got the carrot and now I'm going to squash the bunny.'
- 'What do you want me to do now? Just stay here and watch you? Of course, petal, whatever you want.'
- 'I wonder how you would like me to join in your game. What do you think? Any ideas on what I could get up to?'
- 'You look as though you could do with a mate driving that big lorry. Can I join in?'
- 'When would you like me to start the train off? Tell me what you want me to do next.'

Remember, your one-year-old will be constantly enlarging their vocabulary, so you can expect even more sophisticated commands from them as they near their second birthday. Less chance of mistaking their instructions too, so we have to be on our toes if we are to make the most of these golden opportunities to stimulate our little ones and give them the confidence they need to venture enthusiastically into the unknown.

On good days

You will need to ensure that you keep your ratio in balance at all times – that is, six *Ask to Plays* for every one *Command* (the Baby Directive opposite – see page 212). It could be a case of jogging your own memory, or actually noting down each occasion, to guarantee you achieve your goal.

On a bad day

The main aim on a bad day is to keep the number of *Commands* that you issue down to a minimum. It's all too easy to start pumping out often completely redundant *Commands* when we are feeling stressed. If all else fails, buttoning the lip is much better than machine-gun-like instructions.

Imitation for One-Year-Olds

- 'You have chosen such a lovely colour, poppet, can I do my bus the same green?'
- 'So, you're going to give your teddy some tea. Good idea, sweetheart.'
- 'Your song about the little star was gorgeous. Can I join in next time?'
- 'Right, I understand. You want to wear your wellies, not your slippers. OK, treasure.'
- 'You're such a marvellous dancer, angel, I'm going to copy all your moves!'

Remember, *Imitation* doesn't have to be all action, especially as your one-year-old becomes more verbal. For instance, your tiny treasure will get the same measure of confidence from you repeating back to them what they have just said to you as they would from you emulating their latest bottom wriggling gyrations to their favourite music. Repetition may be rather boring for you but remember, one-year-olds see it quite differently. In fact, they positively love it!

On good days
You can be skilfully reflecting back to your one-year-old their verbal offerings while simultaneously swinging into action on a myriad of other necessary adult activities. By modelling their behaviour a few times they will know themselves to be well loved, while you barely have to break stride.

On a bad day
If you really cannot summon up the energy on a particular day for good quality *Imitations*, give yourself a break and concentrate on dishing up regular helpings of *Praise*, *Smiles* and *Attends*. These three Baby Centred behaviours take rather less effort than hours spent copying your sweet little 'kangaroo' as they leap around the living room.

Ask to Play for Two-Year-Olds
- 'I loved that song you sang the other day, darling. Would you like me to sing one to you? No? Oh! OK, what would you like me to do instead?'
- 'What could I do to cheer you up? Tell daddy, precious.'
- 'When you've decided what you'd like me to do before tea time, let me know. Don't take too long though, sweetie, or our time will run out.'
- 'Would you like to be the one telling me what to do? You would! Right then, my little star, what shall I try next?'
- 'You have made up such a lovely game, poppet, I'd like to join in. Tell me what you want me to do and I'll do it!'

Remember, promises must be honoured as two-year-olds have incredible memories and will be able to recite chapter and verse if we try to wriggle out of something we said we would do. How very much more important then to be sure that when you give your two- to three-year-old the option of dictating your behaviour, you must live up to their expectations – unless of course they are dangerous or so far embedded in the realms of fantasy that even the most cooperative of parents would fail to get lift off.

On good days
You can end up involved in new and pleasurable activities which, in addition to being stimulating for you both, provide your two-year-old with the very valuable psychological experience of calling the shots.

On a bad day
Make sure you keep to your ratio of six Baby Centred behaviours to one Baby Directive behaviour, even if you do feel like something the cat dragged in. It really doesn't matter if the actual numbers are much lower than usual, as long as the ratio holds fast. Give it your best shot for a few minutes, and then take an hour out, but try again later if you can summon up the energy.

Imitation for Two-Year-Olds
- 'Look, angel! I'm making footprints in the sand, just like you.'
- 'What a fabulous dandelion. Can I pick some too, my love?'
- You're so clever, honey. I want to make my tree look just like yours. Will you show me how?'
- 'I can see you are very good at jumping up and down. Let's see if I can do it too.'
- 'You're running around being a super hero. Look at me! I'm just the same as you.'

Remember, there is absolutely no reason why you should give only one Baby Centred behaviour at a time to your two-year-old. In fact, the more you pin together, the more your attachment to them will flourish. So *Imitations* with *Attends* thrown in for good measure are good news not bad. Forget trying to keep them separate and concentrate on providing several at a time.

On good days
You will be able to set things up so both you *and* your two-year-old actively enjoy *Imitation* games. Weave them into outings, meal-times, garden activities, shopping and all special one-to-one times with your toddler.

On a bad day
Remind yourself that no parent is perfect and be as forgiving of your shortcomings as possible. Try to make a supreme effort to get your two-year-old doing something you too enjoy, then insinuate yourself into their activity. Don't be disappointed, though, if you fail to stir up much visible cooperation when you attempt to lure them into lying quietly on the sofa with you!

Well, I hope I've managed to give you some helpful ideas on how to put into practice these stimulation and confidence-boosting Baby Centred behaviours: *Ask to Play* and *Imitation*. Your input is so crucial to your baby and toddler's attempts to understand and participate in the world around them, that I am sure you will be firing on all cylinders as you give your child the chance to tell *you* what to do, for a change! And I hope you find immense joy at reflecting back to your child their amazing behaviour and progress by imitating their efforts.

What Not To Do: Don't Be Negative!

Now I'm going to look at why too much *Teaching* and too many *Commands* will hamper rather than extend your under-three's stimulation and confident exploration opportunities. As in other chapters, we will look at the situation as it occurs in different age groups in the first three years of your tiny tot's life. These are the Baby Directive twins of our highlighted Baby Centred behaviours. So let's examine if and when they are ever a good idea when we are focused on establishing and nurturing a warm, loving and approving bond with our precious under-three. First of all, I want to remind you of the negative emotional effects your Baby Directive behaviours can have on your tiny tots:

Baby Directive Behaviour: Negative Emotional Effect

Questions	Too many questions, however well meaning, make babies and toddlers feel challenged and unapproved of by their mum and/or dad
Criticism	This results in your under-three feeling devalued and lacking in confidence
Negative looks	Babies and toddlers are left feeling scared and threatened when given Negative looks
Teaches	Under-threes can feel unappreciated and unnoticed as an individual if they are always being taught things
Commands	Too many Commands leave under-three-year-olds feeling confused and anxious
Saying 'No'	An excess of 'Nos' can make babies and toddlers rebellious
Negative touches	Under-threes feel unloved and often angry or afraid when they are smacked

So there you have it! If you want your little sweetheart to grow up to be an emotional mess, pile on the Baby Directives! But, of course, you want the exact opposite, don't you? I know that even when I had no real guidelines for bringing up my children, apart from what I had learned at my mother's knee and from reading Dr Spock's book on bringing up babies, I realised I truly wished for all three of them to feel supported, approved of, valued, self-confident, trusting, safe, appreciated, noticed, clear, unafraid, cooperative, loved and loveable. I'm not saying that I was 100 per cent successful, don't think that for a moment. I'm more than happy to settle for 50 per cent or thereabouts because I now know we can ensure our babies and toddlers get a good deal from us if we manage to reach a one-to-one or one-to-two Baby Centred to Baby Directive ratio. They get a very good deal when we shift up a gear to a two-to-one or three-to-one ratio. As I've already pointed out, six to one should be our ultimate goal, so keep shooting for the stars, especially as your bond with your baby and toddler will inevitably become so much stronger and more secure. Just as inevitable is the likelihood that on occasion we will find ourselves coming up with too many Baby Directive behaviours, especially when we are stressed out, for whatever reason.

But there are times when some of these same Baby Directive behaviours are appropriate, including *Teaching* and *Commands*. I am only going to go into the *Teaching* item in this chapter, as good-quality *Commands* will feature later because they are an important part of Balanced Parenting and dealing with disobedience. Right, so when is *Teaching* our under-threes to be encouraged, and when should we be holding our tongues and *Imitating* instead? Let's look at how that applies to the different phases of being under-three.

Babies Aged Under Six Months

Fortunately we don't have to teach newborns how to suck, cry, sleep, smile, look, listen, smell, taste or touch, never mind the nappy filling business. Being fascinated by other people and the world around them also comes without much initiative required from us. Nought to six-month-olds are pretty good at making lots of progress in the motor and sensory development areas, again more or less independent of anything we might have to offer, except opportunity, naturally. Any *Teaching* required at this early stage then? Not as such, no. Not formal teaching anyway.

But under-six-month-olds do need to learn they are noticed and appreciated. So we must give them many more *Imitations* of their own behaviour than *Teaches*. I recently saw a young father explaining to his newborn that the large red column was used for posting mail! Don't bother, Dad! Put your energy into copying the huge yawns of the little scrap in your arms.

Babies Aged Six to Twelve Months

As babies reach the second half of their first year they are becoming so much stronger physically, as well as increasingly mobile, that we need to *Teach* them about the basic rules of personal safety. Pitched at their level of understanding, the 'Hot!', 'Hurt!', 'Dirty!', 'You'll fall!', 'Cut!', 'Sting!', 'Squash!', and 'No! Don't touch!' warnings seem to be the most frequent and effective safety lessons that need to be learned. And who better to act as teacher than us?

But while six- to twelve-month-olds rely on us to coach them in how to avoid the dangers around them, that is by no means the whole picture. They are still unendingly in need of a solid, secure and safe bond with you. It's their emotional and psychological priority and so it must be ours. Imitating their zillions of cute little ways, mimicking their attempts to walk and talk, will give them an undeniable sensation that they are important and precious to you. So next time you scoop them up to rescue them from potential danger, remember to tell them you want them to be safe because you love them to bits.

One-Year-Olds

You thought your baby was pretty mobile before, but it pales into insignificance compared with their ability to whizz around now that they're one, doesn't it? You and your toddler are on a massive learning curve over the course of their second year, and that involves *Teaches*. I'm not talking alphabets and numbers, though, more about how to get a spoonful of food into their lovely little mouths with your assistance. How to step into their wellies, with your help. How to drink from a cup without spilling, with your guidance. How to lift up their arms to slip on their tops, with your input. How to walk upstairs, with your support. The list goes on and on and we haven't even mentioned waving and saying good-bye, playing pat-a-cake or doing painted hand prints.

But while one-year-olds positively thrive on self-help skills as a result of our *Teaches* on topics like feeding, drinking, washing, dressing and stripping off in a trice their socks, shoes, hats and gloves, too much *Teaching* must be avoided. That's because there is always a demand element to every *Teach* that provokes a very different emotional response in a one-year-old toddler than an *Imitation*. *Imitations*, when genuine, are gifts that reassure our offspring of whatever age that we have noticed and approved of their behaviour. Such interactions, where we enthusiastically copy our one-year-olds, improve the quality of their attachment to us. For parents, however, it is more likely to be the caring and teaching elements of our relationship with our toddler that strengthens the bond we experience towards them. So, next time you have been on an intensive exercise to *Teach* your one-year-old the intricacies of putting only one foot into each leg of their trousers, only to have them grab their nether garments and plonk them on their head, pop something incongruous on your head too. The giggles and hugs that follow will without doubt bring you much closer together than properly fitting pants!

Two-Year-Olds

At two to almost three, don't they seem grown-up? They can play next to, if not actually with, other children, they understand so much more of what we say – and can they chatter? Yes! Olympic standard conversationalists aged two are ten a penny. Instead of 'What's that?' being their favourite question, a new query of 'Why?' is beginning to feature more and more often. Both 'What's and 'Why's are powerful triggers for us to show off our superior knowledge. After all, surely we know enough astrophysics to explain why the sun 'goes away' at night, enough marine biology to explain why there are no sharks in the local stream, and enough mechanical engineering to explain why petrol makes cars go. Or do we? I have to say I found dinosaurs taxing enough and was left floundering in the face of the question, 'Why can't I be a dog today?' In fact, my only solution of any interest to my inquisitive two-year-old was to suggest dressing up like a dog and going round on all fours. This suggestion was in fact so successful that we *both* ended up with paper tails and ears! Panting, tummy rubbing and barking also featured! What can I say? The washing up didn't get done until later but we both had a great time. So there you are, a good example of how a question from our two-year-old, inviting us to *Teach* by information giving, transmuted into a truly enjoyable play time for two dogs! Needless to say, when the little doggie wanted a drink, biscuit or pee pee, the mummy doggie followed suit.

That's why, with our two-year-olds, we must always hang on to the notion that even though they seem to be thirsting after knowledge we should, as well as answering their never-ending questions, stir in liberal doses of *Imitation*. It is our Baby Centred modelling on their behaviour and remarks, not the *Teaches* per se, that will cement the bond between yourself and your toddler. It's also a neat trick to reflect back to them, without even attempting an answer, some of their more esoteric queries, particularly as they often come up with most engaging replies. I remember one two-year-old girl looking me straight in the eye and saying, 'Why are the stars in the sky?' and when I said, 'Mmmm, you're wondering why the stars are in the sky', her face lit up and her bunches bounced as she replied, 'To feed the moon, silly!'

Just before finishing the 'What Not To Do' part of this chapter, I want to talk about under-threes and TV. When I was little, television had not been invented. My grandchildren gaze at me with blank incomprehension whenever I mention this fact, usually following this up with a slightly patronising, 'Poor Nana, there, there. Never mind.' It simply does not occur to them there is any possible plus side to not having a TV. When my own children were tiny, we did not have a TV for the first five years after the birth of my oldest child. We eventually acquired one when she complained she could not join in with her classmates' constant references to the programmes they watched at home. 'The box' has been a firm family favourite ever since!

But what do we know about the emotional impact of TV on newborns, three- to six-month-olds, six- to-twelve-month-olds, one-year-olds and two-year-olds? Well, the jury has been in and out on that verdict so many times, it's no wonder that mums and dads get confused when they hear yet another set of research findings. The very latest conclusion from the experts in the field seems to be that the less television our under-threes watch, the better socially adjusted they are. Oh, and intellectually brighter too! It's enough to make you weep, isn't it? Just when we thought that as long as we protected them from violent scenes and too many early morning cartoons, we were doing our duty, it turns out we are supposed to be much more generally restrictive.

I don't personally feel that a suitable DVD for twenty minutes in the morning while you get dressed and make breakfast for your one-year-old is a crime. Nor does an afternoon slot of special children's programmes seem to me to be a likely source of harm to under-three-year-olds. I would be less enthusiastic about the idea of parking babies in front of a television for any length of time, no matter how entranced they might appear to be. We are all warned by any pundit worth their salt about the dangers of using the television as a babysitter. Obviously ignoring your under-threes for hours at a time while they sit alone and 'goggle' would never be a Baby Centred parent's choice. But most of us make pretty consistent efforts to stick to sensible limits in terms of our child's exposure to TV, so I don't think we should overload ourselves with guilt because we tuck them up on the sofa for extra programmes if they, or we, are poorly. Actually, if we snuggle up too, it is more than possible to turn the whole experience into a cosy bonding opportunity. Talk about silver linings!

Special Feature: Developing Baby's Identity

Having a mind of our own is, essentially, what defines our individuality. It's such an obvious notion that we often skip over its importance, if we bother to consider it at all. Exactly how it works is best shown with a real-life example of *Best Guessing*, so let's start there. You remember the stages? Mirror, Validate, Empathise and Resolve.

Imagine the scene: you are sitting on the floor beside your fourteen-month-old, who is engrossed in their attempts to put multi-coloured rings of differing sizes on to a central cone. It's a toy beloved of generations of under-threes and your baby has probably already gone through the stages of mouthing the rings, banging the rings down and dropping them willy-nilly. But here you are, they have finally matured enough to have a go at doing it properly. You watch with baited breath as they successfully slip the red ring on to the cone. You clap, smile and praise. They clap and smile too. Now for the orange ring. But, oh dear! It's got jammed at a slant. Your child looks concerned and tries to force it down. The ring will not move. Your little star turns to look up at you, a fierce frown of frustration printed on their delicate brow. What happens next is crucial if you want to make the most of this opportunity with your toddler. See what *Best Guessing* achieves:

- **Mirror**: 'Poppet! You look as though you're cross because the ring's stuck.'
- **Validate**: 'I'd be cross too if I couldn't get the ring on properly.'
- **Empathise**: 'Sweetie, I know you're feeling fed up. Poor darling!'
- **Resolve**: 'Would you like me to get the ring off for you, treasure? Or do you want to do it yourself?'

See what these steps enable your toddler to do:

When you **Mirror**	Realise you have recognised they have their own feelings
When you **Validate**	Realise you believe those feelings are justified
When you **Empathise**	Realise you are genuinely able to appreciate their feelings
When you **Resolve**	Realise you are on their side in helping them to feel better

The central messages being conveyed to our toddler cannot be in doubt:

YOU ARE AN INDIVIDUAL IN YOUR OWN RIGHT
YOU HAVE YOUR OWN FEELINGS
YOUR FEELINGS MATTER
YOU ARE NOT ALONE

The same goes for our under-threes' thoughts and ideas, so it is important to make sure they realise you credit them with independent intellectual activity, in tandem with reassuring them they can always turn to you for help when they can't manage alone.

So, in order for our newborns, babies, toddlers, one- and two-year-olds to develop their own identity, we must first behave towards them in a way that demonstrates our belief in their individuality. They need us to show we credit them with feelings different from our own:

- ideas of their own
- thought processes separate from ours
- dreams that are their sole preserve

The marvel is that the more clarity in this differentiation between parent and under-three, the more secure the bond. When babies and toddlers are not accorded the dignity of their own identity, it can result in emotional, psychological and attachment problems. But it really is quite easy to avoid such difficulties. All you have to do is get across to your child your view of their unique and marvellous individuality. And you already know how to do that – yes! By being Baby Centred!

Every *Attend, Best Guess, Praise, Smile, Positive Look, Positive Touch, Ask to Play* and *Imitation* tells your baby and toddler, in terms they can really understand, what a special, wonderful, loveable, delightful, valuable, important and individual little person they are. An excessive amount of Baby Directive parenting – as you might guess – can have the opposite effect. Too many *Questions, Criticisms, Negative Looks* and *Negative Touches, Commands, Teaches* and saying 'No' raises the stress level between you and your under-three, making it much more difficult for infants to achieve their own identity.

Remember, too, that a 'Baby Centred' mummy and/or daddy makes babies and toddlers feel safe in scary situations, and that tells our little ones it will be OK to carry on exploring the exciting world around them. This isn't about intellectual prowess. It's about giving our under-three a secure sense of their own unique value as an individual. Being Baby Centred is a sure-fire method of putting this vital message across. Now it's time to move on to the language aspects of attachment.

Let's start by spelling out what 'reciprocity' means in this context. I suppose one way to define it would be to point out the 'taking turns' feature of verbal communication. While this is undoubtedly essential, it doesn't really highlight the emotional aspects of talking with each other, does it? I think both are important if we are to get a proper grasp of how language reciprocity enhances the bond with our under-threes. It is also crucial to emphasise the role of 'active listening', particularly as it's something we parents seem to find a little challenging! I want to take you through these three main components of the language strand of bonding one at a time, though of course in reality they are inextricably interwoven in every communication with our tiny tots.

Taking Turns

We have all met people who obviously find social interaction difficult. One of the major problem signs of this is their odd pattern of eye contact. Either they do not make eye contact at all or they stare in an intimidating manner. The unblinking stare can be particularly spooky, I find. Or perhaps the only time they risk making eye contact is as part of a left to right, right to left head swivelling exercise. They seem to be looking at something floating in the air above your shoulder, or only glance up briefly from under lowered eyelids.

You may by now be asking yourself why I am going on about eye contact when we are supposed to be talking about taking turns in conversation. The answer is that when we are really communicating with someone, certain patterns of eye contact send signals about who is going to stop talking soon and therefore whose turn it will be next. For socially skilled individuals, making these adjustments seems to come naturally, or maybe practice has made perfect. In any case, it's clear to see that emotional closeness between two people is unlikely to flourish unless both participants have developed sophisticated turn-taking skills.

When we look at the attachment between parents and their under-threes, it is not difficult to see that we grown-ups have the edge on our infants when it comes to turn-taking ability! So, once more, it's up to us mums and dads to take the initiative. With newborns that means we are doing at least 90 per cent of the input and imaginatively filling in those gaps when our baby would have taken their turn, if only they could. You know the sort of thing. Your baby is laying on their back along your joined thighs, contented and awake. You lean forward and manoeuvre your head so you can gaze into their open eyes. Your conversation with them probably goes something like this:

- 'Oh! You're awake!'
- 'Hello, my little sweetheart!'
- 'Yes! Your mummy/daddy is talking to you!'
- 'What's that?'
  * 'You're telling me you're a very happy baby!'
- 'Yes you are!'
  * 'And you're saying you need a little nap now!'
- 'Of course you do. Off we go!

The terms marked with an asterisk are those where you have 'filled in' for them. Various versions of this process continue throughout our offspring's first three years, with them progressively able to take their own turn. Of course they butt in, can't wait, stare dreamily into the middle distance, appear to be completely deaf, fall asleep, run off, push their faces right up against yours, yawn, try to pull your hair/nose/earrings/glasses off, kiss you, lick you, wriggle, laugh, cry, frown, sing, shout, and even tell you to be quiet – it's all a part of learning the rules about reciprocal language. So we need to be patient, *very* patient, as well as generous-spirited and warm-hearted towards our miniature but enthusiastic language students.

Emotional Flavour

This is where it becomes clear that enabling our under-threes to acquire turn-taking skills, though necessary, is not sufficient to ensure the language strand of your attachment with your baby and toddler takes root and grows. The emotional flavour that you give to your communications with your under-threes is equally important, if not more so. The actual content of what we say, along with our non-verbal messages, have an enormously powerful impact on the quality of the bond being forged with our babies. And the guidelines to observe? Parent/Baby Game guidelines of course. When you are *Best Guessing*, *Attending*, *Praising*, *Smiling*, *Imitating*, *Asking to Play*, *Positively Looking* and *Positively Touching*, then you are giving your baby and toddler all the sensitive understanding, approval, security, trust, warmth and confidence they could ever need to persuade them that you know and use the language of love. This is the real heart of reciprocal language and your child is thirsting for your offerings long before they can utter a 'mama' or 'dadda'. And as they go on wanting you to provide more of the same throughout their lives, getting in plenty of practice right at the beginning is probably well-spent parental energy!

Active Listening

Talking is one thing lots of us adults find pretty easy to do. Listening is quite another matter! And Active Listening really has to be cultivated if our little ones are to grow up believing they have a 'voice' within the language strand of your relationship with them. That is both literally *and* figuratively speaking. How often have you heard parents say to an under-three clamouring to be heard, 'Be quiet! Can't you see I'm busy talking to Daddy/Mummy/Uncle Joe?'

Another version of this starts off, 'Wait a moment!', said in tones of some irritation. I'm undoubtedly guilty of this myself. Or there is the exasperated, '*I'm* talking!' When your under-three is chattering nineteen to the dozen from dawn to dusk, it's no wonder we feel as though we have to fight for any little scraps of adult conversation available. I remember the stage when I had three children under six as being a time when chatting to the window cleaner was a thrill, simply because it was a chance to indulge in a few minutes' grown-up talk!

None the less, the most common complaint of adolescents is that their parents 'Don't listen'. All too often this coincides with a phase in family life when relationships are strained and communication stressful. So why not get in early on the Active Listening front and start practising with your under-three? This is where we really come full circle on the reciprocal language aspect of attachment, because the core of active listening is about taking turns, good eye contact and emotional sensitivity – plus a healthy dose of Baby Centred or Child Centred behaviours. Oh, and *time*! When I am at the nursery, I try to make sure I provide Active Listening time for each of the under-fives I interact with. That inevitably means I don't get round to all of them, but quality time is really crucial when we are nurturing the reciprocal language aspect of any attachment, so sometimes quantity has to take a back seat. What I urge you to do next time your toddler, one- or two-year-old wants to chat is get down to their eye level, say, 'I'm listening, poppet', and give them your full attention for the fifteen seconds they need to tell you they urgently need a wee/poo/drink/cuddle/biscuit or carrot stick. That's all it takes for them to feel the full force of your love. That's all it takes for the giving and receiving in your bond to blossom.

But what if nobody listened to us? Suppose our own parents were rather strict, 'brooked no nonsense', and would much rather we as children were seen and not heard? Sad to say, some of us have had to grow up under the rule of an authoritarian parent, or even two! How can we make sure we don't re-enact the same damaging parenting style with our own under-threes? Let's move on now to 'Echoes From Our Past' and look for some answers.

Echoes From Our Past: Authoritarian Parenting

This is a style of interacting with children that we probably associate most with a bygone Victorian age when a parent's word

– particularly father's – was law to their offspring. Today, you may see reference made to 'Authoritative' parenting, which is another term for what I call a 'Balanced' style. More details on that in chapter five. Suffice it to say at this point that an 'authoritarian' parenting wins no friends, while 'authoritative' parenting is the goal we should all be aiming for.

My own family history reveals a mixed bag of parenting styles, with my grandparents bringing up their children in quite different ways. On my mother's side, though my grandparents were un-doubtedly products of the Victorian era they were not typical spouses and parents. As I have already mentioned, they cuddled openly in front of my mother and her sister, which was almost unheard of in those bygone days. My father's upbringing was very much less demonstrative and altogether too strict, though quite unexceptional for the times. Discipline was harsh and unbending, which of course left a lasting impression on my father's and his brothers' personalities and attachment styles. Inevitably, my own mother and father's parenting styles differed, which will come as no surprise!

While my mother believed in and enforced consistent guidelines and ground rules for her 'Lulu, Lillybet and Jojo' (that's the pet names she gave me and my siblings), she put them into action in an authoritative rather than authoritarian fashion. In other words, she was Baby and Child Centred and for much of the time used the Attention Rule properly (see page 129). There were exceptions, of course – moments when she would lose her temper and shout instead of ignoring our irritating behaviour, but she too was only human and none of us is a perfect parent!

I remember one occasion when I, usually the goody-two-shoes, had become so carried away with my 'artwork' that I had scribbled across several pages of a treasured story book, in a frenzy of rainbow colours. Now I know that some people believe there is nothing sacred about the written word and books are only 'alive' whilst being read. It all sounds a bit too existential to me! But anyway, my parents set great store by preserving the literature around the house, so my artistic crime was not viewed lightly.

Quite the reverse! I was told off in no uncertain terms, in a scarily loud voice by a mother whose face was contorted with outrage. I wasn't smacked, however, but I was sent to bed to meditate on my sins and not allowed down until I could say sorry, *mean* it and promise never to repeat such desecration. Directly after I had apologised, my mother once more became reassuringly Child Centred – I was about three at the time I believe. The sun shone again and I knew once more I was the apple of Mummy's eye. What a relief!

It was a very different story with my father, though my mother's ameliorating influence undoubtedly diffused the impact of his more authoritarian stance. I am just going to check off the major features of an authoritarian parent and then compare them against my memories and see how he fares! An authoritarian parent is:

- Too directive
- Insufficiently concerned with a child's perspective
- Overly concerned with appearance
- Self-centred
- Rigid
- Dismissive

Dad showed some of these characteristics some of the time, while with Mum it was little and seldom. It's often a matter of degree, isn't it? The all-or-nothing personality profile is really quite rare. However, when the degree of authoritarian parenting is notched up beyond a reasonable threshold, there are all sorts of nasty repercussions for babies and toddlers. Repercussions that can linger for a lifetime, as you might have discovered for yourself, if you had the misfortune to be raised by a harsh disciplinarian. Such authoritarian parenting can lead to emotional, psychological and attachment problems for babies and toddlers. Let me list some of them for you:

- Low self-confidence
- Passivity and over-dependence

- Fear of authority figures
- Anxiety about being spontaneous
- Feelings of not being worth listening to
- Emotional insecurity
- Rebelliousness and defiance
- Bullying, aggressive behaviour

Quite a long list, showing how an under-three's development can be pushed out of the normal, healthy range towards an extreme of either fearfulness or aggression.

In terms of Baby Centred *Ask to Play* and *Imitation*, you can see that authoritarian parents would be loath to use either, because each one involves open acknowledgement that little ones, too, can be accorded a degree of power. When an under-three's mother or father frightens them by being too directive, rigid and dismissive, the baby or toddler's stress levels zoom up into the very uncomfortable zone. One of the effects of this is that their capacity for responding positively to stimulation is diminished, resulting in lack of confident exploration.

When an under-three remains in over-close proximity to their authoritarian parent, they want to reduce the likelihood of mummy or daddy being angry with them. It's as if they hope that by slipping under their parents' guard they will escape punishment. Some babies and toddlers seem to take a diametrically opposite approach and withdraw from any attempt at emotional intimacy. Instead, they seek their stimulation from the material world, which also has an equally damaging impact on the bond with their parents. Another set of problems altogether can arise from an under-three attempting to challenge their mother and father's authoritarian behaviour and instead exercise their own defiant version of bravado. Not a happy scene is it?

What about you? Has reading about authoritarian parenting chimed with any aspect of your own childhood? Do you think, on reflection, your parents were, or indeed still are, authoritarian rather than authoritative? See if any of the scenarios I am going to mention apply to you when you look back at your childhood.

Maybe you remember that you had little confidence in yourself. Perhaps you were afraid of your parents and felt you had no control over events in your life. You might have felt powerless most of the time. If you still feel rather like that now, it could be that your own mother and father, in their attempt to stay in charge of the family, took too much power away from you when you were little. Can you remember occasions when you were overruled without having a chance to put forward your point of view? Were there few opportunities to show you could be independent or make constructive choices? Were you intensely afraid that anyone in authority was bound to be dismissive and critical towards you? Did you ever feel the only safe response was to do exactly as you were told?

Perhaps you continue to have these feelings, even though you are now the parent. Or maybe you find yourself being authoritarian towards your under-three even though it is the last thing you would wish. Of course, we don't want our babies and toddlers to grow up feeling unsure of themselves and of course we don't want them to believe they are powerless and have nothing of value to contribute. If you have the kind of childhood memories I have just mentioned, then, despite your best efforts, you might be experiencing unresolved issues relating to power in your interactions with others, including your under-threes. But take heart, no one has to remain stuck in an attachment style they want to change, and you could already be on the way to handling your power as a parent in a more productive way, simply by recognising that you may have previously been too authoritarian.

When you make the link between your style of parenting and the unresolved issues of power in your relationship with your parents, then you have taken that crucial first step towards a more flexible and balanced way of bringing up your own under-three. So what else might you do to help yourself move on and become less authoritarian? Before I make some suggestions, let me tell you about two families where rigid, disciplinarian, critical and domineering parent behaviour was actively damaging the children's development.

Case Study One

David and Stephanie were, everyone agreed, devoted to their three children: Aaron, two, Catherine, four, and Jane, six. The family were deeply involved in their local community and always attended school and church functions as a group. In fact, it was rare to see any one of them out alone, except David. People always said what a marvellous father he was as, in addition to working full-time from home as an accountant, he also took the children to nursery and school in the morning and collected them later in the day. Jane and Catherine were no trouble to anyone. Indeed, some thought them to be rather too quiet and compliant, even passive on occasion. Aaron, it was clear, was a very different personality! He was big for his age, noisy, extremely active and full of energy. A regular little tornado, in fact. But while Stephanie and David had been thrilled at the birth of a son, Aaron was undoubtedly proving to be a bit of a handful, even at two years of age. Stephanie actually found it almost impossible to maintain a reasonable degree of control over her toddler son's behaviour, to such an extent that she seriously doubted her parenting abilities. David, concerned by his wife's increasingly low mood, decided Aaron needed to be 'taught a few lessons' and so he took charge of keeping Aaron within bounds.

The problems, unfortunately, worsened. The more David clamped down on Aaron, the more the toddler shouted, hit out, ran away, and seemed to take delight in defying his father. David's response was to tighten the rules still further, which resulted in a daily running battle between himself and Aaron. Meanwhile Stephanie and her two daughters were becoming progressively anxious, fearful and unnaturally quiet. Eventually, Stephanie's mother became so worried about her daughter that she called me, hoping for some idea on what to do next. David rang me the next week and I agreed to visit the family at their home. After two hours' observation and discussion it was clear to me that David, with the best will in the world, was responding to Aaron's challenging behaviour by being even more authoritarian than he had ever been.

Apparently, David had always been the controlling force in the family, not surprising when one learned of how rigid and domineering his own father was. All the while David was 'in charge' of his wife and daughters, he had been able to maintain quite a benevolent attitude. However, Aaron had proved to be much less malleable, which led David to become harsh and repressive towards his toddler. Fortunately, helping David to practise the Attention Rule and become much more Baby and Child Centred resulted in pretty rapid progress within the family. This was made all the more possible because David was able to see the link between his father's authoritarian parenting style and his own tendency to be over-controlling, particularly when stressed by challenges to his authority.

Case Study Two

Delia lived alone with her two children, both boys: Danny aged one and Rory, who was nearly seven. The brothers had different fathers, neither of whom were regularly in touch with their sons. Delia felt her responsibilities as a lone parent very acutely indeed, especially as Rory seemed to be right on the line between what could be called extremely lively and that deemed hyperactive. Though visibly smitten with Danny, Delia found coping single-handedly with her two young and demanding sons an almost overwhelming challenge. Reports from school and nursery suggested both boys would benefit from a structured routine, clear behavioural limits and praise for being good. Delia, who had previously taken the line of least resistance with her sons, worked really hard at tightening up on the demands she made on Danny and Rory. Actually, she went way over the top, leaving both boys totally bewildered and angry to boot. I was contacted by Rory's teacher, who said that Rory needed professional help and I became involved shortly afterwards.

I discovered that Delia, at her wits' end attempting to get Danny and Rory to bed at the overly generous hour of 8.30 p.m., had resorted to an inflexible, bullying and dismissive style of interacting with her sons. She also admitted to anger, frustration and occasionally smacking Rory and Danny much harder than she believed right.

It was particularly painful for Delia to acknowledge she was now treating her two boys in just the same way her own mother had behaved towards her and her four younger siblings. This pattern of parenting had sapped her own self-confidence to the point that she had found herself intimately involved with two violent, domineering men – the boys' fathers. Realising she was in the process of becoming the type of parent she had sworn she would never be was upsetting for Delia, although it also motivated her to make significant changes in managing Danny and Rory's behaviour.

As Delia became more able to *Best Guess*, conflicts between herself and her young sons became less frequent and intense. Danny and Rory both became more settled at nursery and school, while a Baby and Child Centred bedtime routine that showed the boys their mother could be firm *and* fond saw the disappearance of the previously nightly rumpus.

Let's get back to some detailed suggestions on how you might help yourself to steer away from being too authoritarian in your parenting style. Firstly, here are some self-instructions you could give yourself as a start towards becoming a more balanced parent:

Say to yourself:
- 'I have a lot to gain by giving up some of my power. My children would not be so afraid of me and we could become more friendly.'
- 'My children need me to allow them some power over their own lives so they can eventually become independent people.'
- 'I will not lose touch with my children by helping them towards independence, because they will want to spend time with me of their own free will.'
- 'I know it feels risky to take more of a back seat, but I could win my children's cooperation and that is quite a prize.'
- 'I can learn to allow myself not to be all powerful.'

Remember, by loosening your repressive control over others, you actually make it more likely that a positive bond will develop.

Being domineering towards your children, on the other hand, will actually drive them away. Don't forget how alienating it felt for you when during your childhood your mother and father were too directive, punitive, rigid and apparently unaware of how that had made you feel. Step back from the position of authoritarian power and control and you will find nothing dire happens. Quite the reverse in fact!

There are other steps you can take to bolster your good intentions. For example:

- Tell your partner or trusted friend that you plan to give your child a little more autonomy
- Talk about your own frightening childhood with someone who has a sympathetic ear and then actively listen in return
- Take the step of confiding that you think there may be a link between your early years and the way in which you have always felt you must run the show

Sharing your growing self-awareness with those you really trust may mean your parents have to be excluded, at least in the beginning. It has to be acknowledged, however, that in some families, the damage done has been so devastating that it will never be safe to take parents into our confidence on this score. You should always try to share your thoughts, feelings and plans with your partner, even though it can sometimes feel tough. I explain how later on.

What about the more practical issues? Most of our difficulties as parents end up with the sometimes anguished cry of 'What shall I *do*?' See how these ideas grab you:

Practical steps you can take:
- Make a list of the areas of your under-threes' lives where you make all the decisions and pick out those where you could safely give them more individual choice
- Listen to and watch out for your baby and toddler's perspective on things

- Work out what activities your little ones could do independently, then let them go ahead and explore and expand their capabilities
- Gradually extend the areas of independence of thought and action you give your under-three
- Plan ahead and reward yourself for each target you achieve

Each of these practical steps can be adapted to suit each phase of your child's development, starting with your utterly dependent newborn right through to the almost three's fearless adventurers. And don't forget, it's not only your baby and toddler's efforts that merit praise and rewards. Your attempts to reach your planned goal of being less overpoweringly in control also deserve recognition and applause. Just in case you haven't been able to arrange for anyone else to be the bringer of gifts, choose your own treats! Anything, from chocs to Chopin, can feature as a sign of your progress, so pick something that really motivates you. When my children were very young, I used to indulge myself in a pamper activity once they were all tucked up in bed. This could be painting my toenails or taking a long hot bubble bath; as long as I felt nurtured at the end of the experience, anything went!

There will be moments, of course, when your best laid plans and intentions simply won't hold. It's at these points in time, when the last thing we want to do is to agree to another's choices, that you may find the anti-authoritarian emergency mantra helpful. See what you think.

BE FLEXIBLE – BE FRIENDLY – BE FUN

I know it may look a little puny on the page, but don't be fooled into underestimating the power of self-instruction. Simply repeating the mantra to yourself, especially at times of maximum stress when you are most likely to revert to old behaviours, will shift your thought patterns into a different gear – one that more easily enables you to find a less controlling answer to the parenting challenges you meet every day. Remember to include lots of *Ask to Plays* and *Imitations*. Adding lots of these Baby Centred behaviours to your repertoire will inevitably make you less authoritarian towards your child. Of course, being Baby Centred will not solve all your problems, because being a parent is just one of your roles; we all have multiple relationships. That's not to say these attachments would not benefit from liberal helpings of 'Person Centred' input! Your most significant adult-to-adult interactions will naturally involve your co-parent, if you have one, whether fiancé, partner, husband or wife.

Special Feature: How To Play With Infants

I want to underline how vital it is that we spend time playing with our children, even though we have a million and one things we should and want to be getting on with. When you are intent on giving the bond between you and your baby or toddler the best chance to flourish, time given to play is like putting money in a bank of happy families. There are several reasons for this that I think it could be useful to jot down, so here goes.

First I am going to highlight the role of fun, humour and good times in the process of establishing and maintaining a secure attachment. I'm not saying let joy be unconfined, but I am pointing out that play and happiness in one another's company go hand-in-hand. With your newborn you can enjoy gentle play with the water drops and bubbles in their bath. Your six- to twelve-month-old will revel in similar activities, only with rather more splash effects! By the time your toddler is one, he or she will delight in your participation while they manipulate more advanced bath-time-toys, and your two-year-old would much rather you joined in with their filling-up and pouring-out games than by sitting on the loo seat staring at them, albeit with a loving eye.

Often we adults regard bath time as a case of getting it over and done with – another item on the daily childcare checklist that must be ticked off. When you are under three it's a very different matter! Bath time then is about pleasant sensations, novel experiences, exploration and experiment – in other words *fun*. And you can be part of that everyday journey into the magic of play when you take time to join in with them. You will be strengthening the positive emotions within your relationship when you look into each other's eyes, touch and giggle together. Think of all those psychologically healthy neural networks you will be building up as you splash away having a fun playtime. It's got to be worth the effort.

Secondly, we need to remember that, for the under-threes especially, play is a very serious business indeed. As adults we associate the word play with the leisure activities we choose to cram into the time available when we have finished the important work duties. For babies and toddlers, play *IS* work. During play our children gradually come to terms with their changeable physical environment. They slowly learn that their actions can cause results in the world around them and they begin to practise interacting in a sociable way with other people, both familiar and unfamiliar. Play is an under-threes' life-skills class and if we opt out we put at risk our bond with them and their ability to cope with the world. This may sound rather extreme but I'm not going to apologise for my remarks because I urgently want you to understand the central importance of play with and for your baby and toddler.

A third point about play for under-threes is how it links in with our child's development as someone who can mix successfully with other babies and toddlers of a similar age. We all want our young children to have friends. It's a natural progression from having fun times with mummy or daddy or brother or sister to looking with interest and in slight trepidation at the other babies and toddlers they encounter. A natural next step is to be near to them and reach out to touch. Then comes the sitting and standing alongside each other, eyeing the other's actions and toys, followed quite swiftly by grabbing and swiping. The sequence moves on to the stage where one toddler will sometimes spontaneously proffer the odd spade, glitter star or cowboy hat to another child nearby. Finally, by the time they are approaching three years of age there may be, just may be, a tiny inkling of what 'sharing' means, though that doesn't necessarily mean they want to do it even when prompted and praised!

Your under-three will need all the help you can give them in learning about give and take, waiting your turn, not always being the winner, and sharing. When you play with them yourself you are giving them valuable opportunities, within the safety of a familiar environment, to practise all sorts of social graces that will stand them in very good stead when they venture to play in parallel with another child, move on to cooperative play and then to full-blown imaginative play. We want our toddlers to be able to sit at a table with three others without keeping all the Play-Doh, stickle bricks or glue pots to themselves.

We want our toddlers to join in alongside others in racing up and down on diminutive bikes, pushing buggies or drawing with water, when they're outside playing. We want to see them enacting group picnics in the Wendy house, running away en masse from an invisible monster, or 'cooking' up a storm together in the home corner whilst dressed as princesses, pirates and penguins. So, play isn't just about forging a mutually rewarding bond with our young children, it's also about giving them the social survival skills that will ensure they have the confidence to enjoy pre-school activities with their peers.

Play is also intimately linked with intellectual and language development, and of course our ability to think things through and talk about our feelings is a central aspect of all relationships, including that between parents and their babies or toddlers. So when your little one is 'pestering', in other words begging, you to play with them, remember that what looks suspiciously like being yet another tediously prolonged period of teddy, dolly or dinosaur going to the doctor's is actually a golden opportunity for your under-three to polish up their potential for empathy, insight and verbal communication. It won't seem nearly such a waste of time!

Actually, there are so many lessons for life being absorbed in these caring and sharing games – that's when you have to be given 'medicine' too! – that it's interesting just to tease some of them out so you can appreciate the full complexity of what is learned during even such early imaginative play. It's almost the equivalent of our trying, in our forties, to get to grips with astrophysics – and that's tough, very tough!

Right, caring and sharing games enable our under-threes to begin to learn how to:

- See things from someone else's perspective: INSIGHT
- Recognise another person's feelings: EMPATHY
- Grasp the likely consequences of their actions on someone else: INSIGHT
- Change their behaviour to protect and nurture another: EM-PATHY
- Understand their own feelings: INSIGHT
- Become emotionally sensitive: EMPATHY
- Develop social awareness: INSIGHT
- Link feelings, thoughts, speech and behaviour together: EM-PATHY, INSIGHT and VERBAL COMMUNICATION

All this intertwines and eventually plays a central role in ensuring our offspring is able to make and maintain mutually rewarding relationships of all types, most significantly with you, their mummy and/or daddy. And you thought you were just playing doctors!

Now let's have a look at the attitudes to play that parents can show. There are some goodies and baddies, of course. Parents are only human too! Look at these lists and see if you can spot yourself:

PARENTAL ATTITUDES TO PLAY

Goodies	Baddies
Good tempered and rewarding	Grumpy and complaining
Joining in enthusiastically	Refusing to join in
Letting your baby or toddler lead the way	Running the show

Allowing your baby or toddler to come first or be the best	'I'm the winner!'
Encouraging your child's contributions and choices	'What I say goes!'
Emotionally involved	Seemingly unaffected and remote
Relaxed and confident	Paralysed with embarrassment
Full of imaginative ideas	No idea what to do

I'm pretty sure that you won't display more than one or two of the baddy attitudes, except on occasion. However, we can all have our off-days, so I'm going to look at each one separately and give you some hints on how to play with your under-three in a style that will cement a strong and rewarding bond between you.

Grumpy and Complaining

We can find ourselves being grumpy playmates if we are tired, poorly, bored or fed up – just like a much taller version of our children! Imagine your baby in the bath with you. It's the end of a long day, you've got soap in one eye and your baby has just managed to jab a tender part of your anatomy. Grumpy mummy? Complaining daddy? You bet! But only sometimes. If you find you are grumpy and complaining all the time, please go and talk to your health visitor or GP because you may need extra help in coping with your under-three. There is absolutely no shame in needing support, advice, or perhaps medication or therapy. Go back to chapter two and read over the Baby Blues and post-natal depression (PND) section if you are worried you might need further help.

Hints on becoming better-tempered and generously rewarding to your little one as a playmate would include the following:

- Make sure you hand your baby or toddler over to someone you trust for a couple of one-hour periods each week.
- Choose to play at a time you have put aside especially for this purpose.

- Decide that because play is so important for the bond between you and your baby or toddler, you will give it priority over less important claims on your time or energy.

Refusing To Join In

Playing with an under-three often involves quite literally getting down to their level and that means the floor, surrounded by the fascinating array of noise-making toys you have lovingly supplied. Unsurprisingly, you are more comfortable on a sofa or chair, and it's tempting to believe we are taking a proper part in our baby or toddler's play activities by leaning down on occasion to talk to them, stretching out an arm to point something out or coming up with the odd praise or two. However, from this position we can only make a contribution to our child's play and that just isn't the same as joining in.

Hints on how to join in enthusiastically:

- Get right down on the floor and sit facing your baby so you can see their enjoyment and concentration as they battle to slot the red circle into the right hole.
- Tell yourself that playing together is really beneficial to the bond between you.
- Recognise the significance of play in helping your infant develop into a caring and sharing personality who will be popular at school and later at work.

Running The Show

It can be tempting to believe that we always know what's best for our under-threes. After all, we are the adults in the family! While this sentiment is understandably a feature of good responsible parenting, it isn't always productive to have it blatantly on show. Imagine taking your child to the local pond to feed the ducks. You will have primed them with stories about ducks and how they love to eat bread. You will have involved them in putting pieces of bread in a bag just for the ducks. Anticipation is running high. You picture your toddler looking adorable as they confidently scatter crumbs for the appreciative ducks. Alas, it is not to be!

Your one-year-old is made really quite anxious by the ducks and in any case wants to eat the bread themselves, stoutly refusing all blandishments to the contrary. You are disappointed that the trip did not work out as planned and you wonder if your young child's anxiety near the ducks shows that you are not a good-enough parent. In other words, you found it difficult to step back from running the show without feeling at least a little negative.

In order to avoid unwelcome sensations such as this you need to take positive steps to allow your under-three to lead the way. Try these tips and you will find playtime much more rewarding for both of you:

- Acknowledge that nought to threes need to be given the chance to set the tempo for various activities if they are to gain in self-confidence.
- Read up on the fears that many under-threes experience and be accepting, calm and reassuring when they surface.
- Remember that letting your little son or daughter lead the way at playtimes will strengthen their love for you because you are in essence giving them a message of approval that says you find them loveable.

'I'm The Winner!'

It's a competitive world out there and although graceful losers are applauded it's the winner who receives the loudest 'Bravo!' No wonder, then, that when playing a competitive game with your child, it's so tempting to give in to the urge to demonstrate your superior prowess. You have all seen jubilant fathers punching the air when playing beach cricket with their toddler, as they take a wicket or slam the tennis ball into the sea for a six. We know that some mums cannot resist pointing out to their toddler that they, the mother, have fashioned the best Easter/Christmas/Birthday card.

When we allow ourselves to become trapped by the need to win we are really acting out unresolved issues of self-confidence from our childhood. We probably all suffer from these attachment gaps to one degree or another. After all, our parents weren't perfect either. The most significant fact to hold on to when we're being tempted in this direction is that we grown-ups are much more able than our two-year-old to influence our emotions by involving our powers of reasoning. To feel is not necessarily to act when you are twenty-four years old, but at twenty-four months they are still one and the same thing. Hold back on your wish to be the winner and you will be boosting your toddler's self-esteem and enabling them to bask in your approval and love.

Try these tips if you need to pull back from racing ahead, either literally or figuratively:

- Remember that boosting and not boasting is the way to strengthen the security of the bond between yourself and your under-three.
- Ask yourself why you need to triumph over your little son or daughter. If the answer is related to your own childhood experiences, repeat this little mantra: 'My baby or toddler deserves the best, so let's make sure they are the winners.'
- Look at your under-three's face when they realise you have acknowledged them as the winner. Their moment of joyful triumph is well worth the position of being second, third or even last, now isn't it?

'What I Say Goes'

Parents who want to make all the choices when playing with their children are unlikely to be using Baby Centred behaviour with their under-threes. That's because telling children what to do and issuing commands left, right and centre is Baby Directive behaviour. Of course, as responsible adults there will be times when a clear *Command* is imperative, but generally speaking we would all be well advised to dramatically reduce the number of instructions with which we pepper our babies and toddlers. (Much, much more about *Commands* on page 289.)

I realise that we might rather stay indoors when it's raining, but the fact of the matter is that lots of under-threes just love splashing about in puddles. For them, jumping up and down in water is an especially exciting game. The fact that it leaves us cold is actually irrelevant if we are putting the quality of our bond with our toddler in pride of place over our own visions of soaking socks and shoes. Remember, they are not gleeful because you'll have more washing to cope with. They are gleeful because jumping in puddles is *fun*. Nurture the bond between you by giving your under-three an *Attend*, and see them blossom in the glow of your approval.

You might find these hints helpful when trying to give your child choices and increase their contribution to their playtimes with you:

- Say 'What would you like us to do next?' Be brave! You can always decline and ask them to choose again.
- Stop trying to move things on all the time. Watch your child with an affectionate eye, enthusiastically describe out loud their behaviour and live in the moment.
- You can give your child limited choices when you want to narrow the field of play, so say, 'You can jump in the puddle or we can have a race to the slide.' You have to stick by the outcome though!

Seemingly Unaffected And Remote

It can be difficult sometimes to put your heart into playing with your infant, especially if you are exhausted, worried or ill. We have all had those moments when we say, 'Mmmm – lovely', without paying any real attention to our child's antics or requests. It's not that we don't care. It's not that we don't find our baby or toddler delightful. It's just that we are preoccupied with adult concerns. The trouble is, from our under-three's perspective, because we are not listening to them, not noticing them, and above all not responding by playing with them, they may well feel ignored and unloved. What they really need is a parent who can strike a constructive balance between nurturing the bond with their under-three through play, and dealing with the rest of life. They only know that they feel safe and secure when you give them your undivided attention, and discounted when they see you whizzing about with an assortment of papers clutched in one hand and a biro gripped between your teeth. You can tell which one strengthens the bond, can't you?

When you begin to feel overwhelmed by the demands of adult life, to the detriment of your relationship with your under-three, try these tips:

- Say, 'Mummy/daddy has to do these papers now, so I'm going to set you up with this game and a snack. I'll be quick, and then we can go out in the garden together.'
- Rapidly work out another time slot for focusing on your adult responsibilities, and then give yourself over to the game with your little one.
- Say, 'Hang the jobs! Playtime with my baby and toddler brings us closer together so the washing up/clearing up/telephone calls/letters/milkman's money and the guinea pig hutch can wait!'

Paralysed With Embarrassment

We can all feel anxious about making a fool of ourselves, some more often than others. If, for instance, you are on the quiet, shy side then you are much more likely to worry about embarrassing yourself in front of others than a more extrovert personality would. It doesn't make one style of interacting with others right and the other wrong. They are just individual differences and probably based on how we were wired up neurologically at birth. Let's give thanks for such variation. It would be a very sad planet indeed if we were all of identical temperament.

One of the things that can make anyone nervous is novelty. You know, your first day at a new job, first driving lesson, meeting your partner's parents for the first time, or running your first marathon. Being a first-time parent is right up there with all the other activities that can be a major source of apprehension, filled with innumerable opportunities for us to fall flat on our faces in front of all and sundry.

One of those opportunities rears its ugly head when we think about playing with our toddler. We don't mind doing a few 'Wheeee . . .!' lifts with our under-one. We don't mind a little bit of squealing and chasing when they are one, nor digging in the sand with them at two. What we can't let ourselves relax into is being childlike along-side our under-threes. By childlike, I mean the ability to temporarily divest yourself of your adult dignity in order that you can become the horse, princess, dragon, doctor, superhero, monkey or postie your little treasure needs in order to complete their game plan.

A real killer is when they require a baby for their scenario, and that baby is *you*! We don't want to disappoint them, but equally we don't want to end up with egg on our faces. Some of our social inhibitions are so strong that even when there are no observers around, we still can't shrug off our mantle of hard-earned maturity and 'descend' to our baby or toddler's level. That is such a shame because, not only are we denying our precious child rich bond-building opportunities, we are excluding ourselves from a whole category of interaction with our offspring. If you want to feel more comfortable about playing imaginative games with your child try these ideas. Hints to help you feel relaxed and confident when playing games, especially imaginative ones, include:

- Tell yourself you want to be a really good mummy or daddy, and the best parents are those who can join in with their under-three's explorations of the outer reaches of their fantasies. I mean, how difficult is it to be a bus/orangutan/wicked witch/poorly teddy for five minutes? Put aside your dignity and have *fun*!
- Keep the games in which you look completely wacky for private consumption only. Tell your child that though when at home you love being a caterpillar giving birth to lots of little Easter eggs (yes, this was one of my children's requests!) doing it in the park/high street/baker's is a definite no-no.
- Have a list of incarnations you feel able to manage – growly tiger, apple tree, teacher or shop assistant – and should your under-three request something totally outside your range – a baby wearing a nappy only, a doggie who has pee-peed on the carpet, a monster who hangs from the lights, or a fighter plane – tell them quite calmly and firmly that you don't do that.

Follow this up immediately with. 'I know! What about your favourite? Do you want to be Batman/Barbie or should I? *You* choose.'

No Idea What To Do

Just as our own attachment history – that's our relationships with our parents when we were children and teenagers, as well as adults – heavily influences the sort of parent we turn out to be (see Echoes From Our Past – page 158), so our play history functions in a similar way. For example, I was extremely fortunate in that my mother not only encouraged imaginative games, she also joined in with our flights of fancy. My father was rather less adventurous, though he was happy to let us dress him up while he pretended to be asleep!

Many are not so lucky and have had little personal experience of play prior to the arrival of their baby. The trouble is that while there are books, DVDs and classes on many aspects of parenting, not much is said about how to join in games with a small child. So, if you don't have any useful experience or ideas to fall back on, give the following tips a try:

- Watch the infants' TV programmes with your child so that you can get some ideas on interactive games suitable for their age group.
- Watch your baby or toddler watching TV and notice which bits make them spontaneously laugh, clap or generally wriggle about with pleasure, then use them as a starting point in playing with your under-three.
- Buy a book of nursery rhymes and songs with associated movements. 'The Wheels on the Bus' is a classic, or 'Round and Round the Haystack' for the really tiny – and sing along. Believe me, you will soon have learned by heart any number of toe-tappers and your baby and toddler will find you an endless source of amusement and fun.

That brings us to the end of our look at the play and socialisation strands of attachment. I hope you are now as convinced as myself

that time spent playing with your under-three is a valuable investment in your bond with them. The fact that you can enjoy
interacting with your child while you socialise them is another
major bonus. So please take the plunge and let your hair down a
little, especially when you are required to do your furry bear
impression.

Special Feature: Relationships Under Strain

I suppose the sorts of adjustment challenges that face new parents
as a couple are not, in essence, that different from those we were
trying to tackle prior to the arrival of our baby. But there is one
difference – and it's a big one. There are now *three* people involved:
Mummy, Daddy *and* Baby! In your previous life, BBL – that is,
Before Baby Life – and, yes, the cut-off point *is* that clear – you may
have struggled to sort out priorities, to achieve a healthy balance
between work and play, to assign domestic and financial responsibilities, and inhabit appropriate roles.

As a couple you may have felt there was too little time to talk,
make love, go out for dinner, watch sport or wash your hair. These
issues do not simply alter in character after we become parents,
they become so much bigger that, in whichever direction we try to
look, there they are, staring us right in the face. And to make
already bad matters even worse, we are reeling from the shock of
the birth, wasted by fatigue, laid low by the Baby Blues or post-
natal depression, and struggling with a crying baby who doesn't
seem to need much sleep and has a voracious appetite! It probably
feels as though you are drowning rather than waving to one
another. Be reassured, you *will* survive and your baby *will* thrive,
but will your intimate relationship with your beloved also be
thriving when you next get the chance to say hello?

Actually, the odds are good for all three, but we can all do with
as much help as possible in negotiating the slings and arrows of
outrageous parenthood, so I am going to try to suggest some
solutions to the obstacles and vulnerabilities that can arise.

Time and Priorities

First, I am going to list several scenarios, any one of which could be the story of your ABL – After Baby Life – bringing the vulnerabilities right to the forefront. Then we are going to tease out how to avoid falling into these troublesome traps or, alternatively, how to dig our way out once we're in.

Scene One: *No Time, No Energy and Changed Priorities about Work*

BBL Weekday mornings always used to be a bit of a rush as you both had to leave the house by 7.45 a.m. in order to get to work on time. You had it down to a fine art: the cuddle and kiss, coffee, toast, shower, dress and bingo, you were on your way! Cheerful exchanges about friends and workmates, a chat about potential plans for the evening, and promises to stay in touch during the day. This functioned as a relatively lively, definitely mutual and emotional strand of communication, as you both approached lift off. A goodbye kiss and 'I love you' completed your very satisfactory early morning routine and made a really positive start to the day.

THEN YOU HAVE A BABY!

ABL It's another weekday morning and *everything* has changed! Only one of you is in a rush to get out, the other one is knee deep in nappies and up to their eyes in baby posset. There is a distinct lack of friendly joshing and a decided surplus of resentment. Resentment is focused on how one of you is escaping the responsibilities of parenting for a whole day, while the other must remain shackled to the tiny newborn you both adore. How can that be *fair*? What happened to the plan for job sharing so you each spent equal amounts of time at home? The escapee, casting an appalled eye around at the mountains of baby equipment strewn about what used to be an aesthetically pleasing living space, experiences a pang of guilt, but only for a moment. Once out of the front door, relief takes over. But can it be *fair* to feel like this? What happened to the idea of sharing the practical parenting side of caring for your child? Meanwhile, back at baby bath time, adult conversation seems a distant dream, outings with colleagues from another era, crisp decision-making a lost art. And nobody has said 'I love you' in what seems like an age!

WHERE DID IT ALL GO WRONG?

Re-adjustment tip: Make a Date

Remember how you used to enjoy going out together? Well, now you can conjure up that romantic twosome feeling when staying in together. Once a week, have a pre-planned 'date' evening – well, couple of hours! Or you could try lunchtime if that's a reliable snooze time for your baby. Order in a takeaway, light the candles, put on some background music and prepare to gaze into each other's eyes.

Scene Two: *No Time, No Energy and Changed Priorities regarding Sex*

BBL   It's Sunday morning, the special day of the week when you lie in bed together, talk, laugh and probably make love. Just the two of you, being emotionally and sexually intimate. Reaffirming your joy in a commitment to being a couple. Maybe you had breakfast in bed, read the paper, shared a shower and then had a leisurely late lunch followed by a pleasant stroll hand-in-hand by the river.

THEN YOU HAVE A BABY!

ABL   It's another Sunday morning, but everything has changed! There are three of you in the bed, at least two of you are sleep deprived and functioning on automatic pilot. You can't see across the bed for nappies, Babygros, breast pads, formula, cotton wool, baby lotion, tiny hats and snuggle suits. One of you is wearing a huge maternity nightie and sitting propped up against pillows with your eyes shut, trying to decide whether the long-awaited baby is actually finally asleep or just pretending. The other grown-up is sprawled across what's left of the bed – allowing for the Moses basket, baby and partner – and in a deep slumber, no doubt caused by thirty-six consecutive interrupted nights' rest. What do you think of emotional and sexual intimacy now? Are you looking forward to peacefully reading the papers, larking about with your beloved and ending up with an athletic bout of 'rumpy pumpy'? With no pause for thought, your answer is a swift and emphatic 'No!' Instead you poke your sleeping partner and hiss a demand for tea right *now*. After a total lack of response, you gingerly ease yourself out of bed, trying not to disturb the angel in the Moses basket, and begin to creep towards the door, heading for the kitchen. As you silently open the door, the biggest one left in the bed stirs, jogs the Moses basket and sits bolt upright looking wild-eyed as your tiny infant starts yelling. Emotional harmony? Sexual intimacy? What are you talking about?

WHERE DID IT ALL GO WRONG?

Re-adjustment tip: Share a Bath

Showers are invigorating, baths are sensuous. Choose a time of day when your newborn baby is most likely to be peace-fully asleep, light the scented candles, pour in the essential oils and slide gratefully into the relaxing water. So neither of you are the sylph-like creatures of the past! So what? Remember that it was your physical passion and emotional intimacy that created your baby. Get back in touch with those feelings while you lovingly caress each other's toes, knees, shoulders and any other bits you can reach.

Scene Three: *No Time, No Energy and Changed Priorities about Money*

BBL Couples who work hard are entitled to play hard, you both agree. You share a passion for travel, music, sailing, dancing or darts. It is also understood between you that there are separate activities you enjoy pursuing by yourselves. For her, it's visiting glorious gardens and for him, playing cricket. You budget with your interests in mind, allowing for sun-soaked breaks, concert events, weekends on the river, torrid tangos and trips out with the pub's Golden Arrows darts team. You feel a deep sense of satisfaction that your joint finances more than adequately support your active social life. It is a positive pleasure to indulge in having just the right gear for every event. Diamantés for dancing and tip-top luggage for travel are well within your financial grasp. You even buy little, or sometimes big, surprise gifts for one another, safe in the knowledge that it won't break the bank. No doubt about it, life is good when you have no money worries.

THEN YOU HAVE A BABY!

ABL   You are suddenly faced with the reality of just one salary, and managing money is not the doddle you had anticipated. No one is starving, but you are having to budget quite tightly in order to meet your regular commitments and plan for a holiday – even a modest one at the seaside. Pressure builds up and it is making you snappy! You find yourself muttering darkly about your needs not being given any sort of priority when the funds were being shared out. It's just not fair. Tempers are short and tiffs seem to escalate into rows of mutual recrimination with sickening regularity. One evening it all boils over and angry emotions flood what should have been a tranquil scene. A crisis erupts and your intimate relationship feels deeply wounded.

WHERE DID IT ALL GO WRONG?

Re-adjustment tip: Take a Break

Don't vanish from the family scene! Just make time to take a break from being parents so you can talk about still being a couple. Although you are actually a threesome, or even foursome, making sure your tiny tots are given the kind of family environment that will allow them to form a secure bond with mummy and daddy means paying quality attention to your co-parent. Plan ahead and put aside a particular time each day, only fifteen minutes or so, when each of you guarantees to listen to the other's gripes, hopes and fears with a generous heart. Sharing your feelings like this on a frequent basis will take the sting out of those new financial priorities, so give it a try. You could even find you have a previously untapped ability to relish the joys of rather less expensive treats, such as a CD instead of a concert, a tree fern instead of a trip to a tropical isle, or a single night out at the cinema instead of a season at the opera.

Another problem couples can encounter post-baby are to do with changes in their roles and responsibilities. I think it would be helpful if we looked at these inevitable challenges to our previous positions in terms of the two Scary Lists, starting with the Official List.

Relationships, Roles and Responsibilities

OFFICIAL SCARY LIST

Hers	His
I look like the back end of a bus	I'm worried she doesn't want me
I'm just a milk machine	I'm just a money machine
There's no time for me	I feel shut out
I can't face the thought of sex	I'm too tired to feel sexy

Roughly translated, these Official Scary List items reflect the apprehensions we can experience about the transition from being a lover, worker and leisure companion who can react spontaneously and is responsible only for him- or herself, to being a **PARENT** and *all* that entails. Things like a drop in libido, the conviction that we are no longer sexually attractive, missing out on the buzz of work or feeling stressed by being the only breadwinner, finding time away from parenting to look after ourselves or indulge in once-loved pastimes, becoming submerged by the role of parent to such an extent that the responsibilities involved feel as though they have formed a wedge between us and our partner in this taxing venture. Though mothers and fathers share many of these anxieties, there are concerns specific to each role.

Fathers may focus on feelings of exclusion from the tightly knit mother-and-baby couple. This can be particularly intense if the newborn is being fed by breasts that previously featured as objects of sexual arousal. It seems relatively few men are either willing or able to enter into the spirit of breastfeeding to the level of being part of a nursing threesome!

The new mother's concerns frequently centre around the changes that pregnancy, childbirth and lactation have wrought on her body, especially in terms of her physical attractiveness. Anxieties about our no-longer-streamlined form plague many mums, though there can also be long periods in each day when we are so centred on caring for our little miracle that we couldn't care less.

The tensions linked to the inner conflict generated by the changes in roles and responsibilities that inevitably accompany the move to parenthood can be a potential minefield for couples. There can be times when our fears reach such a pitch, we realise we have an Unofficial Scary List too! Items like this would probably include:

Relationships, Roles and Responsibilities

UNOFFICIAL SCARY LIST

Hers	His
I will never get my figure back again so he won't fancy me anymore	I just don't seem to fancy her any more
I will be left to cope with the baby alone because he will leave me	I'm not cut out to be a father so I might have to leave
I'm not a person anymore, I've been taken over by the baby	I'm not important as a person anymore
I have gone off sex completely, and I will never fancy him again	I'm afraid our sex life is over for good

Of course, some couples *don't* experience this degree of confusion, disillusion, desperation and despair, so let's ask ourselves how they manage to avoid these painful pitfalls. As with most questions about what makes us tick, the answer is at once simple and incredibly complex! The simple bit? It is that couples who *stay in touch* and *communicate* beat the odds. And the complex? How to make sure you can do the same!

Well, why not take a leaf out of the Parent/Baby Game and play the Me/You Game? Here are a few pointers to being Partner Centred rather than Parent Centred:

- Give your partner *Attends* that are to do with how you notice and enjoy their physical company:
    'You smell lovely.'
    'Your smile really lights up your face.'
    'I love your touch.'
    'I love the colour of your eyes.'
- *Best Guess* your partner about stressful issues relating to their feelings as a person. Mirror, Validate, Empathise and Resolve issues like:
    Self-confidence
    Self-worth
    Self-presentation
    Self-image
    Resolution mostly means *reassurance* here.
- Give your partner *Praise* for their personality traits:
    'You are incredibly trustworthy.'
    'You are so supportive.'
    'You are a great listener.'
    'You're the most patient person I've ever known.'
- *Smile, Look at* and *Touch* your partner *Positively* every chance you get:
    As you pass in the kitchen
    When sitting in the living room
    In the shower and bath
    Out in the car

- *Imitate* your partner's remarks and actions in relation to adult-only topics:
  Be genuine
  Be enthusiastic
  Be subtle
  Be warm
- Try your partner with an *Ask to Play*, not only when they seem harassed but at calmer times too:
  'What can I do for you now, darling?'
  'Is there anything special you want me to do now?'
  'Would you like me to make you a drink/a meal/a comfy seat/anything at all?'
  'Why don't you tell me how I can help?'
- *Ignore* 90 per cent of your partner's annoying little personal habits.
  Look away
  Keep quiet
  Tell yourself it's not important
  Only resume communications once you are calm

You may find it quite an effort at times to come up with a steady flow of Partner Centred inputs for your beloved, but remember, they take no more time or energy than being Partner Directive. And they're a good deal more constructive for your relationship as an adult couple! That's because, just as being Baby Centred rather than Baby Directive nurtures the emotional bond between parent and infant, so being Partner Centred will bring you two closer together. Put all that together and you are on the right route for the future happiness of the whole family.

The huge changes in time, energy and priorities, roles and responsibilities brought about by becoming parents are bound to effect some pretty major shifts in your intimate adult relationship with one another. That cannot be avoided and, in any case, this forced transition from carefree independence to circumscribed duties can also kick-start a whole new surge of maturity, which is no bad thing. And after all, when you compare the past pleasure of reading the Sunday papers with the exquisite joys of drinking in the beauty of your baby's smile, well, there *is* no comparison is there? So, yes there are sacrifices as well as delights involved in becoming responsible parents. As long as you make time to give priority to your role as part of an adult relationship, then everyone in your family should benefit from the strong, reassuring and secure bonds you will all enjoy.

Sometimes, however, things can get so bad between you that there is real danger your relationship with your partner will not survive. This can happen when one or both of you finds the adjustment from adult to parent particularly difficult, for whatever reason. If this happens to you then I would strongly suggest you seek the help of professionals offering some form of couples' therapy. There is little to be gained by hanging on until it's too late for a very important relationship to be revived. Your local Relate would be a good first stop and they are always listed in the telephone book for your area.

What To Do Next: Am I Overstimulating My Baby?

It is time now to take a look at the challenges associated with making sure our babies and toddlers are provided with just the right amount of stimulation – not too little and not too much. When we get that on the button, our next task is to protect our under-threes from any dangers associated with their joyful exploration activities. So I will also cover parents' emotional experiences in facing the challenge of dealing with this very important part of infant development, including some practical tips on keeping anxiety and stress at manageable levels.

Scenario One: Babies Under Six Months

Supposing you are really intent on giving your baby lots of stimulation right from the word go. You are so enthusiastic about intellectual stimulation that you are constantly playing them Mozart. Let's face it, we have all so often heard that this unparalleled genius's work is the equivalent of brain food for babies that it must be true! You are so keen on social stimulation that you introduce them to at least three new people a day, all of whom want to hold your newborn and chat to them, whether the baby is interested or not. You are so determined to give lashings of language stimulation that you find yourself interacting in a kind of verbal frenzy, even as your infant nods off to sleep, full to the blissful brim with marvellous milk. And emotional stimulation? You both agree it's an absolute must and consequently load your facial and vocal efforts with masses of smiles, surprise and wide-eyed 'Oooh! What's that?' looks. That's not to mention vastly exaggerated expressions of sympathy and concern over the tiniest tear or snuffle.

I imagine you might be feeling just a weeny bit irritated with me at this point in time. After all, haven't I just been going on about how stimulating your baby is a crucial part of their development and one we must not neglect? And now I'm hinting that it's possible to go over the top! Cheek! Ah, but it's all a matter of *degree*, and as my dear old granny used to caution, 'Everything in moderation'. She also used to sing a Victorian music hall song called 'A little bit of what you fancy does you good!', so it wasn't all bad news! Getting the degree of stimulation just right for an under-six-month-old can therefore be tricky. You could, for instance, err on the other side and experience a scenario like this:

You have rightly sensed your newborn at first needs food and sleep rather than exposure to the delights of a baby gym. You might even be feeling very much the same yourself! Very gradually, you introduce a musical toy, a shiny red mobile, and the ubiquitous bunch of plastic keys for them to rattle and chew on. You restrict the number of visitors, switch the television off when they are in the room and strictly limit the number of outings when Baby goes too.

Am I now saying that this is a much better way of going on in the stimulation stakes? Well, no, because the two scenarios set out are both rather extreme. Your main aim would be to stay on top of your baby's *evolving* stimulation needs over the first half of year one. But we must try to remain sensitive to our baby's stimulation needs. Most newborns are going to need increasing amounts of intellectual, social, language and emotional input from you as time goes by, so we have to gauge what to provide almost on a daily basis.

I well remember bone teething rings, with silver bunny bell attachment, and the uncertainty I felt about exactly how much rattling of said contraption I should be doing in my baby's first weeks. There is, of course, no absolute set of rules that can be applied to each and every under-six-month-old. Their development and temperaments vary so much that what would be stunningly appropriate for one is boredom or clamour for another. No wonder we can feel anxious about either overprotecting or over-exposing our incredibly young offspring to the various types of stimulation.

Overprotection

Overprotecting our under-six-month-old from too much stimulation is a common reaction of many parents. Understandably, because their very lives depend upon mummy and daddy keeping them safe and comfortable. Such tiny babies have no notion of danger, so we are well aware we must be vigilant on their behalf. That naturally includes shielding them from becoming overexcited due to too much noise, movement and carers. However, in our anxiety to prevent any harm befalling our most precious jewel, we can veer too far away from the happy medium of stimulation that they need. Remember, what a one-month-old regards as blissful peace is akin to sensory deprivation five months later by the time they are sitting up and taking lots of notice! Handling our own apprehensions, therefore, becomes a priority if we are to meet the demands of ensuring the level of stimulation is spot on.

Suggested methods of keeping stress levels down would include spelling out your fears and then challenging them, in the same style as dealing with Negative Automatic Thoughts. You could also remind yourself that a trifle too much exposure to stimulation is probably better for your under-six-month-old than too little. In practical terms, remember that your baby needs a variety of stimulating experiences, covering physical interactions with the material world, social and emotional input, language and intellectual opportunities for exploration. You can also remind yourself to look out for the signs your infant is under-aroused by the world around them.

Signs of Under-Stimulation: Babies Under Six Months

- Excessively long periods of sleep; for example, more than five hours at a stretch, except at night.
- Too much passive observation as opposed to an active wish to interact with you.
- Niggling, whining and reaching out repeatedly for something they can see, all at the same time.

Overstimulation

But supposing, in your enthusiasm to promote your under-six-month-old's confident exploration of the sights, sounds and social life surrounding them you overdo it? You know, those occasions when your baby might just as well be wrapped up in brown paper and tied with string, it so resembles a parcel being passed between eager hands! Your intentions, and those of your baby's admiring audience, are beyond question, there's no doubt about that. However, in your desire to show off and push along your baby's ever-increasing prowess, it is possible to lose your focus on your infant's experience of the situation. If we want to get the right balance of stimulation in those first precious months, we may need to deal with the little matter of you being just a tad too energetic in meeting your baby's stimulation and exploration needs.

To ensure you are not displaying too much parental enthusiasm it is important to focus on empathising with your under-six-month-old. You can do this really easily by simply thinking yourself into their position. Imagine giant beings are constantly passing you around when all you want is to be left alone. Think what it would be like to be bombarded with an excess of loud music, a surfeit of swirling colours and an overdose of in-your-face nosy parkers all trying to kiss you. Not something we would be queuing up for, is it? As for practical tips, remember to put in place a few precautions against overstimulation. Things like limiting the number of people who interact with your little sweetheart to, say, three in any one day. Make especially sure to arrange for quiet times between you and your under-six-month-old, including when they are awake and alert. Simply *Imitating* them while you *Ask to Play* by wondering out loud what they would like you to do helps strengthen the bond between you, even at the earliest of ages. You can also take care to be fully aware of any signs that your baby is feeling overstimulated.

Signs of Overstimulation: Babies Under Six Months Old

- Closing their eyes or trying to look away, plus fretful whimpering.
- Turning their heads away from the source of stimulation.
- Crying in a fractious way and pushing away the overstimulating person or object.

Always be ready to alter the amount of input your baby is receiving, by watching out for the clues they provide by their reactions to your efforts at stimulation. Of course, because of the phenomenal pace of development in our under-three's first year of life, the six- to twelve-month-old presents a rather different challenge to our attempts to encourage them in exploring their world. Our emotional reactions alter too!

Scenario Two: Babies Aged Six To Twelve Months

You have always known your baby loves to look at you, smile and 'talk' with you. They obviously enjoy your touch, as you have been devoted to making sure you are getting the six to one Baby Centred to Baby Directive ratio sorted. You are absolutely thrilled by their progress, especially that they seem so insatiably inquisitive. They want to investigate every aspect of their environment, including their own cute little toes and fingers, as well as perpetually using their mouths to taste anything and everything within their grasp. Literally. And there's the rub, because, of course, your own fingers and toes can easily become irresistible for your child to investigate. But it doesn't end there, does it? Naturally not, particularly when your infant has learned to crawl and cruise their way around the magical delights of a baby-friendly living room. I remember being astounded at the sheer determination of my six- to twelve-month-olds in their pursuit of novelty. Scrunching, banging and then mouthing paper, fabric, cutlery, furnishings, not to mention the other unmentionables they unerringly spy out on the carpet! If only I had been blessed with eyes in the back of my head, life would have been a great deal calmer. Suddenly, stimulating my under-one-year-olds became a matter of attempting to rein in some of their untrammelled enthusiasm for exploration, rather than making sure I presented them with a carefully judged amount of input.

Perhaps the most intrusive example of my six- to twelve-month-olds' fascination for anything within reach occurred when my face became a focus for active excavation on their part. I know you too will have suffered the enthusiastic eye-poking, nose-twisting and lip-grabbing exploits of your adoring baby. Faces are always a prime source of stimulation for infants, so no wonder they can't think of anything more delightful than a handful of cheek or a mouthful of chin. Your cheek! Your chin! I expect you have also noticed that their dimpled arms can reach further than you can bend your neck backwards away from their grasp. You have? Welcome to the club! It's not that we want them to keep their hands to themselves, we just can't help feeling a little irritated by these unstoppable face invaders, especially if they make our eyes water or force us to cry out in tones of surprised outrage: 'Ouch! That hurt!' I remember on one occasion being thwacked smartly across the nose by a ten-month-old wielding a plastic flute. It hurt, albeit momentarily, a great deal, and it was quite a job resisting the urge to retaliate in kind. Parents are only human, after all. On the other hand, if we could be assured that indulging our baby's latest journey of exploration would not involve a painful experience on our part, we might be very much more amenable to being so personally involved in their unending search for novel sensations. Sadly, that's out of the question and trying to explain to six- to twelve-month-olds about the distress of having one's individual space violated is not an option. So, what to do?

One of the things you can do in order to avoid being drawn into acting out your annoyance at having your face chomped on by a toothy one-year-old is to take charge of the situation by modelling gentle touching, physically guiding and then praising your baby's attempts to imitate your behaviour. It is at times like this that a spot of emotional coaching is definitely called for, so go ahead and *Teach* rather than *Imitate* your tiny tot this time. You will also need to set limits on the amount of contact with your face that you are willing to allow. Decisions will vary from parent to parent, of course. Some mums will be quite happy to have small, but sturdy fingers popped into their mouths and ears, but draw the line at nostril poking. Dads might tolerate chin gnawing but draw a line at nose sucking. No doubt you have your own idiosyncrasies, though no one has ever told me they actively enjoy being poked in the eye or smacked across the bridge of the nose! Make sure, too, that you put into practice all you know about reducing your irritation instead of reacting in the heat of the moment.

In practical terms, you will be nurturing a secure bond with your baby if, rather than snapping, you simply put the infant down somewhere safe and walk away, while you wipe off the dribble or blink away the tears and calm down. You could also be doing other people a good turn by warning them that spectacles, earrings and necklaces are bound to provoke the infamous grab, hold fast and pull response from your under-one-year-old. You can also comfort yourself by referring to a book on a baby's developmental ages and stages, because this will reassure you that the snatch-and-grab game is just another phase your offspring is passing through. Neither should you spend a second worrying about their having any intentions at all about hurting anyone, most especially not their adored mummy or daddy. It is just a case of your face being such an exciting source of stimulation that for them the urge to explore it is irresistible. Six- to twelve-month-olds simply cannot foresee what the consequences of their actions will have on the object of their attention, so they need our help to learn. This means putting sensible limits in place. I go into some detail on limit setting, giving clear commands and using time out in the next chapter, when I tackle disobedience, so I am concentrating here on other aspects of coping with the challenges to do with stimulation and exploration that show up in the first three years of our baby and toddler's life. Let's move on then to the one-year-old toddlers themselves.

Scenario Three: One-Year-Olds

One of the most astonishing things about one-year-olds is the speed with which they can move around. They go from being unsteady cruisers one minute to Olympic sprinters the next in what seems like moments. Of course, it's a joy to behold, especially as it's a uniquely human accomplishment. There's a downside, though, and it's called rampant anxiety or, to be really honest about it, terror! Here's a little scene I witnessed whilst writing this book, although it is doubtless happening across the globe thousands if not millions of times a day.

A sturdy toddler is out for an afternoon walk along the promenade beside the sea. It is cold but bright and our toddler has on a small pair of denim jeans, a red furry jacket and a navy woollen beanie hat pulled well down over his ears. He is springing from foot to foot rather than just walking, with every few steps a bigger bounce and an explosion of laughter. His smiles and chuckles seem to stem purely from the joy of his own triumphs. His mood certainly isn't the least infected by the potential dangers that surround him on his innocent and peaceful outing. Dangers like the low, flimsy fencing around the edge of the esplanade, the unguarded railway crossing, the threatening-looking dog, the steep slope down to the sea, and the jagged rocks below the fence. Thank heavens his attentive, vigilant and protective mother is with him! You certainly could not trust him to look after himself for more than a second or two, mostly because he darts here and there at such speed. First the fence, then the dog, back to the fence, over to the steep slope and then right up to the rail crossing. And then there is his fascination with the overflowing rubbish bin and its contents!

All this is taking place faster than it takes to write it down! Meanwhile, his mummy is having to trot behind him, dive sideways to grasp him, leap forward to forestall him, whilst explaining that not all doggies are friendly and little boys mustn't play with rubbish because it's dirty.

Just remembering what I saw makes me breathless. The toddler's mother certainly needed to be fit and fast on her feet in order to keep him safe, despite his joyful and confident exploration of this stimulating seaside environment. And her emotional reaction to her one-year-old's behaviour? As you might expect, one part pleasure and five parts anxiety, with the occasional flash of real fear. No wonder you can't let them out of your sight for a moment at this age. It would be crazy to think otherwise, so us parents are caught nicely in a trap between our primary responsibility to keep our offspring safe from harm and our attempts to ensure the under-threes' thirst for new experiences is not squashed out of them. The tension created by this conflict of interests can generate quite a stock of irritation along with the inevitable anxieties. Given a toddler's passion for all things new to them – and that's a *lot* of things – we can expect to find it pretty difficult to relax when in their company. Constantly being in a state of high alert is no joke and, as a result, if we are to be able to enjoy time spent with our daring one-year-old adventurers, we need to reduce our feelings of tension – whilst not risking their safety. So how best to handle our own emotional reactions while effectively safeguarding our tiny bundles of energy? A mixture of psychological manoeuvres in combination with practical steps seems to be the best solution.

One important path to relaxation is preparation, taking into account even some slightly unlikely contingencies that could occur. I am sure we have all faced stressful times when we have had to throw a party, take a driving test, cook our first three-course meal or even give a presentation. How did we feel beforehand? Anxious, and much more so if we were not properly prepared. We have all suffered the consequences of leaving things too late. A damp squib of a party, an incorrect driving manoeuvre, inedible food, or a muddled talk. Of course we live and learn and try again. But we don't have this option when we are responsible for a one-year-old's moment-to-moment safety.

So, in order to be able to relax, safe in the knowledge that our one- to two-year-old can come to no real harm, we have to put in place practical precautions before we can relax our vigilance. This means we have to anticipate the dangers that our toddlers quite literally don't see, and exclude them from the agenda. It can be quite rewarding to go through the list of steps needed to protect our toddlers, put plans into action and then, if we have been thorough, sit back and enjoy the show. Once fearless fourteen-month-olds are on reins in busy streets, sixteen-month-old mountaineers are prevented by gates from unsupervised stair-climbing, eighteen-month-old would-be high divers prevented by locks from flying out of windows, twenty-month-old daredevil cyclists saved from injury by stabilisers and a parent's steadying hand, twenty-two-month-old jungle explorers corralled in a toxin-free baby-and-toddler zone, and so prevented from eating noxious plants, and two-year-old champion swimmers kept afloat by water wings – only *then* can we really relax! Apart from developing an extra pair of hands, that's probably the best we can do to maintain a healthy balance between our anxieties and their freedom to explore with confidence. In terms of the bond between you and your one-year-old, it will be much more constructive, too, because you will both be able to enjoy the pleasure of spending time together without the tensions associated with being constantly apprehensive. If I had been the mother of the seaside toddler? You've guessed it: he would have been in reins!

Scenario Four: Two-Year-Olds

Two-year-olds are, to my mind, an utter delight, but then I don't live with one any more! When I had a three-year-old *and* a two-year-old at home, I suspect I might have been a little less dewy-eyed. What about you? You have probably arranged for one or two half days, or two-hour sessions at least, at your local nursery every week so that both you and your two- to three-year-old can each have a change of scene. You have chosen a playgroup very carefully indeed, canvassing the opinion of parents who already use the centre as well as visiting several times with your toddler. I know it's a cause of considerable anxiety, ensuring your two-year-old will be safe *and* stimulated. There has been an ongoing debate for many years now, all centred on answering the question of whether under-threes do better if kept at home with a parent all day, or show more progress if sent to a nursery, playgroup, pre-school or looked after by a childminder. Increasingly, it seems, studies show that spending most time at home with mummy or daddy may be the most helpful set-up for under-threes. That's not to say little ones who receive a good deal of input from parent substitutes of one kind or another are affected negatively. And let's face it, the days when most women gave up work for good after the birth of their first baby have long since become history.

My own position, looking back over forty-plus years of parenting, is that I was fortunate to be able to combine full-time motherhood with studying in the evenings for a busy but extremely rewarding eleven years. On the other hand, I can also recall moments during that period when I could cheerfully have torn my hair out with the tedium of day after day devoted to wiping bottoms and making dip-in eggs with bread and butter soldiers! It is never going to be an easy call. Parents need stimulation and opportunities for exploration too!

However, no matter what arrangements you make, you will still be spending enough time with your two-year-old to recognise the following scene. Your toddler has been up since dawn, full of beans and twice as lively. So far today (and it's only 10.45 a.m.!) they have breezed through the following activities: bed bouncing, bath splashing, a getting-dressed romp-and-tickle, sixteen nursery rhymes *with* actions, two short child-friendly DVDs, four drinks, a breakfast and mid-morning snack, running round in circles arms out-stretched, squealing 'Look at me! Look at me!' plus painting, Play-Doh towers, washing doll's hair, pretend shopping, farm, hospital and post office, being a baby in a blanket . . . shall I go on? I don't think so! We all know where the day is heading – parental exhaustion by coffee time and unbounded energy, invention and exploration by the two-year-old right up to bedtime. Should we be joining in every imaginative escapade they cook up? Are we bad parents because we flag well before they do? Do they have any idea of the mixture of wonder and fatigue we experience merely watching them go through their paces? No, no and no, to all three. When our two-year-old seems so sophisticated we can barely believe in the magical transformation that has occurred, it's difficult to remember they still have only a pretty rudimentary grasp on the consequences of their actions. Especially in terms of their impact on other people, and that includes us parents!

How can we cope most constructively with the emotional impact on us of our two-year-old's apparently insatiable thirst for stimulation and exploration opportunities? I suggest going with the flow, whether that means agreeing to dress up as a princess or pony after a generous *Ask to Play* or laying on the sofa chiming in with verbal *Imitations* as you try to snatch a moment's rest. The main feeling to hold on to is your wonderment at your two-year-old's burgeoning ability to initiate their own search for novelty and pursue their unending quest to explore the world around them. Remember, too, that you don't have to be *Asking to Play* or *Imitating all* the time, just ensuring you do six times more of these Baby Centred behaviours than their Baby Directive opposites *Commands* and *Teaches*. Also, try to hold on to that delicate balance between over-encouraging your little darlings to progress and swaddling them in cotton wool. That's part of what allows our two-year-olds to retain the emotional safety of their bond with us. Then we can relax in the knowledge that we have provided them with the all-important Secure Base from which to make confident forays into their fascinating environment, exploring as they go.

As far as practical tips are concerned, I think I would see providing an inexhaustible supply of creative materials as a top priority. Planning ahead so 'messy play' can take place in an atmosphere uncoloured by the fear – *our* fear – that carpets and cushion covers will be ruined is another must. But don't forget to enjoy any time you may have to yourself, rather than cramming in a thousand and one jobs that will still be there tomorrow. And remember, just because our two-year-old is ecstatic about making rainbow-coloured Play-Doh spaghetti, that doesn't mean we have to find it a scintillating activity! It is perfectly all right to read a magazine that interests you while you give your two-year-old toddler a string of *Attends*, *Praises*, *Smiles* and *Imitations* while they enthusiastically investigate the play materials you have so thoughtfully provided.

I hope this whole chapter on babies and toddlers' need for stimulation so they can learn to explore their world with self-confidence has been useful, informative and even fun at certain points. Here are the seven Golden Bullets to help you refresh your memory on the main issues covered.

GOLDEN BULLETS

• **No. 1. My Baby Needs . . . Stimulation**
All babies and toddlers need plenty of novel experiences, and they rely on their parents to provide them. Using frequent *Ask to Plays* and *Imitations* with your under-three, instead of *Commands* and *Teaches*, will provide the stimulation they crave, while also strengthening the security of the bond between you. Give your under-three the chance to tell you what they would like you to do, even if you have to guess because they are too tiny to speak properly. This gives the message that you recognise their individuality. Use often. Copy your baby and toddler's actions, noises, behaviour, words and play ideas. They will learn that you notice and admire them. Use often.
• **No. 2. What Not To Do: Don't Be Negative**
Too many *Commands* – telling babies and toddlers what to do – can leave them feeling confused and anxious. Use as seldom as possible. Similarly, overdoing the *Teaches* – providing your under-threes with facts – can make them believe you are unappreciative of their efforts. Use sparingly. Too many of these Baby Directive behaviours undermine your

baby and toddler's potential to form a warm, loving, secure and rewarding bond with you, their parent. Don't sap your under-three's self confidence. Instead give them the *Ask to Plays* and *Imitations* that will enable them to explore their world with happy enthusiasm. Remember, Baby Centred parents don't need to do lots of *Commands* and *Teaches*, because they are having too much fun being flexible with their offspring. Aim for six *Ask to Plays* and *Imitations* for every one *Command* and *Teach*. Concentrating on these Baby Centred behaviours will strengthen the bond between you and your baby and toddler.

• **No. 3. Special Feature: Developing Baby's Identity**
Take turns and interact with your baby and toddler in a way that credits them with a mind of their own, and helps build up the language and intellectual strands of your attachment.

• **No. 4. Echoes From Our Past: Authoritarian Parenting**
Even if you had authoritarian parents yourself, you can make progress towards being flexible, friendly and fun with your under-three. This will allow them to develop as self-confident, independent and cooperative individuals. Nourish your relationship by giving frequent *Ask to Plays* and *Imitations* while cutting down on their opposite behaviours, *Commands* and *Teaches*. You, your baby and toddler will experience a much more rewarding bond when you let go of all the power.

• **No. 5. Special Feature: How To Play With Infants**
Baby and toddler play, especially with parents, is an important part of developing the abilities necessary for building best quality bonds, and encouraging a positive self-image and becoming sociable.

• **No. 6. Special Feature: Relationships Under Strain**
Having a baby means making adaptations in adult relationships. Roles and responsibilities have to be re-negotiated. It is very important for your under-three that you and your partner are a loving couple. It can be tough going, but a little emotional tolerance and practical support can go a long way, especially on a bad day.

• **No. 7. What To Do Next: Am I Overstimulating My Baby?**
Meeting the challenge of providing the right type and level of stimulation for your under-three as they progress from newborn to active two-year-old can be quite demanding. Don't be apprehensive, though, because there are lots of psychological and practical tips for you in this section.

Chapter Five

Responding Sensitively to Your Baby

WHAT THIS CHAPTER IS ABOUT

The main focus for this chapter is that your baby needs . . . Sensitivity and how you can make sure they stay in touch with you both physically and emotionally. You could say that, when we are managing to be sensitively responsive to our under-threes, we have cracked the parenting code. But don't feel anxious about being able to cope with so much responsibility, because you have the key to the code in your own capable hands: it's the Parent/Baby Game of course! The Baby Centred behaviours highlighted are *Ignoring Minor Naughtiness* and *Giving Clear Commands*.

Also in this chapter:
- What Not To Do: Don't Give Fuzzy Commands – page 289.
- Echoes From Our Past: Balanced Parenting – page 317.
- Special Features: Displaying Physical Affection – page 310; When Grandparents Undermine – page 331.
- What To Do Next: Troubleshooting – page 298.
- Golden Bullets – page 341.

My Baby Needs . . . Sensitivity

Babies and toddlers don't just need their mummies and daddies to handle them gently. Nor will listening closely or watching with an eagle eye suffice to meet the under-three's need for sensitivity to their physical needs. There is emotional sensitivity, too, when we must make valiant efforts to stay tuned into our under-threes if we truly want them to develop a deep and trusting bond with us. Being 'in tune' with your infant is a vital first step in being able to meet your child's need for sensitivity. The kind of sensitivity necessary to ensure your little one's physical and emotional requirements are met has to be *responsive*. That means parents have to not only constantly monitor what their under-three is doing, they also have to *interpret* what they observe and then come up with a relevant, constructive *reaction*. When parents succeed in being *sensitively responsive* to their baby and toddler, under-threes experience a wide range of benefits, including a sense . . .

- of being closely in touch with us
- that they are really important to us
- that physical closeness is safe
- that emotional intimacy is to be welcomed
- that their comfort is a matter of concern to us
- of being valuable in their own right
- of being understood
- of being cared for
- that reciprocal communication is vital
- that we will keep them safe when they are afraid or in pain
- of their own identity
- of the fun in play and interactions with us
- of their place in the family and eventually in the wider world

In fact, a sense of . . . well, just about everything significant in terms of their progress from totally independent newborn to sparky, chatty and mobile almost three-year-old.

When I am observing parents and their babies or toddlers, my paramount objective is to focus on the grown-ups' sensitivity in responding to the constant stream of messages from their under-threes about their fluctuating needs. That is, emotional needs, intellectual needs, social needs, play needs, attachment needs, behavioural needs, language and communication needs, psychological needs, personality or temperament needs – it's a long, long list! I will be spelling out a detailed plan, how best to be Sensitively Responsive at each phase of your under-threes' first few years. That means clarifying what to do so that your infant stays comfortingly in touch with you, both physically and emotionally, as they mature from passive infant to action-hero toddler.

I can't really stress heavily enough the central role that parents' Sensitive Responses play in a baby and toddler's development into a confident, alert, inquisitive and emotionally stable three-year-old. Without such attunement by their mummy and/or daddy, the little one's progress in almost every area, from neural connections to number counting, crying to crawling, and walking to talking, will be undermined. In my work with deeply troubled families, I have seen small babies who have learned to become purple in the face with distress and frustration in order to elicit a response, sensitive or otherwise, from their mother or father. Parents who pay too much attention to their infants and make under-threes unnecessarily anxious are also missing the boat.

The red-faced infant can grow to believe they are of so little importance to their mummy and daddy, they are not worth noticing until crisis point. The over-cosseted toddler is likely to feel there is something deeply unsafe in just being themselves. Follow their progress for a few years and you'll find either unlikeable little bullies, or small, passive nervous wrecks. Mind you, under-threes like this are the exception, but they are made – *not* born – so we have to keep our wits about us and make sure to practise being Sensitively Responsive (SR) every minute we can manage. So, on to the promised details on exactly how to become SR mums and dads:

In getting the right balance between being either undersensitive or oversensitive when we respond to our babies and toddlers,

Ignoring Minor Naughtiness is key, especially in conjunction with giving *Clear Commands*. Naturally, newborns, infants and small babies are incapable of any sort of naughtiness, so we won't be doing much, if any, *Ignoring* with them. And, of course, for the first few months, because they are not independently mobile, there are very few moments for giving a *Command*, clear or fuzzy.

I suppose the point I am trying to make is that we don't actually need these child-management techniques until our under-three is in a position to bend or challenge the rules for acceptable behaviour that we are busy trying to lay down as part of that major parental preoccupation – socialising the infant into a civilised individual. As you will no doubt have realised from points I have made in previous chapters, I believe it is vital to the growth of a healthy bond between ourselves and our under-threes to keep at the forefront of our thinking the notion that babies under three months old do not *intend* to annoy us. They simply aren't clever enough. Neither are the three- to six-, six- to nine-, or nine- to twelve-month-olds. In their first year of life our precious treasures have only a fragile grasp on cause and effect sequences compared with our own sophisticated abilities, and virtually no comprehension in terms of planning ahead with the *intention* of irritating or defying us.

We really must not burden the under-one-year-old with the emotional fallout from the shock, fatigue, Baby Blues, post-natal depression, anxieties about feeding, intimate adult relationship adjustments, or family tensions that can swamp us at times during their first year. So instead, I strongly suggest you spend that first year accepting that your life as an independent adult and/or part of a couple has changed *for ever*. Your emotional antennae are now tuned to your baby rather than yourself, and that there will be no let-up in demands on you to be Sensitively Responsive; no matter how you might be feeling at any given moment. However, by making a continuously SR attitude the main guide to your inter-actions with your under-one, and reminding yourself their beha-viour is driven by their need for warmth, approval, trust and confidence, and *not* any intention to tax you beyond your limits of patience, you will find yourself able to ignore the annoying elements of your under-one-year-old's behaviour. Use only the very few *Clear Commands* needed at this early age, without losing your focus on being an SR mummy and/or daddy.

But what about the ones and twos? I hear you cry! Surely they will need more guidance on how to behave! Yes, of course you are right. As babies mature into toddlers it becomes more and more appropriate to *Ignore Minor Naughtiness* and give *Clear Commands* because in their constant search for new experiences and their ever-present urge to explore their world, they will inevitably push boundaries and break rules. It cannot be any other way as their priority is to test out new skills and expand their horizons, while ours is to keep them safe, protect them from harm and gradually turn them into acceptable members of society. No wonder there are clashes! That's why we must make sure to be Sensitively Responsive when we are setting, and then sticking to, reasonable ground rules for our one- to three-year-olds' behaviour in various situations. Getting the Attention Rule (page 129) right is only part of the battle. To be a SR parent, *when* to use it is just as important.

Once we add *Ignoring Minor Naughtiness* and *Giving Clear Commands* to our Baby Centred behaviours, we have nearly all the main ingredients we need to encourage compliance and reduce disobedience in our under-threes – but not quite all. To hold a full hand in terms of parenting and managing baby and toddler difficult behaviours, we need to add in techniques such as Distraction, Time Out and Withdrawing Privileges. Therefore a further topic for discussion will be what to do when your one- and two-year-olds come up with dangerous or destructive actions that it is not safe to ignore. But first let's define our two chosen Baby Centred behaviours.

Ignoring Minor Naughtiness
You will find that *Ignoring Minor Naughtiness* reduces such annoying behaviour in the future. That's because it takes away something our infant truly thirsts for: our attention. However,

ignoring is very much more difficult to do properly than you might imagine. That is why I have packed this chapter with all that you might need to know about how to ignore your tiny tot's irritating behaviour. I shall include some useful suggestions on how to decide what comes under the heading of annoying but harmless, as opposed to thoroughly objectionable and dangerous.

Giving Clear Commands

I would completely understand if you had lost patience with me on this one! First, I say don't, then I say do! Actually, the fact of the matter is that while peppering our under-threes with a multitude of unclear and unnecessary instructions is bad news for bonding, issuing a few crisp instructions at just the right moment is an important part of sensitive parenting. And sensitive parents, it is widely acknowledged, create secure attachments with their babies and toddlers. We are not talking sergeant-major shouting, nor a complicated string of instructions. A *Clear Command* is one where we grown-ups follow a set sequence of actions and words that vastly increase the chances that the one- or two-year-old on the receiving end *will* do as they are told. That's got to be exceedingly good news. Again, we are excluding the under-six-month-old from the exercise of instructing them to do or stop doing whatever it is they are up to, because it's a pretty pointless waste of time and energy when they are that young.

Ignoring Minor 'Naughtiness' by Babies Aged Under Six Months

I have put 'Naughtiness' in inverted commas here because as we have already agreed, newborns and infants under six months of age aren't actually capable of 'bad' or 'unacceptable' behaviour. That doesn't mean to say they never irritate, annoy or frustrate us, particularly when we cannot soothe their crying or get them to sleep. It does mean, though, they do not intend to wind us up, ruin our day or spoil our sleep. So, what might happen when we are being Sensitively Responsive to our newborn, despite them being a tiny bit troublesome? Let's look at some examples.

- Because your expectations of your newborn and infant are properly aligned with their individual profile of development, when they bring back their milk or spit out their baby rice, you are CONCERNED and/or TOLERANT and do *not* blame them for the mess they have made.
- Because you know your under-six-month-old does not intend to drive you to distraction by crying non-stop for an hour when they can't be comforted by you, you hand them to someone else while you take a breather. You reclaim your baby as soon as possible and do *not* resent them for being distressed. Instead you are UNDERSTANDING and FORGIVING.
- Because your grasp on what your under-six-year-old needs is Sensitive, and you interpret their clues swiftly and accurately when they are frightened or uncomfortably surprised by a sudden shock, you are SOOTHING and SUPPORTIVE and do *not* belittle them for their vulnerability.

On good days
Your SR rating will be sky high, so remember to give yourself a mini-treat or three for being a maxi mummy or daddy.

On a bad day
You will feel rumblings of discontent that so much is asked of a SR mum or dad and so little given. Which means it's reward time again for the big people in the family. When you feel emotionally nourished, even if it takes chocolate to get you there, have another go at *Ignoring* your baby's unintentionally stressful ways, whilst simultaneously catering to their needs.

Remember, your under-six-month-old is totally dependent on you for their supply of emotionally sensitive responses to their needs. When they are this tiny we must be responsible for interpreting their behaviour in a Baby Centred fashion. That means *Ignoring* any irritation they might inadvertently cause us and focusing on providing the emotional intimacy they so urgently need if a secure bond is to blossom between parent and baby.

Ignoring Minor 'Naughtiness' by Babies Aged Six to Twelve Months

You will still need to do lots of interpreting with this age range, though don't forget that they are learning fast.

- When your baby seems to drop things over the side of their buggy, chair or cot merely for the fun of watching you retrieve it, INTERPRET this sometimes annoying behaviour as a delightful game in their experience and *not* the meticulously planned attempt to send you stark, staring bonkers that you fear.
- When your rising one-year-old crawls rapidly and repeatedly towards the very object you want them to avoid, apparently as yet another attack on your sanity, INTERPRET this irritating persistence on their part as the current manifestation of their unstoppable quest for novelty and adventure and *not* a concerted effort to make you implode. Saying 'No' or 'Don't touch', in ever-increasing frustration as they continue to reach for their goal, will not work because you are actually giving them attention, albeit critical, for a behaviour you want them to stop. Far better to *Ignore* their *Minor 'Naughtiness'*, physically remove either the object or your baby from the scene and put into practice the hints on good quality *Ignoring* we looked at in chapter one.
- When your six- to twelve-month-old has become a practised 'cruiser', INTERPRET their slightly wobbly lunges at whatever might be in reach from their new vantage point as a welcome sign they are enjoying their first moments of independent, upright mobility and *not* a concerted campaign to smash up the happy home. A spot of instant *Ignoring* of *Minor 'Naughtiness'* by whipping them up into the air for a little tango together, while casually retrieving the threatened knitting, nuts or novel, often does the trick.

Remember, always give *Praise, Attends, Smiles, Positive Looks* and *Touches* and *Imitations* to those behaviours you want your almost one-year-old to repeat in the future. Ignoring undesirable actions only works well if you are plugging in the other Baby Centred input when your six- to twelve-month-old comes up with the goods. Being a Sensitively Responsive parent to babies in this age range, at the same time as ensuring their consuming passion for adventure is not crushed, is quite a balancing act.

On good days
Glory in your ability to see the world from your inquisitive rising one-year-old's perspective. See if you can let some of their wonderment at the relatively simple things in life rub off on you too.

On a bad day
Give yourself permission to be less than 100 per cent Sensitively Responsive for once. Just don't expect your six- to twelve-month-old to interpret *your* behaviour! Share the demands with your co-parent or another carer, if possible, and treat yourself to a couple of half-hour 'me time's.

Ignoring Minor Naughtiness by One-Year-Olds
It is now time for you to start to establish some meaningful limits on your toddler's enthusiastic forays into, well, everything! It really is Attention Rule time at last.

- Should your one-year-old, now fully and determinedly mobile, decide to investigate how it feels to push over a tiny friend, then as a SR parent you would not be *Ignoring* this embryonic anti-social act, would you? No. You would want to comfort the victim and prompt your little tearaway to kiss and make up. But what about their attempts to create a tidal wave in the bath? If you have covered the surrounding floor with towels and put a capacious sou'wester over your party gear, then it's 'Yes' to *Ignoring*. It would be insensitive to expect your one-year-old to inhibit their joyous splashing, so taking sensible precautions beforehand and *Ignoring* the water droplets on your clothes would seem to be the most SR way to react.

- Should your one-year-old be found dreamily staring into space, while squatting behind the settee obviously filling their nappy, would this behaviour be labelled naughty? At this age, of course not, so you would grant them their privacy. Mind you, if they were still doing it at four you would begin to wonder! But what about if they start to annoy you because they are spraying lovely red poster paint around the room by conducting an invisible orchestra with their dripping brush? Should you *Ignore* this rather destructive behaviour, however innocent? Probably not, though from what I see around me, putting one-year-olds and paint together really is asking for trouble unless everyone is kitted up in wet weather gear before you start. So what would you class as a *Minor Naughtiness* at this age? What about squishing food in their hands? What about trying to blow bubbles in their drink? What about pulling off their nappy and scampering around naked? If your answers, like mine, are in the affirmative then you know what to do – *Ignore* them!
- Should your eighteen- to twenty-four-month-old produce a fit of epic proportions when refused a second helping of gooey pudding, then being Sensitively Responsive would mean *Ignoring* their tantrum rather than *Criticising*. Telling off a one-year-old for this sort of behaviour is absolutely pointless. Worse than pointless, it actually fuels their frustration, with more impassioned yelling guaranteed – that's them, *not* us! So the golden rule here is the Attention Rule: *Ignore* your one-year-old's tantrums and only return your focus to them when they are behaving peacefully.

On good days
You can afford to really go to town in the 'creative arts' department when you feel on top of things. Join your one-year-old in the fun of glueing, painting and being a bit messy. You can always have a bath together afterwards!

On a bad day

When your one-year-old has run you ragged and trashed the living room three times in a row, admit you are beaten! Call for emergency family/friend support, go fun shopping or take a walk in the park. A change of scene will do you both good. Remember, *Ignoring* your one-year-old's undesirable antics does not make you an insensitive mummy or daddy. Actually, *Ignoring Minor Naughtiness* is an incredibly Sensitive Response because you are getting across the message about what behaviours you find unacceptable without constantly *Saying No*, *Criticising*, or issuing a stream of *Unclear Commands*.

Ignoring Minor Naughtiness by Two-Year-Olds

Astonishingly, your once utterly dependent newborn is now roaring about the garden at a potentially lethal pace, brandishing a nearly bald teddy and shrieking, 'He's a monster Ted! He'll get you!' Can this be? Oh, yes! Time to notch up the screws in the Attention Rule.

- When your two-year-old pokes a pal with a stick, swipes a friend's special toy or bites a newcomer at nursery class, should you *Ignore* their anti-social behaviour? Definitely not. Being Sensitively Responsive to your toddler's emotional needs to stay in touch with you translates into having clear ideas on which of their actions merit your active intervention. Beastliness to buddies definitely fits the bill. Making a mess accidentally, wetting their pants or giving off a 'pop' at a party, do not. So make a list, and stick to it. That way you don't have to reinvent the wheel every time your two-year-old confronts you with a particular behaviour.
- When your two-year-old throws themselves down at the supermarket checkout because they can't have another little packet of chocolate-covered raisins, *Ignoring* their tantrum is your strongest weapon against their acting out. It's also going to help them learn about how to behave socially, which makes you an enormously Sensitive and Responsive parent. You

really are being kind by taking this stance, though others might look at you as if you're being 'cruel'. *Ignore* them too!

- When your almost three-year-old bangs their spoon rhythmically on the table at mealtimes, kicks their chair incessantly, persists in laughing into their drink and therefore spraying all and sundry with an unappetising mixture of juice and spit, you might be forgiven for thinking they are doing it on purpose. After all, they have chosen to taunt you with those very behaviours that you find particularly irritating. Should you let them get away with it? It all depends, doesn't it? Depends on what you mean by 'letting them get away with it'. Pouncing and telling them off seems to be the thing to do if they are ever going to be acceptable company at mealtimes. Unfortunately it doesn't really work and breakfast, lunch and tea can descend into a screaming match that upsets everybody's digestion. The best and most Sensitively Responsive reaction is to completely *Ignore* their attempts to gain your attention by pressing your buttons. You know the routine – turn your head away, talk to someone else (but not about the miscreant) or keep silent. The moment they behave properly, catch them in the headlights of your approval and give them a *Praise*, *Attend* and *Smile*. Honestly, it works like a dream – so long as you persist. But prepare for them to 'up the ante' temporarily because they can't quite believe what's happening.

On good days

You will notice that you are managing to *Ignore Minor Naughtiness* without any visible strain. And your efforts will be successful because you are being calm, consistent and caring. Pat yourself on the back and spread the news to other parents who are struggling to deal with similar challenges to their pack-leader status.

On a bad day

You may well need to grit your teeth, leave the room or give yourself an emergency treat because your little rascal really is getting to you! Don't despair – *everyone* has bad days when frustration and irritation are pretty constantly at boiling point. You could even explain to your two-year-old that you are tired, poorly or worried, as they can be surprisingly sensitive. Praise yourself for your successes rather than berate yourself for your failures in *Ignoring*.

Ignoring Minor Naughtiness only works when you constantly use *Attends*, *Praise*, *Smiles*, *Positive Looks* and *Positive Touches*, *Imitation* and *Ask to Plays* following your child's sociable, co-operative, compliant and unbelievably cute behaviours. You simply cannot have one without the other. And above all, apply the *Attention Rule*:

ATTENTION RULE

1. *Ignore* 99 per cent of annoying behaviour
2. *Praise* all good behaviour
3. *Intervene* early to stop dangerous behaviour
4. When necessary, give *Clear Commands*

This may all sound a bit too cut and dried as an approach to fulfilling your baby and toddler's need for sensitivity and staying in touch emotionally, but that really is not the case. It's only when we confuse being sensitive with being excessively indulgent that we find it difficult to respond with sensitivity to our under-three's overarching need for a secure bond. We must include helping them to learn which behaviours can and cannot be tolerated in their family and, later on, society in general. In pointing them in the right direction on this score, modifying your approach to accommodate their rapid development from one stage to the next, you are consistently demonstrating that you are closely in touch with their changing needs. Here is a mini-list just to remind you how to be sensitive, responsive and in touch with your under-threes:

- Listen carefully
- Look closely
- Touch gently
- Learn all you can about your own special baby
- Be available to identify your baby's needs
- Be ready to solve problems

Babies who experience their parents as being sensitive to their quickly varying needs are learning one of the most powerful psychological, emotional and attachment lessons of all – that being in touch with other people, especially mummy and/or daddy, pays big dividends. They realise they can successfully get their parents' active attention and this really enhances their sense of their own importance to you. Babies and toddlers also begin to flex their own psychological muscle. Even under-threes need to know they can make things happen! They learn to trust that letting others know how you are feeling actually provokes a sensitive response. While it might not always work quite like that at playgroup, none the less it is the best way to start finding out about how to communicate needs, wants and desires to others.

That said, let's move on to the business of issuing orders and giving instructions to the under-threes. As attempting to tell under-six-month-olds what to do is pretty pointless, I'm going to jump straight to the second half of the first year. It's then that we begin to want to say things like this, isn't it?

'*No*! Take that out of your mouth this instant!'
'Don't touch! I said *don't touch*!'
'Spit it out into my hand, *now*!'
'Leave that alone! You *know* it's hot!'
'Sit still! You can *see* I'm trying to get your socks on!'
'Stop it! Stop that *at once*!'

Clear Commands for Babies
Aged Six to Twelve Months

Looking at the list of commands just presented, do you think they are clear? And do you think your six- to twelve-month-old is capable of complying even if they wanted to, which simply cannot be guaranteed? Chew over your answers to those two questions while I set out what I consider to be some *Clear Commands* appropriate for this age group:

- 'Charley – eat up all your pudding.'
- 'Alex – give that plum to me.'
- 'Kieran – stroke the pussycat gently.'
- 'Maddy – put that fork down.'
- 'Sophie – look at your book.'
- 'Daniel – put the bricks in the box.'

Of course, they probably *won't*, because they often *can't*, at least not without a good deal of input from you! The sentences are pretty sophisticated too, but that's really a matter of choice as we might as well have said:

- 'Eat'
- 'Give'
- 'Stroke'
- 'Down'
- 'Look'
- 'In'

That's because they are the operative words and work surprisingly well, especially when accompanied by the obvious gestures. So what's the point of actually spelling it all out? Twofold really. First to give yourself early practice in using *Clear Commands* and second to expose your communication-mad six- to twelve-month-old to the wonders of fully elaborated sentences. It's up to you to take your pick, or you could swap between shorter and longer versions.

Commands, like other Baby Directive behaviours, should always be kept to the minimum. Listening to mums and dads of six- to twelve-month-olds, it's obvious none of us realise just how many *Commands* we issue. *Commands* that call for more advanced skills than our tiny almost ones can manage. So be Sensitively Responsive about telling these little ones what to do, and choose guidance, example and *Praise, Praise, Praise* instead.

On good days

Practise leaving out as many 'Pleases' as possible. It's bad news to be asking, pleading or even begging your little treasure to do as they are told, particularly if you start off with:

> Could you . . .
> Would you . . .
> Can you . . .
> If you could . . .
> Might you just . . .

Why? Because phrasing a command as a question implies *Choice* on the recipient's part. You don't want that to happen if you are aiming for compliance with your instructions.

On a bad day

Cut right down on the number of *Commands*, whether clear or fuzzy! If you're feeling stressed, the last thing you want to provoke is a confrontation. Save your energy for the important stuff like keeping your crawler safe and amused. Life is much calmer the fewer instructions we issue. Try it and see.

Clear Commands for One-Year-Olds

In order to ensure you are specific when giving *Clear Commands* to your one-year-old, you need to know the rules that make for a good-quality instruction. I'll pop them down for you in a minute, but first some examples:

- 'Stevie – I want you to drink up all your juice.'
- 'Katie – I want you to give me that pencil.'
- 'Alan – I want you to pat Matthew gently.'
- 'Mickey – I want you to put that cup down on your table.'
- 'Kelvin – I want you to sit and read your book.'

- 'Tilly – I want you to put the dolly back in her bed.'

You notice the difference between these *Clear Commands* and those set out for the almost ones. Yes, it's the '*I want you to*' phrase, and it's the best way of making your instruction irresistible that I have ever come across. It's virtually failsafe with ones and twos, and it works with grown-ups too! Try it and see! Always use your one- to two-year-olds' name at the beginning of your *Clear Command*, as we are all immediately alert the moment we hear this most vital of words. Try, 'I want you to', because it's firm, it's fair and it's formidable. Also important, limit your instructions to one-step commands. That is, do not ask your child to do more than one thing at a time.

On good days
Give some attention to being Sensitively Responsive to your one-year-old and don't give a command *unless*:

- You have checked that it's truly necessary
- You have asked yourself if your child has the skills needed to do it
- You are prepared to make sure your child carries out your command

On a bad day
Instead of trying to stay in control of the situation by coming down hard with masses of unnecessary, inappropriate and ineffective commands, tell yourself it's much better to let go, relax and do something fun with your one-year-old. Bad days can quite often improve once we modify our expectations of ourselves and our bond buddies.

Clear Commands for Two-Year-Olds
You can now start to experiment with two-step commands, and even add in an explanation for your increasingly brilliant two- to three-year-old.

- 'Miranda – it's nearly time for lunch so I want you to come and wash your hands.'
- 'Donna – it's rainy today so I want you to wear your boots.'
- 'Nicky – you look upset so I want you to put your car down and come here for a cuddle.'
- 'Maggie – I can see you're thirsty. I want you to come and sit in your chair to drink all your juice up.'
- 'Ronan – it's bedtime now so I want you to come upstairs for your story.'
- 'Joey – sand can sting people's eyes so I want you to stop throwing it about and put the spade back in the bucket, *now*.'

As you can see, for two-year-olds, giving the explanation first and the *Clear Command* second really gets across the message of what behaviour you expect of them next. I know that might sound counterintuitive, but at two to three years old our child is less interested in the explanation than we are! They need the *Clear Command* to be the last things ringing in their ears.

If you want your instruction to be effective, you must get eye contact as you say their name. That obviously means all my shouts from the bottom of the stairs of 'Teatime. Come down now!' and 'Time for school!' could safely be ignored by my three offspring. And ignored they were! It is also vital to *Praise* and give an *Attend* IMMEDIATELY YOUR TWO-YEAR-OLD *STARTS* TO OBEY YOUR COMMAND. Keep them coming as your tiny tot proceeds to complete your instruction and you'll be awash with willing cooperation.

On good days
You could take this opportunity to test out whether your two-year-old can manage a three-step command. Keep it simple and you could both be delighted with the results.

On a bad day
Go back to one-step commands and keep them very simple. Two-year-olds use a special kiddie-radar to tune into our moods, so if we

are feeling below par they can reflect this by being extra sensitive to the number of demands we are making on them.

What Not To Do: Don't Give Fuzzy Commands

So far we have been highlighting *Ignoring Minor Naughtiness* and *Giving Clear Commands*, the two last Baby Centred behaviours to feature in *The Parent/Baby Game*. Now it's time for their Baby Directive opposites, *Saying No* and *Fuzzy Commands*. What I want to do is show you how *Saying No* and giving *Fuzzy Commands* actually increases the amount of defiant opposition you will see in your toddler. This issue also involves the thorny problem of disobedience and how to deal with it using the techniques of Distraction, Withdrawing Privileges and Time Out.

So what do we mean by disobedience? 'Playing up', 'Not listening', 'Taking no notice', 'Deliberately breaking the ground rules', 'Misbehaving', 'Being defiant/bad/wicked/naughty/a pest/a nuisance' or 'out of order'. These are all remarks made by parents when criticising their children's lack of compliance with instructions or flouting of established behavioural limits. By the time our child has reached toddler status, you will have noticed they don't always do as they are told! Neither do they always want to abide by the ground rules you have worked so hard to establish. They throw things when they know they shouldn't. They bounce on things when they've been told not to. They run off despite strict instructions to the contrary.

You are mortified. It seems your efforts to socialise your little darling have failed and you fear you may have lost control of the situation. It's all a bit of a disaster! But don't worry, help is at hand and over the next few pages I'm going to spell out for you the tried and tested combination of child management techniques that will restore order, *most* of the time! I'm going to start off with 'What Not to Do' if you want your toddler to take notice of your rules and instructions. Let's look at a common situation.

You have just come out of the pool with your toddler. The under-threes' swimming lesson has been a delight, with your own infant the star of the show, at least in your opinion! It's off to the changing room for a shower and towel down, to be followed by a visit to the café for an enormous hot chocolate with all the trimmings. It's in the shower that the incident occurs. You have sluiced off your toddler and rinsed their hair. In essence they are finished. However, you are still struggling to get out of your cossie and your hair is a wreck. As you persist in trying to shower, your daredevil under-three starts rattling the cubicle door. You are naked, and chummy though the family changing room might be, you don't fancy stepping out stark staring! What follows goes like this:

You	'No, don't *do that, poppet!*'
Toddler	Rattles door again and looks round with an impish grin.
You	'*Sweetie, I said don't* do *that! No. No!*'
Toddler	More rattling and more grins, plus a chuckle.
You	'*I said* stop *it!*'
Toddler	Pauses for a fraction of a second, then gives a final shove and stops.
You	'*I wonder where your little friend is? She might be having a shower too.*'
Toddler	Gazes at you thoughtfully before bending double and attempting to see out from under the shower door.
You	'*Careful, darling, you'll bump your head. No.*'
Toddler	Tries to squeeze whole body through the gap.
You	'*No, don't* do *that, poppet!*'
Toddler	Squeezes harder.
You	'*Sweetie, I said don't* do *that! No. No! NO!*'

You can see where this is going can't you? That's right, a sequence of *Saying No* and *Fuzzy Commands*. See how many of each you can count up in the shower scene. I make it eight nos and six fuzzies. 'So what's wrong with that?' you might ask. 'My toddler did as they were told.' *Saying No* works and they *knew* what I meant when I said stop it. OK, but what do you think will happen next time you are in the shower? I'd bet on it being a repeat performance from your toddler. Why? Because they earned a good deal of attention for door rattling and trying to squeeze under the door and none for complying. Let's run the scene again but use the Attention Rule when handling the situation:

You	*'Poppet! Come and stand next to me.'*
Toddler	Gives one last little rattle and then skips over to you and takes your hand.
You	*'Brilliant! You're my special treasure. I love it when you hold my hand.'*
Toddler	Smiles broadly and does a little jump on the spot.
You	*'I want you to help me get finished quickly. You hold the shampoo.'*
Toddler	Holds shampoo. Gives it a few squeezes.
You	Ignore squeezes.

Ask yourself, which cubicle would you rather be in? Which scenario is likely to undermine the quality of your bond with your baby, and which add to its security? Just to make sure I am not guilty of any fuzziness, I will put down final tips on what not to do when aiming for obedience from your toddler.

What Not To Do When You Want Toddler Obedience

- **Don't say 'no'**
  It's vague and pointless and can even be both warning *and* provocation
- **Don't frame a command as if it was a question**
  Under-threes know they can drive a horse and cart through this one, answering either yes or no
- **Don't give commands on what to *stop* doing**
  Your toddler won't know what to do instead
- **Don't ignore compliance**
  It's equivalent to punishing obedience so give immediate *praise*

- **Don't ignore good behaviour**
  It's equivalent to punishment so give immediate *praise*
- **Don't save your attention for disobedience**
  You will be rewarding bad behaviour
- **Don't shout**
  You will lose your under-three's trust and respect
- **Don't make threats you have no intention of keeping**
  Your toddler will learn you don't mean what you say

You won't believe how effective this approach can be and you'll be thrilled with the decrease in those tense, embattled moments that can sour your relationship with your precious toddler. There are, of course, other things you can put in place that will increase the chances of your under-three being obedient, or at any rate less disobedient. When I'm talking about what can be called parental 'discipline', I am naturally excluding all babies under the age of one year or so. It really would be unreasonable to expect them to be capable of controlling, which usually means inhibiting, their own behaviour until they are into their second year. That said, let's move on to sorting out the kinds of things we can do to increase the likelihood a toddler will do *what* we want, roughly *when* we want. Unless you are running a military boot camp for one- and two-year-olds, it would be sensible not to rely on them 'jumping to it!' Right. Here we go.

What To Do When You Want Toddler Obedience
There are three main types of behaviour involved. First is Planning For Success; second is On-the-Spot Reactions; and third, Mopping Up. Let's take them in that order, because that's how they usually happen.

Planning For Success
One- and two-year-olds aren't particularly interested in being obedient. In fact they have almost no concept of obedience or doing what they're told. That's why they can give every appearance of listening closely while we try to come up with *Clear Commands*, and then do the exact opposite! So we need to face up to the fact

that we are the driving force in these matters. OK, time for the nuts and bolts. These bullet points show where we must put our energy if we want positive results.

- Top priority must be given to **always rewarding good behaviour** with a Baby Centred response
- Next in importance is **reducing the number of baby directives you use**
- A close third is aiming for the **six to one ratio**
- It's necessary to give **Clear Commands on what you want your toddler to do**, rather than *stop* doing
- Next, you must make sure your **Clear Commands**:
  - are given in a firm voice, slightly louder than usual
  - start with your toddler's name and do not proceed until you have eye contact
  - Use only a one- or two-step activity
  - have any explanation as to 'why' before the command itself
  - are only ever used when you are fully prepared to follow through with unpopular consequences if your toddler does not comply. By this I mean, a magic stair/chair/cushion/rug/corner. This has to be explained to your toddler as the place they will have to go to if and when they don't do as they are told. Tell them it's magic because it will help them to be good. This must all be agreed in a calm moment and not left until there is trouble brewing

On-the-Spot Reactions

It's all very well having planned for and achieved obedience, but it will never be 100 per cent, so we need contingency arrangements in mind to guide us when our toddler refuses to do as they are told. Here are tips for staying in control of the situation when you are on the spot:

- Make an immediate decision on whether this defiance can be *Ignored* as a *Minor Naughtiness* or not
- If it can, go ahead and *Ignore*

- If it can't, quickly work out what you want your toddler to do next
- Give your *Clear Command*
- Wait five seconds, you can count to five out loud, to see if they start to comply
- If your toddler begins to obey, give *Immediate praise*
- If they disobey, give a warning. The warning goes like this: repeat the *Clear Command* and add, 'If you haven't started by the time I count to five, you will have to sit on the Magic Stair/Chair/Cushion/Spot'
- If your toddler begins to obey, give *Immediate Praise*
- If they still fail to start to obey, take them to the Magic Spot.
- Say only, 'You can come off the Magic Spot when you are ready to', then repeat your *Clear Command*. When they either say they will do what you wanted or start to do it, say, 'You can come off the Magic Spot now', and start to *Praise* at once
- For one- and two-year-olds, *no more* than one or two minutes should be needed for the Magic Spot to work
- If your toddler is protesting about being on the Magic Spot, tell them they cannot come off until they are quiet
- When they are quiet for around ten seconds, say, 'You can come off now'. Then repeat your *Clear Command*. And off you go again!

This technique is often called Time Out, which is the shortened form of Time Out from Positive Reinforcement. It's often referred to as a more extreme form of *Ignoring*. I like to call it the Magic Spot these days, a name given by a four-year-old who said it helped him to be good! It really does work and you can use it even before your toddler understands the words used. It's a great alternative for one-year-olds to *Taking Away Privileges*, which I think should be reserved for more sophisticated thinkers aged two and upwards. It's also ace for when your toddler is biting, smacking, pinching, kicking, running riot or throwing themselves about in a furious temper because *they* don't want to do what *you* want them to!

Mopping Up

This may involve the use of tissues, so be prepared! Your one- and two-year-old will have been experiencing some unpleasant feelings when disobeying you, even if they seem to be incandescent with mischief at the time. You yourself have probably noticed your heart rate increase as adrenaline pumps round your body during the clash of wills with your tiny mite. Of course, once you give your *Clear Command*, battle has been joined! You *have* to win if your toddler is to trust you can keep them safe by meaning what you say and saying what you mean. So there you are, maybe panting a little and looking a trifle flushed after your success. What to do next is Mop Up!

- Have a heartfelt cuddle
- Have more cuddles
- Say, 'You must do what I tell you, darling'
- Say, 'I love you, sweetheart. I always love you'
- Have a last cuddle
- Say, 'You look thirsty, angel. Would you like me to get you a drink?'
- Have a final hug
- Say, 'Let's both have a drink together, poppet'

It all takes much, much longer to write down than it does to happen, so take heart! Anyway, it really is worth the effort you put into it because it works! But what about the under-ones? How can we avoid trouble spots when they are so very young?

My best bet would be distraction or nipping 'it' in the bud – 'it' being the behaviour you don't rate at all highly. Things like screaming loudly because your six- to twelve-month-old does not want to come out of the bath, put on their night clothes, take off their nappy or wear a hat. You know these mini activities simply have to happen, but you'd much rather you both didn't end up disgruntled and red in the face because of the conflict involved. Using Distraction and Nipping it in the Bud with our babies of under-one seems to come almost naturally. I suspect it's been going on from around the beginning of time! Why? Because it works like a dream, if we put some energy into it. We have all seen babies' tears dry miraculously on their eyelashes as we tempt them to 'Look at the pussycat!' or 'Feel the bubbles!', 'Have a drink' or 'Dance with mummy or daddy!' The storm of passionate resistance vanishes, to be immediately replaced with a sparkling smile and looks of interest and pleasure.

Timing is all important with Distraction and Nipping it in the Bud. If you wait too long to start, it can end up as a reward for tears and tantrums! I suppose the most helpful way of looking at these approaches is to view them as two parts of the same process – Nipping it in the Bud by Distraction. The sequence might go like this:

- Your under-one swipes their food on to the floor and opens their mouth ready to yell, presumably to protest at pasta and cheese again
- You make a snap decision to *Ignore* the lunch disposal behaviour and move in fast to nip the threatening tears and tantrums in the bud by distracting the infant
- Before they can give voice, you scoop them up out of their chair, twirl them around for a moment singing a favourite nursery rhyme, and then pounce on a brilliantly coloured musical toy and activate it within their reach
- Their mouth closes, their eyes brighten and widen with excitement
- You gracefully skirt round the pasta-strewn area of the floor, conjure up some finger food and a tasty dessert, and order is restored

I know it all sounds a bit manic but with this minute or so's energetic input you have completely avoided what would probably have been a distressing and unnecessary interruption of your connection with your infant. Of course, as your six- to twelve-month-old becomes a one-year-old, it becomes more difficult to side-track them because they develop an increasingly focused determination to finish what they have started. I remember seeing a very patient daddy repeatedly try to lure his eighteen-month-old away from the fascinating business of poking a small twig into an even smaller hole. Seven times! In the end he swept his child into his arms and strode off singing 'Humpty Dumpty'. Thankfully, under-ones are much less persistent so nipping undesirable behaviour in the bud by distraction is a winner almost every time.

There is only one other strategy for dealing with disobedience, and as long as you follow through on consequences, it's a very useful addition to your armoury. As your two-year-old toddler becomes more articulate – and they can usually understand distinctly more than they can say – you can begin to use Withdrawal of Privileges. It's a version of punishment that has been tried and passed the test. But only if you actually *do* it. It's all too easy to say, 'Right! No trip to the park today, because you have just been really spiteful to your little friend. Poor Caroline!' in the first flush of outrage at your angelic toddler's unprincipled attack on an innocent bystander. It is very much more difficult to put this statement into effect. You forget. They fall asleep. You regret having been so swingeing. They are so enchanting after their nap that you simply cannot bring yourself to put your punishment into action. You know the sort of thing. All of these reasons are a demonstration of your fondness towards your two-year-old and, as such, laudable. But toddlers don't just need fondness, they need firmness too. If you are aiming to be a balanced parent, you will want to be Sensitively Responsive to both these requirements and will therefore do your best to resist capitulating.

Let's just check out a few essential guidelines for taking away privileges as a way of dealing with behaviour by a two-year-old that cannot be *Ignored* because it is dangerous, aggressive or destructive.

Withdrawing Privileges – Dos And Don'ts

- **DO** follow through: your predictability is an important source of security for your toddler
- **DON'T** make promises you have no intention of keeping: your two-year-old will just continue to test limits with even more determination

- **DO** make the punishment fit the crime: your fairness will be a good model of reasonable behaviour for your under-three
- **DON'T** overdose on revenge punishment: your aim is to get your toddler to stop a particular behaviour, not make their life a misery
- **DO** pick privileges that are under your control: it's no good promising to take away things that are not in your gift
- **DON'T** involve food: you, food, love and your bond with your two-year-old are all inextricably interwoven, so steer clear of this one
- **DO** involve 'treats': these can be anything from piggy-back rides to jelly babies
- **DON'T** involve anything further away than teatime the same day: you might well forget and they will never remember
- **DO** stay calm when issuing your promise: this will have much more impact than ranting and raving

What To Do Next: Troubleshooting

This is the part of each chapter where the focus is on coping with the challenges thrown up by trying to meet our baby's need for Warmth, Approval, Security, Stimulation and now Sensitivity. I cover the various scenarios you could face as your newborn moves towards the grand old age of almost three, your emotional reactions and how to handle them, as well as some practical ideas on coping. I tackle topics such as under- and over-sensitivity with the under-six-month-olds, the ferociously rapid development of six- to twelve-month-olds and how it can stretch our resources, the 'what about time for me?' issue during our toddler's second year, and trying to balance work schedules against quality time with our two- to three-year-olds. I cover your emotional reactions to the stresses and strains inherent in trying to be sensitive to the cues of your under-threes, plus any practical solutions you might try.

Scenario One: Babies Under Six Months

We all want to be really sensitive to our newborn's every need. The difficult bit is pitching our awareness of each breath, burp, sneeze and snuffle at a level that is neither anxiously intrusive nor neglectfully vague. There can be a further dilemma for caring new mummies and daddies, in that in trying to avoid one extreme we fear we may stray too close to the other. What an incredibly anxious and doubt-ridden business it is being responsible for tiny mites aged under six months. Plus, of course, we are absolutely drained by lack of sleep for much of this period, which doesn't help one little bit.

So there you are. It is 5 a.m. and your baby is finally asleep after a two-hour wakeful stint. As you flop back into bed you wonder why they want to 'play' during the hours of darkness as well as when the sun is shining. Could you be missing something? Is there a clue you have failed to pick up? Are they bored? Poorly? Hungry? Upset? You fall asleep before any answers present themselves. Later in the day you gaze thoughtfully at your beloved baby's face as they sneeze a huge bubble of mucus from one tiny nostril. Ah! That's why they're fractious! Cross bored, hungry and upset off the list and focus on poorly!

When you think about it, being sensitive to and staying in touch with the many and varied – not to mention changeable – needs of the under-six-month-old is rather like being on a quiz show where your specialist subject is 'Everything Anyone Ever Wanted to Know About Babies'. It's no wonder we find ourselves conducting ceaseless internal monologues – and not always so internal – on the eternally fascinating topic of 'what should I be doing *now*, or at least *next*, to ensure my baby is comfortable?' I have an idea that much of human behaviour is actually devoted to the search for our own personal version of comfort, so it is no surprise we focus so much time and energy on providing the same for our baby. I certainly remember an enormous amount of 'Let's try' moments when my children were babies. You know, 'Let's try winding/feeding/rocking/singing/changing/pat-a-cake/driving round the streets' sequence of experiments to see if we can settle them comfortably. That's just another way of saying 'getting them to stop crying', isn't it?

Crying is the biggest clue an infant can give to indicate that they need our sensitive intervention right *now*. It is designed to alert us, a purpose-built siren to grab our attention and get us activated on their behalf. Parents often respond to their first baby's signals with a degree of alacrity, while signals from their second and third or more babies may well receive a more leisurely response. It all appears to be closely related to the amount of anxiety we are experiencing at any one moment. How worried we are that we might not be reading our infant's cries accurately. After all, we would never forgive ourselves if we mistook a life-threatening rash for heat spots, and rightly so. Can you imagine? I can feel goose bumps just contemplating the horror of what could follow from a moment's insensitivity. But none of us can live in a constant state of super vigilance. We would soon fall prey to the carer's equivalent of battle fatigue. So what can be done to help us get a healthy balance? Here are some ideas that might prove useful.

First of all, it is probably constructive to view hypersensitivity as roughly equivalent to anxiety, and low sensitivity as associated with a degree of depression. Once we have done that, we can focus on the fact that in this book we have already covered lots of techniques for reaching a steady emotional state rather than one extreme or the other.

Remember, there are self-instructions that can reduce anxiety, there are breathing exercises that can reduce anxiety, and there is a myriad of distractions that can reduce anxiety. Just tap into these when you feel that you are maybe a bit 'hyper' and, even more importantly, forgive yourself for getting so wound up! It's natural to be super-sensitive, because for the first six months of your baby's life they are exceptionally dependent on your ministrations. I'm not suggesting you switch off your continuous monitoring of your under-six-month-old's functioning and development. I *am* suggesting you'll actually be *more* sensitive to their needs if your anxieties are kept at a manageable level, as opposed to running riot.

On the other hand, should you be experiencing low mood, you would need to tease out the Negative Automatic Thoughts (NATs) fuelling your rather depressing take on things. It's often quite difficult to distinguish which comes first when you find yourself suffering from a dip in motivation, terminal fatigue and a negative perspective. Has lack of sleep been the root cause? Are you just a selfish parent who hasn't got the energy to be sensitive to their baby? Why are you the only one feeling like this? Personally, I would opt for sleep deprivation being the main culprit, with my strongest NAT challenge being that if I could wangle eight hours' solid sleep, my view of the world might be very different indeed. Being low on sleep, low on sensitivity, and low in mood can all be part of a common trio of troubles in those first six months, so forgive yourself straightaway! You aren't neglectful. You aren't insensitive. You are exhausted.

You could employ several practical problem-solving techniques alongside the psychological ones. If you are *hypersensitive*, it's helpful to:

- Limit the number of times you check on your baby when they are sleeping.
- Swap checking duties with your co-parent.
- Install a baby alarm.
- Put yourself on a little reward programme for gazing at your baby without feeling anxious.

If you feel you are *low in sensitivity*, try:

- Taking a nap each time your baby drops off.
- Drafting in a trusted grown-up to take over your baby responsibilities for three afternoons on the trot.
- Taking turns with your co-parent so you are only on night duty on alternate days.

Before you can turn around, those first demanding six months will have flashed by and you will find your sensitivity chip being taxed by the wild rate of development shown by your six- to twelve-month-old.

Scenario Two: Babies Aged Six To Twelve Months

Imagine, only a few months ago your baby was still safely tucked up in a Moses basket for a good portion of every twenty-four hours. Now look at them! They can sit, they can crawl, they can reach and grasp, they can transfer things from hand-to-hand, they can pull themselves up to standing, and they cruise around the furniture. And that's just the physical stuff! For playtimes, they like 'talking' with you. They smile and clap. They enjoy looking at books. They sway to music, and take pleasure in favourite toys. There is no end to their social and emotional accomplishments. They laugh. They look surprised. They love kisses and tickles. They hug, pat and squeeze. They get grizzly when they are tired, and throw themselves around a bit when over-excited. In short, your little bundle is swiftly emerging as a multi-talented genius.

How on earth are you going to keep up with being sensitive to their every need when it's all changing so quickly? That's the first thing that hits us, swiftly followed by a sense of being overwhelmed, swept away and almost drowned by the flood of demands for sensitivity and staying-in touch with our six- to twelve-month-old marvel. The second thing that hits us is the distinct possibility that we may go off the rails unless 'things' slow down quite significantly. By 'things' we often mean our baby. If only they would just stop for a moment. You offer it up almost as a prayer when everything is, yet again, hectic beyond belief. But the fact of the matter is they don't stop, won't stop and can't stop. They are so busy exploring their world and extending their skills during the second half of the first year they haven't got a millisecond to spare. We wonder, with a mixture of joy and fear, how it will be when they are walking!

Once more, an important step to take when coping with these reactions to our six- to twelve-month-old's development drive is to forgive yourself for not being up to constant sensitivity and staying in touch. Don't berate yourself for being unable to concentrate on any one thing for longer than a moment. There are few sources of distraction more powerful than your six- to twelve-month-old. Try these on-the-spot rapid-relaxation exercises when you are feeling particularly frazzled round the edges. They only take fifteen seconds.

1. Tense up every muscle in your body as tightly as you can. Include feet, hands, legs and arms, bottom, tummy, shoulders, neck and face. It won't look pretty, but who cares?
2. Hold your tension and your breath for a count of five to ten. Don't go over ten. I don't want you seeing stars!
3. Exhale as you let your body go floppy. Try not to sink to the floor if you're doing this in public. Otherwise, go ahead!
4. Stand tall, head high, eyes open and *FOCUS*.

It sounds a trifle military but, believe me, it works! In addition, to help you relax and focus, take a lovely bath with your bouncing baby so that you can gaze and touch, listen and chat to your heart's content in the warm watery environment. Baths really are a prime location for emotional and physical intimacy, sensitivity and staying in touch. And you don't have to wait until bedtime. Anytime can be bathtime when you and your infant need some soft focus time.

Moving on to the more practical side of things, let me suggest you limit yourself to one particular area of development per day as the target for sensitive staying in touch. Naturally, you will be flexible, up to a point, in order to keep up with any especially startling events in your baby's behaviour. To help you structure your sensitivity activities even more, try making a list. Lists are there to free-up brain space and once it's on the fridge door, millions of neurons can breathe a sigh of relief! The list could look like this:

Monday	Play development: provide utensils or toys for banging
Tuesday	Mobility progress: arrange living room for safe cruising
Wednesday	Attachment process: sing and dance together
Thursday	Speech and language development: imitate babble
Friday	Social ability progress: arrange a game of sharing tiny pieces of chocolate
Saturday	Emotional functioning: play peek-a-boo
Sunday	Intellectual development: look at books together

If you also stir in loads of Baby Centred *Attends*, *Best Guesses*, *Praise*, *Smiles*, *Imitation*, *Positive Looks* and *Positive Touches*, and remember the Attention Rule at least some of the time, then your six- to twelve-month-old will be getting all the Sensitive Responsiveness they need. You will be staying in such close touch emotionally and physically that your bond will be burgeoning with more security each day. And, a real bonus this, you'll have retained your sanity! OK, time for the one-year-olds.

Scenario Three: One-Year-Olds

Brace yourself! The one-year-olds are even busier explorers than the six- to twelve-month-olds, and with a vengeance. Add their independent mobility to the picture and what you see is a blur of coloured light as they scoot about at top speed. We can only watch in open-mouthed amazement. Well, no actually, we can't. We are far too busy trying to keep up with our one-year-old to have any time for simply 'watching'. Watching would be a luxury. We don't even have time to think about the indulgence of 'Me Time', never mind arranging any! Note that hint of resentment creeping in? So, the one-year-old's scenario goes something like this:

It's sunny and warm. As you look out into the garden you wistfully imagine sitting on the garden bench in the dappled shade, drinking a cool glass of fruit juice. Perhaps with ice? Your thoughts are interrupted by your one-year-old master escapologist, who has managed to dislodge the safety gate into the kitchen and is even now making their way with astonishing rapidity towards the half-open dishwasher. As you hurtle after them, images of toddlers trapped in domestic appliances flash before your eyes. Fortunately, you scoop them up well before any danger threatens. Clutching the precious little body to you, you decide now is the time for that cool drink. With a hefty, wriggling one-year-old on one hip, you prepare a feeder cup for them and a plastic mug for yourself. In no time at all you are both sitting on the bench. It's blissful – for about twenty seconds – and then they're off, chucking the feeder cup into the pot of geraniums as they go. As they slide to the ground you lunge, trying to prevent them from bruising anything. Accidentally, you catch your juice a glancing blow and by some cruel trick of gravity the liquid manages to flow upwards into your sleeve. But no time to focus on yourself, as dangerous toddler adventures are afoot by the rockery. Diving at your venturesome one-year-old, you inadvertently stumble on the feeder cup and stub your toe. It's the last straw! 'All I wanted was a drink,' you howl. 'But no! There's no time for *me*!'

It's not that you don't love your infant, you do. It's not that you have stopped being Sensitively Responsive, you haven't. It's not that you don't give your child top priority, you do. But, and it's a big but, 'What about *me*?' The thing is, your one-year-old has no notion whatsoever about you needing individual time as an adult. At one to two years old they are still living almost entirely in the present and not really equipped to see things from anyone else's perspective but their own. You know that, you understand completely *and* you must have 'Me Time' too. Meanwhile you feel shocked at the degree and intensity of your resentment towards your tiny tot.

Surely it must mean you are an unnatural and cold-hearted parent? No. Not at all. It simply means you definitely do need some time to yourself. If you were to be Sensitively Responsive to your own needs, you would probably have acknowledged this several weeks previously. As it is, you have been so preoccupied with looking after your one-year-old, you have neglected to nurture yourself. Those old clichés have some basis, after all. The ones about not being able to give, give, give unless we too are being nourished. All true! So what can be done in circumstances such as these? How can you help yourself, psychologically, to deal with these sour feelings of resentment?

Why not try some self-instruction? Tell yourself you are worth 'Me Time'. Say it over and over. Say it out loud to others. Write it down. Work at convincing yourself it's true. You can also do the old fridge magnet business, too. Spell out a 'Me Time' message to yourself and surround it with stars. Your real task here is to convince yourself, rather than others, that it is absolutely *normal* to want time for yourself. Not only normal but desirable, because when you get the balance right, every member of your family benefits. The feelings of resentment are completely understandable too. They occur due to the imbalance between parent time and toddler time. So best to accept the feelings, acknowledge they will disappear when you do have some 'Me Time' and get on with sorting out the necessary practicalities to achieve your entirely reasonable goal.

Some of the practical steps parents find useful include, first of all, identifying what you want to use the 'Me Time' for. Is it one hour's yoga weekly, plus a swim at the local leisure centre? Or an afternoon's outing once a fortnight? What about thirty minutes every other evening to just flop on the bed? Maybe an evening class once a week? The choice will be yours, though you'll have to accept that some activities may simply not be feasible. Having picked something that's rewarding for *you*, set about drawing up a timetable. Remember, with an active one-year-old, you will need a substitute to cover if you are planning to take 'Me Time' during their waking hours. However, most one-year-olds are still having at least one nap during the day, giving you one to two hours' break from the constant toddler involvement that is your life. Only catch up on chores if you really must. Otherwise, earmark three or four nap times a week as 'Me Time' and decide ahead of the event what you plan to do. Sleep is always a good bet!

I made the classic mistake with my first baby of putting on the laundry before lapsing into snooze time, with the result that everyone was feeling ratty by teatime. By babies number two and three I was much wiser and even if I didn't actually drop off, I certainly wound down! Take turns with your co-parent, if possible, to have one evening to yourself a week. One night out per week can be blissfully free of separation anxiety when we know our little treasure has been left in the capable hands of their mummy or daddy. Personally I would reserve grandparents – or another suitable babysitter you can trust – for very special occasions when mummies and daddies get to go out together, as a *couple*! What larks! Whatever next? Well, what's next is your one-year-old morphing into a two-year-old. A two-year-old who talks and asks squillions of questions. What price sensitivity and staying in touch now?

Scenario Four: Two-Year-Olds

Spending time at my local nursery has allowed me to observe, and sometimes take part in, masses of greetings and partings between two-year-olds and their parents. The 'separation' period is two-and-a-half hours, which we might regard as hardly time to get home, make a phone call, have a coffee and bingo! your time-off is up. I can remember pedalling home like fury on my bike, equipped with a child-seat on the back, so I could get on with my drawing of an earthworm for A-Level zoology. Ah, happy days! But what do our two-year-olds make of these partings from their secure base? Remember, the secure base isn't home, it's *you*. As long as you are within their reach they can be brave and adventurous. Remove yourself, no matter how imperative the need, and their little world can collapse in seconds unless the separation is handled sensitively. Even then, it can be a tough call for the two- to three-year-old. Let me set the scene for you.

You have decided to go back to work for three half days a week. On two of those days your child can stay at home with a trusted grandparent. On the third day, a morning session at nursery will be needed, with your co-parent dropping your precious treasure off and you picking them up at lunchtime. Your two-year-old enthusiastically waves goodbye to you from your co-parent's arms. It's smiles all the way. You speak briefly later in the morning and are reassured the little sweetheart skipped into pre-school without a backward glance. Congratulations all round and general relief the programme of six introductory visits has had the desired effect. After a hectic morning at work, you manage to take your place in the queue of parents waiting to collect their own particular star from the story room. When your turn arrives, you see your poor darling is looking flushed, tearful, and wearing an entirely different set of clothes from the ones they had on when you last saw them. Explanations are made, a damp outfit handed to you along with your hiccuping offspring. No bones broken. No cut knees. So why are you feeling so guilty?

Guilt is a crippling emotion. It makes us feel bad about ourselves. Labels like 'selfish', 'uncaring', 'insensitive' dance around in our heads. We seriously consider giving up the part-time job/morning at the gym/visiting a pal. We must be a really bad mother or bad father to desert our beloved toddler and leave them in the care of people who, with the best will in the world, can't possibly understand them the way we do! Guilt eats away at self-confidence. Guilt can keep you awake at night. Guilt seems to be part of the package for every parent who aims to spend a regular amount of time pursuing their own interests away from their two-year-old toddler. How can we best deal with such a potentially corrosive emotion? Well, what about some good old self-instruction along these lines:

> 'My two-year-old needs some practice at parting from me for short periods of time.'
>
> 'My two-year-old needs a wider choice of social interactions now.'
>
> 'My two-year-old needs to learn I will always come and collect them.'

And it's all true! Two-year-olds actually benefit from a limited number of such opportunities. One two-and-a-half-hour session per week at pre-school helps to introduce toddlers to a source of enriching play and social experiences.

Another psychological tactic you can try is to challenge the Negative Automatic Thoughts (NATs) that feed our guilt. Thoughts like 'I am a selfish parent.' 'I am an uncaring parent.' 'I am an insensitive parent.' 'I am a bad parent.' I think *not*! You are simply trying to get some balance in your life between your responsibilities to your toddler and your responsibilities to yourself. That's part of being a balanced parent. Part of being warm, approving, stimulating and sensitive. Part of being Baby Centred. Once more, you must work hard at forgiving yourself for being human!

In my own efforts to get that balance right, I found I had to have *all* practicalities of any substitute care worked out to the finest degree. Whether it was play group, babysitters, or handing the parenting baton over to my husband as he arrived home and I left, I knew I would not be able to focus properly unless I knew my toddlers were safe. I cannot stress too heavily the importance of sound, practical toddler-care arrangements for my peace of mind. And I know I am not alone in this. Work colleagues, friends and relatives alike, the same rule applies. Sort out the parent substitute, and the rest takes care of itself. This includes being so relaxed in the knowledge that your two-year-old is safe and well, that you can actually 'switch off' and concentrate on your own activity.

Of course you will want to stay in touch during the day. Of course you'll be thrilled when you sweep your tiny tot up into your arms the moment you are reunited. And of course your secure bond with the light of your life will be unharmed, because you can be Sensitively Responsive about your brief separations just as you are when you're together. It can also help you both to acclimatise to a new routine if you earmark a short period each day, fifteen to twenty minutes would be fine, when it's just you two together. By focusing solely on your little one for that time you have the opportunity to expiate any residue of guilt that has escaped your other efforts to stay balanced.

Meeting your baby and toddler's needs for Sensitivity and Staying in Touch is one of a parent's biggest challenges. So remember to forgive yourself when you temporarily lose your balance! OK, we seem to have negotiated our way through being Sensitively Responsive to an under-three's need for us to be attuned to their cues about the emotional aspects of being in touch. But, of course, the physical strands of attachment are also vital, so I am going to focus on the tactile elements of your bond with your under-three next, in the following special feature.

Special Feature: Displaying Physical Affection

Although I am talking separately about being in touch physically, this aspect of your bond with your baby and toddler is inextricably entwined with the emotional strand of all relationships. Babies who are handled roughly or not at all, toddlers who are hit or ignored when being 'good', any under-three who is physically mistreated or neglected by their parents, in each of these cases the child's attachment to their mother or father will be seriously damaged – sometimes beyond repair. But that refers only to the most flagrantly dysfunctional of families of the kind seen in some specialist clinics. In your case, thankfully, such harmful extremes will not apply. The power of the interdependence between the physical and emotional aspects of our relationship with our babies and toddlers can never be overestimated. So, in this section, I would like to focus on the whole issue of *Physical Touch* and how the very basic nature of caring for our under-threes might affect our reactions. I'm going to start with the touchy-feely end of things and then look at the 'hands-off' brigade.

Touchy-Feely Families
Do you love to cuddle up with your intimate partner? Do you enjoy hugging and kissing friends and family? Do you stroke, squeeze and pat the person you are talking to? Do you feel deprived in some way if you aren't getting enough in the tactile department? Answering yes to these queries makes it very likely indeed you will have come from a touchy-feely family, and that means you will have received a full quota of tactile affection from your own parents. But it isn't just the bare fact of physical contact that

leaves such a lasting impact on our style of relating to others. Emotional warmth has to be given and received for the touching to be truly Sensitively Responsive and therefore beneficial to your bond with your baby and toddlers.

Physical affection is a very precious commodity when we are talking about forming close, secure bonds with our little children. Come to that, it's pretty important in all relationships of any emotional significance. Now I'm not suggesting you career around approaching complete strangers with outstretched arms and the offer of an on-the-spot hug. I am suggesting that if you come from a touchy-feely family then you should be able to dish out to your beloved infants lashings of vital physical affection. Why do I say it is vital? Put simply, without it almost every area of an under-three's development can be jeopardised and undermined. This is how things could work out:

IMPACT OF SEVERELY LIMITED PHYSICAL AFFECTION

Development area	Impact
Health	Immune system can be compromised
Growth	Growth-rate limitation can occur
Motor	Mobility can be delayed
Sensory	Unusual reactions to touch
Cognitive	Intellectual development can be diminished
Language	Communication skills may be delayed
Education	Poor response to the educational environment
Play	Cooperative play may be delayed
Social	Peer group and other relationships can be disturbed
Personality	Low self-confidence can be a feature
Emotional	Abnormal mood states can develop
Behavioural	Behavioural problems can occur
*Attachment	*Family relationships can be disturbed

Even if we ignore everything in these two lists but the last item, 'Attachment' (marked with an asterisk), that is still more than enough reason to carry on your touchy-feely heritage down the generations by giving your own under-three loads of physical affection. You are in the very fortunate position of finding it easy to provide for your baby and toddler's fundamental need to stay literally in touch with their mummy and daddy. All you have to do to be a big success on this score is to give in to your desires to stroke, kiss, cuddle, hug, rock, nibble, sniff and cradle your tiny offspring. You will doubtless be touching them with tender, gentle, warm assurance and murmuring sweet nothings to them at the same time. In fact, the only conscious effort you may have to make is in the direction of not drowning your little treasure with the sheer volume of physical affection you have to offer! But seriously, the chances of this latter eventuality are virtually nil, so keep on cuddling as a sure-fire method of letting your under-three know you love them with all your heart.

After all, it's hardly charity work when we ourselves reap so much pleasure from these caresses, is it? No. We in return are able to experience the joys of being the object of our own under-three's spontaneous and responsive efforts at staying in touch with us. The kisses that land in your eye, the fierce hugs round the neck, the cuddle on the end of their jet-propelled launch towards you, the little pats and strokes. When we, as well as our children, are touchy-feely, the reciprocal physical affection we share between us is one of the most unequivocal signs of love. It can only benefit your bond together to stay so closely in touch. Long live the Touchy Feelies! But what if your family roots weren't like that? What then?

Hands-off Families

Were open displays of physical affection a rare event in your family? Was holding hands, kissing and cuddling frowned upon? Were your parents never to be seen in any public embrace apart from a small peck on the cheek? If your answers to queries like these are in the affirmative, then you probably come from a hands-off family. This is not to say you were not loved, simply that your parents' style of demonstrating their feelings is at the other end of the scale to those from the touchy-feely gang. Maybe you still believe that such restraint is the best way to behave. Or maybe you have determined to jettison this rather distant fashion of interacting with others because you feel it damages relationships between parents and their babies and toddlers. Or perhaps you find yourself torn between the two. Whatever your position, when you read this, please allow yourself to be more open in giving your under-threes the physical affection they need in order to develop into self-assured, confident, stable and sociable individuals. Did you notice I put 'please' in there just now? It shows you how insidious our so-called good manners can be! What I really meant was, 'I *want* you to . . .', because the mutual benefits can be absolutely enormous, while the hurt from being deprived of loving touch is extremely painful.

When we are hardly touched at all, except in anger, we are being taught that being close to someone else is dangerous. Other people are not to be trusted. Emotional intimacy is equated with fear, avoidance and self-defensiveness. You can see how this has happened to some of the people you know, some of the people you meet, perhaps even to yourself. It can be really difficult for hands-off mums and dads to get in touch physically with their none the less much-loved young offspring. If you believe this might apply to you, then I urge you to look back at the chapter about *Smiles*, *Positive Looks* and *Positive Touches* because it contains a variety of suggestions on how to become more physically expressive of the deep affection and love you feel for your recent arrival. Talk with your co-parent, who may be more touchy-feely than you. You may even have chosen your partner for that very reason! It really does help to share memories and ideas about our own childhood experiences of being given physical affection by our mother and father, whichever type of family we grew up in. You may well find it is the starting point of a much more relaxed and demonstrative attitude to those you love. You might feel a bit weird and unsafe at first, but do press on. There is nothing to be afraid of with your baby and toddler. They are like little sponges, soaking up your displays of love and affection

A word to the wise, though. If you think you could be damaging your bond with your under-three due to your own difficulty in physically expressing the love you feel, don't hesitate to track down professional help. You and your tiny tot have a whole lifetime's relationship ahead of you, one that can only be enhanced by breaking down the psychological and emotional barriers that prevent us from staying in touch. There is no need to feel ashamed if you are having problems of this nature, none of us is to blame for the way our parents brought us up. But we are responsible for our own behaviour as mummies and daddies, so take whatever steps are needed to ensure that the bond between you and your infant features masses more touchy-feely encounters than hands-off.

Before moving on to Attachment Theory and Echoes From Our Past, I want to make it very clear that I am by no means labelling all women touchy-feely and all men hands-off. I know that in some cultures men are required to exercise the equivalent of the 'stiff upper lip' of Victorian manhood. That's not denied. Neither am I agreeing with the widespread assumption that women are often seen as the more overtly emotional sex. What I do want to get across is the idea that all humans, including most importantly the baby and toddler variety, thrive on a steady diet of loving touches. As mummies and daddies, we are in prime position to make sure our particular infant learns there is nothing to be feared from the physical closeness that you shower on them. This in turn will convert into bond-building material of exceptional strength. You will also have made great strides towards your goal of being a balanced parent. That's balanced, *not* perfect! So throw yourself into the sheer joy of the physical contact that is inevitable when you are bringing up your much-loved under-three. You and they can only benefit, especially in terms of building a secure attachment between the two of you. Let's take a look at Attachment Theory now.

ATTACHMENT THEORY

In many ways Attachment Theory can be seen as the study of the psychological background against which we play out our interactions with others. It is a framework for understanding relationships and bonds that has its roots in psychoanalytical theory rather than cognitive behaviour therapy. John Bowlby, a British psychologist working at the Tavistock Clinic in north London, first began to build up the basics of Attachment Theory in the early to mid 1900s. Not all his colleagues agreed with his ideas, but despite this his notions have steadily gained credence over the decades. It is now accepted on a world-wide scale and continues to be researched and written about by academics and clinicians alike. Personally, I see Attachment Theory and cognitive behaviour therapy as productive partners rather than mutually exclusive entities, though not everyone would agree I know. I have found combining the two, along with child development theory, a most constructive mix for helping families, parents and children to tackle any problems they may have.

Attachment Theory proponents claim our personality profile, emotions, behaviour patterns, psychological make up and, above all else, our style of interacting with others, is unavoidably and heavily influenced by our experiences within our family of origin as a baby and toddler, pre-schooler and child. So, according to the attachment style of our parents when bringing us up, we can develop a similar way of relating to others. It's not quite as simple as that of course, because parents may have differing attachment profiles; family crises can occur, and other factors like illness, poverty and disability have a role to play. One way of understanding how the differing categories of attachment style relate to each other is to study the tables below.

ATTACHMENT STYLE CATEGORIES: ADULTS

Healthy
FREE/INDEPENDENT

Normal   Normal
DISMISSIVE/DISTANT   ENMESHED/PREOCCUPIED

Damaged
UNRESOLVED LOSS AND TRAUMA

ATTACHMENT STYLE CATEGORIES: CHILDREN

Healthy
SECURE

Normal   Normal
AVOIDANT   AMBIVALENT

Damaged
DISORGANISED

You can see how being brought up by parents who were themselves able to make and sustain secure, independent healthy relationships would increase the likelihood of their children being able to pass on the compliment when they in turn become mummies and daddies. Unfortunately, the same goes for the dismissive/distant and enmeshed/preoccupied styles of attachment as they can be passed down the generations. But don't worry, all the types of interaction I have already mentioned in terms of parenting styles are within the normal range. So when I'm talking about unresolved issues from our pasts, I do *not* mean you have an attachment category of the damaged unresolved loss and trauma type. And just because you may find on occasion your toddler is quite literally 'all over the place', this does *not* show they have a disorganised attachment style.

Of course, the best way to ensure your under-three grows up feeling secure in your love for them is to push ahead in the Baby Centred stakes. When we manage that six-to-one Baby Centred to Baby Directive ratio and use the Attention Rule across the board, we are actively protecting our newborns, babies, toddlers, one- and two-year-olds from those aspects of family life, which can so damage their self-confidence. In other words, you have it in your power to make sure you and your under-three have a beneficial, strong and lasting bond between you. My advice is to go for it!, whatever sort of attachment history you yourself have.

Echoes From Our Past: Balanced Parenting

We have at last reached the part of the chapter where balanced parenting will be the style of interacting with your under-three-year-olds to be highlighted. I see it as the type of parenting to which we all aspire, though my definition of what is involved may, of course, differ from yours. See what you think by the end of this section. When you hear about 'Positive Parenting', many of the ideas expressed will be similar to those found in my descriptions of the Parent/Baby Game, and my previous book *The Parent/Child Game*. Whatever its name, the principles and approaches involved all aim to provide helpful guidance for parents who long to give their under-threes just the right mix of warmth, approval, physical affection, stimulation and sensitivity, sensible limits and boundaries, security and safety. Some challenge! It's no wonder we can often feel we are not coming up to scratch! But try to remind yourself that being a balanced parent is not some impossible dream. If you are being Baby Centred with your under-three, you are *already* being balanced, positive and authoritative.

When I look back at how my parents brought me up, I can clearly see how hard they worked at providing myself and my two siblings with good parenting. Their notions on what this entailed were naturally heavily influenced by their own upbringing, and as they came from quite dissimilar backgrounds each had an individual take on the business of parenting. As I have discussed in previous chapters, my maternal grandparents were much more flexible towards their three daughters than were my paternal grandparents towards their two sons. The impact on myself of this discrepancy, via my own mum and dad's parenting efforts, is undeniable.

My earliest memories are of a father who, though very much loved by his wife and children and despite his unlimited fund of funny stories and jokes, none the less had to be given due respect because of his position as the only wage earner. This fed in quite nicely to his more reserved, didactic and slightly rigid style of parenting. For example, I remember that late afternoons revolved around making sure all was fully prepared for his arrival at 6 p.m. sharp. When we were little, we would already be bathed and in our night-clothes when he came home. We would also be engaged in quiet, sitting-down activities, having previously exhausted ourselves during 'The Mad Half Hour' when we were allowed to career around the room on top of the furniture! My mother would be washed and changed, with Dad's evening meal already cooked and waiting to be served. He ate alone at the table though there was quite a bit of clustering round to tell him of our triumphs and tragedies. He listened with a certain degree of sympathy though his comments were likely to be focused on our achievements rather than our efforts. Constructive criticism was another of his favoured responses. It was Mum, however, who called us to order by saying, 'Leave your father to eat his meal in peace now', when Dad was almost unable to get his fork into his mouth for the press of enthusiastic offspring.

My mother was much more flexible in her approach to parenting, almost always willing to negotiate alternatives to her own suggestions and overflowing with an endless stream of really good ideas on what we could do next. It was she who organised our games of dolls' hospital, post offices, picnics, blowing bubbles, painting cut-out dollies, washing teddy, putting on a concert, making a camp, decorating mud pies – plus a million more! Mum didn't actually join in with our play, though after she had 'set us up' she maintained what I now know to be a constant flow of *Praises, Smiles, Attends, Imitations* and the occasional *Ask to Play*. She would easily enter into our flights of imagination and allow us to splash in the bath. She also encouraged dressing-up, cooking and outings, making her a genuinely fun mummy to us three children.

The interesting thing is, looking back I see a slightly stern father who never the less had us in stitches with his witty humour, and a spontaneous, rewarding mother who none the less maintained sensible parent–child boundaries and behaviour ground rules. I guess they made a good pair of parents in that their separate contributions, though different in style, combined to provide myself and my younger siblings with a pretty balanced parenting package. I also notice that I carried on many of my mother's habits when I too became a mother, and my own children have similarly decided to adopt some of my own approaches with my grand-children. I say 'decided', but I wonder if it's really that conscious a process. It's probably no surprise that it was a good few years before I became fully aware that the Christmas celebrations I orchestrated were dead ringers for those I experienced as a child in my own home. Hardly a coincidence!

What about you? When you recall your early years, do you see images of balanced parenting? Do you see one parent who was balanced and one who was not? Was there very little balance because your parents were too often distant, inconsistent, over-involved or authoritarian? If you have memories of a mostly balanced parent and intend to be balanced yourself, take a look at this check list:

Balanced Parents
- Lovingly take control
- Are fond and firm where appropriate
- Are warm and approving

- Set clear behaviour limits
- Keep proper interpersonal boundaries
- Show and tell their babies and toddlers they love them come what may
- Ignore *Minor Naughtiness*
- Praise at every opportunity
- Are flexible and reasonable
- Only punish when behaviour is dangerous or totally out of bounds
- Have occasional bad days when they slip

You will see that balanced mums and dads are probably ace at *Ignoring* and giving *Clear Commands*, as well as all the other Baby Centred behaviours we have talked about in the previous chapters. It's a bit of a relief to note that these very successful parents have bad days too, just like us. I know my mother and father, mostly balanced though they might have been, definitely lost it at times. There was the time when my sister Lizzie trod in the huge home-made rice pudding originally earmarked to feed fifteen at a big family picnic in the countryside! The infamous occasion when my little brother Jon smashed a treasured ornament, not to mention my own early transgressions, which I seem to remember featured a good deal of manic scribbling in library books – *red* scribbling! My own 'slips' as a parent desperately trying not to lose what little balance I had number among them the following charming incidents:

- Screeching – 'If I catch you doing that again, I'll *snap*! I said stop spitting!'
- Growling – 'I can't do *everything* at once! I'm not a cowboy *or* a dragon!'
- Crying – 'It's all too much for me! Look at all those corn flakes stuck in the carpet.'
- Whining – 'Why can't you let me have five minutes' peace? I haven't sat down since six o'clock this morning!'
- Begging – 'Please, please, just be good for ten minutes while I unpack the groceries!'

And that's by no means the whole story! Keeping our balanced parenting going 365 days per year is *impossible*, so don't even try it. Instead, accept there will be times when you slide into a less Baby Centred style of interacting with your baby or toddler and put your efforts into limiting them in number, duration and intensity. We are all prey to stress, illness, anxieties, irritation, emotional outbursts and stabs of disenchantment with our lot, it's unavoidable. So thank heavens that being Baby Centred just half of the time is good enough. I'm going to make sure you notice this because it can save our sanity:

BEING BABY CENTRED HALF THE TIME IS GOOD-ENOUGH PARENTING

Mind you, that's not an open invitation to go berserk the rest of the time! So what kind of existence do our under-threes enjoy when we are being balanced?

- Our under-threes are secure in the knowledge that they are loved and loveable
- Our under-threes are self-confident and communicative
- Our under-threes are able to cope with emotional intimacy
- Our under-threes are full of creative and adventurous energy
- Our under-threes have stable personalities and can learn to deal with life's inevitable disappointments
- Our under-threes are able to empathise with others and be supportive
- Our under-threes are – sometimes – willing to try to curb the need for instant gratification
- Our under-threes are unashamed of tears and have adorable smiles
- Our under-threes are trying to learn how to deal with their own anger

Naturally, our under-three's progress on these will vary with their stage of development. Nobody is suggesting that newborns are able to learn to wait, and neither should they have to. But what this list shows is how when we are predominantly Baby Centred, including doing lots of *Ignoring Minor Naughtiness* and giving *Clear Commands*, as opposed to Baby Directive, then our under-threes are going to learn they can rely on their mummy and/or daddy to provide sensitive responses. Being able to predict this type of reaction by their parents is an enormous bonus for our tiny tots because it means they know how to activate our approval. And our approval directly increases their experience of themselves as loved and loveable. By the same token, as their parents exercise sensible limits and boundaries, the one- and two-year-olds will build up a picture of the behaviours that provoke a withdrawal of their mum's and/or dad's attention, and so learn to avoid their parents' disappointment and perhaps anger. When baby and toddler behaviour is regulated in this way, their relationship with us improves enormously as they suffer much less confusion and anxiety and much more security of attachment.

Let's take a closer look now at how things were when you were a child if your mother or father lacked the self-confidence to be a balanced parent. You may remember them as distant, over-involved, inconsistent or authoritarian and therefore unable to give you that sense of self-worth and inner confidence that we all need if we are to care for our own under-threes in a balanced way. Being a balanced parent is something the vast majority of mummies and/or daddies urgently want to achieve, so why do we sometimes find it almost impossible to come up with the goods? Think back. See if any of the items below conjure up images from your childhood:

- Being unsure about how to gain your parents' approval
- Being unable to find the space and assurance to be yourself
- Feeling afraid you had no right to power over your own actions
- Fearing even your very best efforts would not bring warmth or focused attention from your parents

If this sounds familiar then it may be the case that you still have issues about self-confidence that continue to plague you, stemming from your childhood. When we are unsure of ourselves it interferes with all our interactions, including those with our children. But don't despair! By becoming aware you lack sufficient self-confidence to become a balanced mummy or daddy, and never the less deciding that's the sort of parenting you aspire to, you have already taken a giant step in the right direction. Remember, everyone has the capacity to make positive changes in their style of parenting. Don't forget, either, we all make mistakes. No one is a perfect parent because life is far too complex and demanding for that to ever happen. We are only too aware of our shortcomings when we measure ourselves against the standards of other balanced parents, aren't we? Even if we are beginning to understand much more clearly how our own difficulties as parents may be linked to our early experiences, we can feel pretty much stumped when it comes to working out exactly what to do about it. It isn't always easy to convert insight into action either, is it? In a moment, I will be giving you some hints on how to move forward towards a more balanced parenting style. But first let me tell you about two families where, despite some really positive factors, parents felt a lack of self-confidence about their ability to meet their babies and toddlers' needs.

Case Study One

Eileen and Magnus, both successful solicitors, had barely returned from their extended honeymoon when they discovered they were expecting a child. Although not a planned pregnancy, the couple agreed it felt right to go ahead. Both had enjoyed making preparations for the arrival of their baby and were given every help by both sets of grandparents, who were agog with excitement about the birth of their first grandchild. Eileen and Magnus attended ante-natal classes together, painted a nursery together, and even assembled the cot together. Eileen sailed through pregnancy and childbirth, returning home from hospital within twenty-four hours of their baby boy Milo's entrance into the world. Magnus proved to be a devoted father and Eileen an extremely capable mother. Lashings of support, practical and emotional, was constantly available from their own parents for the new mummy and daddy. Then Magnus, who had been very briefly hospitalised after breaking a leg playing rugby, had to spend several months at home recuperating. His cases at work taken over by a colleague, Magnus focused even more on Milo and the way in which Eileen was bringing him up on a day-to-day basis. Eileen found his interest at first enjoyable, then irksome and finally undermining, but Magnus insisted. The couple decided to seek my help after finding themselves in a frighteningly intense fight over whether Milo (now a bonny ten-month-old) always had to take his afternoon sleep in his cot.

It sounds a simple enough topic to negotiate, but Eileen's self-confidence had been so shaken by Magnus's 'destructive interference' (her words) that she found she barely knew which decision would be best for Milo. After our first two sessions, Magnus's leg was sufficiently healed for him to return to work, a move which the couple both welcomed as their respective roles within their family were once more clearly differentiated. However, I continued to see both Eileen and Magnus for six more sessions as they believed, quite rightly in my opinion, that each had suffered a crisis of confidence about their ability to match up to the high standards they set themselves and each other. During our discussions it became apparent that when she was just three years old, Eileen's father had spent three years at home due to a back injury. Eileen's mother had found this a great trial, especially as her husband was highly critical of her daily routine. She had not hesitated to let people know of her feelings. Magnus's accident had provoked in Eileen the same sense of unease she had experienced as a child, always anxious about whether her omnipresent father would approve of what she was doing. Once this link with the past had emerged, Eileen and Magnus were able to reach a constructive understanding of why, when everything had been going so well, a more than competent new mum had lost her self-confidence.

Case Study Two

The story with Martin and Brenda was quite different. Though still only in their mid-twenties, they had already been together for ten years. Over that time, Brenda had discovered a distinct flair for property management, whilst Martin had trained as a nurse and then specialised in midwifery. Both were thrilled when they conceived and spent long hours discussing joint parenting, job-sharing and how parents were people first and role models second. When baby Davina arrived, Martin was at once absolutely besotted with his tiny daughter. The couple renegotiated their roles and decided Brenda would go back to work full-time, while Martin, who was after all experienced with babies, would be at home with Davina. It seemed to be an arrangement made in heaven. Until little Davina started to crawl, that is. Brenda began to dread finding Martin in yet another bad mood when she returned from work. They had always enjoyed an occasional bottle of wine, but now Martin drank several bottles a week. The crisis came just before Davina's first birthday, when Brenda found Martin in tears because he had frightened himself by wanting to smack his beloved infant.

Martin and Brenda came to see me only three times. The issues were quite obvious to the couple. A brave attempt at role reversal had not worked out and yet neither parent had been able to admit to themselves or each other that things were going seriously wrong. Once they were able to share the fears that had led to Martin's crisis of confidence in his full-time hands-on parenting role, Brenda was able to talk about her side of the situation. I learned both her and Martin's families had been very distant, cool, and dismissive. So neither Davina's mummy nor daddy had any positive model of how to communicate their feelings, most especially when they lost the sense of self-confidence they had built up in their occupations. It seems both these young people came from quite impoverished family backgrounds and each had invested a great deal of their sense of self-worth in their careers. However, when Brenda became the only breadwinner, she realised her job could not give her the emotional satisfaction she craved, whereas time spent with Davina most certainly did.

Meanwhile, Martin's view of himself as an expert on babies was severely eroded once his daughter became mobile. A speeding crawler and cruiser is quite a different challenge when compared with a stationary newborn! Martin was also finding lack of contact with other adults a particularly isolating and depressing business. Thankfully, once they began to talk to each other about their feelings, these competent, bright new parents were able to sort out the daily practicalities of looking after their little girl. A year later Brenda rang up to say she was pregnant again. She said she intended to breastfeed her second baby, stay at home for the foreseeable future and start up her own company working as a consultant. I hope it worked out!

But what about your own levels of self-confidence? What about those bad days? No doubt you would like to move on so that your slips and slides away from a steady balance become less and less frequent. Here are some ideas on how you can help yourself:

Say to Yourself
- 'The more balanced I am in my parenting, the better it is for my precious angel.'
- 'When I am getting it right for my under-three, I am doing myself a big favour too.'
- 'Families are more fun when parents get the balance right.'
- 'I know it takes time, energy and determination to be a balanced parent, but so does being distant, over-involved, inconsistent and authoritarian. At least this way I know my efforts are really benefiting my little one.'
- 'Being balanced is the best way to build a secure, deep and strong bond with my treasured poppet.'
- 'I can learn to have even more confidence in myself.'

Remember, we *all* have room for improvement when it comes to parenting, and I include myself on that list! Even if you feel you have dealt fairly successfully with any unresolved issues of trust, love, loss and power left over from your childhood, when we embark on our new role as a parent it's likely we will experience at least a tad less self-confidence than usual. And it is always helpful to express those feelings, so why not try these approaches?

Other Moves

- Swap ideas with other parents about how you are trying to be an even more balanced mummy or daddy.
- Explain about being Baby Centred instead of Baby Directive to a friend who is also a parent. Tell them it's hard work and ask what they think of your aims. They might like to try it too.
- Discuss with your partner or closest friend your struggle to deal with the unresolved issues from your past. Emphasise that although you are pleased with your progress, you realise it's part of an ongoing, long-term process.
- Talk about any links you can see between your own childhood and the kind of parent you fear you may be – then move on to discuss the type of parenting you *intend* to provide for your little sweetheart.

We are not expecting overnight, magical transformations from 'Bad Mum' or 'Bad Dad' to 'Perfect Parent'. For a start, *very* few new mothers and fathers are 'Bad'. We are much more likely to be anxious about our uncertainties and failing to give sufficient weight to our successes. Do try to share your misgivings with a sympathetic listener. Keeping your worries to yourself can undermine the quality of the bond you are able to form with your baby – so spit them out!

How about the practicalities though? Try these suggestions on for size:

Practical Steps You Can Take

- Make sure you tell your baby and toddler you love them. Make it loud and clear
- Check you are praising your under-three's efforts and activities as often as you can

- Ensure you are giving your child enough personal space to develop their very own sense of identity
- Watch out in case you are not allowing them sufficient independence or that you are not actively listening to what they have to say
- Set up treats for all the family and have fun together
- Congratulate yourself and your spouse or partner on being good-enough parents and make sure you get some time to yourselves to be grown-ups together
- Remind yourself that your infant needs parents who know how to enjoy themselves as a couple, as well as when they are in mummy and daddy mode!
- Write out this emergency self-help line and stick it on the fridge to read when times are tough:

I'M DOING OK AND MY BABY AND TODDLER NEED BALANCED PARENTING – NOT PERFECTION

Your aim is to be Baby Centred in your style of interaction with your newborn, under-one, one- and two-year-old. Baby Centred Parenting equals Balanced Parenting. So it's not an impossible goal and you are not being asked to tap into a mysterious vein of parenting wisdom every time your under-three needs you. It is much more simple than that. All you need to do is remember the six-to-one Baby Centred to Baby Directive ratio and take aim. At six to one you wouldn't just be good-enough as a parent, you would be the absolute tops! If only I'd known all about being Baby Centred when my children were young I might have asked them fewer *Questions*, *Criticised* less, not shot off so many frowns and *Negative Looks*, held back on the *Teaching*, *Commands* and *Saying No* and avoided the few smacks I succumbed to!

My own saving grace was my mother. Her largely balanced, warm, stimulating, nurturing, approving and sensitive mothering made possible the growth of a secure, trusting bond between us. I guess my hope is that I too managed to come up with something not too dissimilar when it was my turn to be mummy. If my Mothering Day cards are anything to go by, I think I may have made it! There's self-confidence for you! When I think about the young parents in my now very extended family, I am full of admiration for their dedication to meeting their children's needs, from birth through to young adulthood. A final mantra to help you and them keep their balance would go something like this:

BE FOND – BE FIRM – BE FAIR

We could all use the same mantra when thinking about ourselves and our other relationships, couldn't we? For instance, being fond of *yourself* is an acknowledged first step to giving affection and feeling compassion towards others. When it comes to being firm we might usefully focus on making sure we stick to plans for 'Me Time', despite the latest mini crisis on the laundry/cooking/shopping/car maintenance front. And fair? Fairness is a notion dear to the hearts of all children, up to and including adolescents who seem to view themselves as continuously hard done by. It should be important to mums and dads too. Always putting yourself last, taking the smallest portion, giving in to others, and generally playing the martyr is not a loveable personality trait. Our offspring do not in the end thank us for our self-sacrifice, so best to start out at the beginning being as fair to yourself as you are to your child. Of course, you may find that your way of doing things does not necessarily meet with general approval, including your baby and toddler's grandparents! So listen in to what they may have to say, but stick to your guns – it's your infant after all.

I think it could be very constructive for the emotional quality of your bond with your infant, if you were able to more easily identify your own, your parents', and your baby and toddler's attachment style – their way of relating to other people. The categories were:

- **Secure** in a child and **Free** for an adult: the ones we are all aiming for.
- **Avoidant** in a child and **Dismissive** for an adult: common but full of uncertainties.
- **Ambivalent** in a child and **Enmeshed** for an adult: common but full of conflict.

One way to get an inkling of which is your own style of relating to others is to try to listen to yourself next time you are talking to someone about your relationships, particularly those with your parents.

If, for instance, you seem to be giving a coherent account of your early childhood, bringing in memories of events and relationships on which topics you can maintain a mature, reflective and psychological perspective, whether they were good or bad, could indicate you have a *Free* adult attachment style. It would be clear you value attachments and bonds.

On the other hand, were you to hear yourself talking brusquely, briefly or hardly at all, then you may have a *Dismissive* attachment style, finding it difficult to describe specific memories, instead providing rather general recollections and feeling very uncomfortable on the subject of emotions and relations. It would seem you did not especially value attachments or bonds. Or it may be you can hear angry tones in your voice as you talk at great length about the problems in your relationships with your mother and father. Sometimes you notice you have been veering off the point. If so, you could be someone with an *Enmeshed* style of relating to others and likely to be preoccupied with attachments and bonds.

As you have no doubt realised, adult attachment styles and parenting styles are not poles apart. Mummies and daddies with a *Free* attachment category could be the balanced ones, those with a *Dismissive* type might be the distant parents, and mums and dads who are themselves of an *Enmeshed* personality may be over-involved. That leaves us with the inconsistent and authoritarian parenting style yet to account for. My sense of how they may fit into the picture is that inconsistent parents probably tend towards the *Enmeshed* attachment category, while the authoritarian could be more on the *Dismissive* side. Mind you, I am just thinking aloud here, so you must view these last comments as my own and not part of Attachment Theory per se.

There is however a link I would like to bring to your attention. It's the one between parenting styles, attachment styles, and being Baby Centred. Basically, I suppose what I am trying to say is this:

WHATEVER YOUR OWN ATTACHMENT HISTORY, WHATEVER YOUR PARENTING STYLE, YOU *CAN* MAKE YOUR BOND WITH YOUR INFANT MORE SECURE BY BEING BABY CENTRED

So remember, nothing is set in stone and you personally *can* be the one in your family to break the mould! Even after generations of distant, inconsistent, over-involved or authoritarian parenting, it is still quite within your capacity to move towards being significantly more balanced when you put the Parent/Baby Game into action. But will 'they' let you? They? Yes, they – your very own mum and dad! Time to think about those important family relationships which include Nana and Grandad, Grandma and Pops, Grammy and Gramps. Call them what you will, there's no getting away from the significance of their roles in your baby's life.

On that note, it seems a good time to move along to our next section, which will focus on, amongst other things, those issues in your wider family that can expose vulnerabilities due to tensions across the generations.

Special Feature: When Grandparents Undermine

During the course of my professional and personal life, I have encountered families of all shapes and sizes. Families with double editions of grandparents. Families devoid of any members of an older generation. Families where grandparents ruled the roost, and others where they dare not utter a word. Each family's situation is unique, if only because of the quality of the relationships involved and the differing personalities. Then there's the matter of how much contact goes on between the generations. Sadly, some new mums and dads have been so bruised by the experience of being raised by their parents that they feel they must either cut off all communication or at least limit it extensively. Alternatively, there are couples who, on becoming parents, demand the presence of grandparents seven days a week. Right, so we are clear on at least one thing: when it comes to families, anything is possible!

Without going into each single family pattern, which would take a whole new book, I want to cover some of the most common tensions that can arise once the two generations become three. And guess what? It's all about bonds, bonds and more bonds! You might find it useful if we included topics like these, all of which feature transgenerational tensions to one degree or another:

- When your mum and dad are more loving to your baby than they ever were to you.
- When your mum and dad's attachment style is different from your in-laws'.
- When your mum and dad don't realise you're a parent now.

Let's take them one at a time.

When Your Mum and Dad are More Loving to Your Baby Than They Ever Were to You

A new baby's arrival in the family is often a source of delight. Parents are weak with relief and joy, and grandparents feel the same way too. But the birth of another member of the family also transforms what may have become – through the death of your grandparents – a two-generation set-up into a three-generation set-up once more. Memories of your own babyhood are trotted out for purposes of comparison, and with them recollections of the sort of baby you once were. Or at least, as portrayed by your own mum and dad.

It can prove to be quite a jolt, hearing ourselves described as 'Always crying', 'Always hungry', 'Always difficult to get to sleep', or 'Always fussy'. Of course, if we are fortunate enough to be described as 'Always smiling' or 'Always such a good baby' then it is totally different, isn't it? What seems quite certain, though, is that we can be swamped, not only by all the new and powerful emotions surrounding the achievement of becoming mummy and daddy, but also deluged with reactivated feelings about our own parents' treatment of us and the type of bond we had with them when we were tiny ourselves. If we are lucky, the reactivated emotions will contain a warm glow, the knowledge of being loved and approved of by our mother and father. The less fortunate may experience resentment, anger or bitterness.

All this is brought into very sharp focus when we watch our parents' interactions with our baby or toddler and conclude they are much more affectionate and caring towards the new addition than they managed to be with us. It takes a good solid dose of mature, reflective psychological thinking in order to deal with such feelings, and we may not be feeling up to it in the early months. So many novel challenges and only the bare twenty-four hours a day to get to grips with them! But supposing your infant is now a busy crawler, approaching one year of age. The negative emotions still swirl around inside you. They simply are not subsiding as you had hoped. What can you do to deal with them constructively? You might choose to:

- Tackle your parents directly, explaining to them how sad, jealous and resentful you are of all the love and affection they are showering on your baby
- Write out your feelings in a letter or card to your parents
- Set out the Negative Automatic Thoughts (NATs) associated with these painful emotions, and then challenge them

- Make up a mantra for yourself and see whether repeating it numerous times per day helps you to unblock your feelings. Try: 'I am loveable – I am loved – I am lovely'
- Talk it all through with your co-parent or a close friend
- Focus on the here-and-now rather than the past, and remind yourself that to your baby and toddler *you* are the most adored being in the cosmos

I suppose there may be some families where the hurt and rejection experienced by the new parents runs so deep that the only course open seems to be to cut off most – or even all – contact with Nana and Grandad. Clearly this is a last resort as a fond grandparent is very important in an under-three's life. But should you decide to take such drastic action, I am sure you would have good grounds, however depressing it may be to acknowledge the facts. So I want to offer my support for you as you take this difficult route and let you know I have direct experience of young families who actively thrived after achieving serious degrees of distance from the grand-parent generation. Remind yourself:

YOUR BOND WITH YOUR BABY AND TODDLER MUST BE TOP PRIORITY

On the other hand, there is my own personal experience of being a grandparent and step-grandparent, which I have to say has been extraordinarily rich and rewarding. What would my children and stepchildren say, I wonder, about my level of involvement? I suspect for some I was not available enough and for others perhaps too frequent a visitor! Suffice it to say we are still all in touch. No one has complained that I gave more affection to their children than themselves, so I presume I must have got it right enough the first time round. Or are they all out there desperately repeating their mantras? I may never know! Let's move on to our second potential source of tension across the generations.

When Your Mum and Dad's Attachment Style is Different From Your In-Laws'

We have all come across extended families where one side is jolly but distinctly haphazard and the other quite prim and organised. I always think wedding receptions are a mine of fascinating information on an issue like this, because just about everybody's attachment style is on show. Of course, while we can all wend our way home after the evening disco, happily talking about the strange relatives we hope we'll never meet again, the situation is very different for the bride and groom and their two sets of parents. Any clashes visible at the wedding will doubtless continue to be evident when the first baby arrives.

So how can we resolve the discomfort stirred up by such discrepancies? Or do we simply have to live with them? Well, in my opinion, we can only fight our own corner. Attachment styles are deeply ingrained and to attempt to modify your in-laws' style would probably be completely fruitless. It is much more realistic to aim at focusing on your attachment with your baby or toddler. Bear in mind:

YOUR BOND WITH YOUR BABY AND TODDLER MUST BE TOP PRIORITY

That could mean involving yourself in an ever-so-sensitive balancing act, trying to keep your in-laws sweet while you protect your baby from the less likeable features of their attachment style. Simultaneously, you will need to maintain open communications with your partner about your position, without completely alienating them. It's their parents you are criticising, after all. If you find yourself in this delicate situation, see if any of the ideas in the list below are of help in your dilemma:

- Make sure you are the one who decides when to end visits from doting, but perhaps rather distant, in-law grandparents. *Be fond but firm.*

- Stand up for your baby or toddler's right to a consistent emotional and behavioural environment. Do not allow in-law grandparents to set new rules or routines for your child. *Be assertive but sensitive.*
- Protect your baby or toddler from too much time with in-law grandparents who are too inconsistent, over-involved, distant or authoritarian. *Be positive but not too patient.*
- Don't say, 'Always' or 'Never' when talking with your co-parent about aspects of relating to their mother and father that you find difficult. *Be generous but not passive.*
- Remind yourself and your partner of your joint hopes and aspirations for your baby's development into a self-confident, happy and sociable little being. Don't let anyone put them down, especially not grandparents. *Be clear but committed.*
- Take time off to visit your own parents with your baby and toddler. At the very least, you'll be on familiar territory! *Be relaxed and robust.*

You may be fortunate in that both sets of grandparents are capable of the free and independent attachment style, which means they will be able to foster a balanced and mutually rewarding relationship with your infant. You'd have to be exceptionally lucky to get a break like that, but I am assured it can happen! Meanwhile, the rest of us flounder about trying to juggle the mismatches in our family caused by differing attachment styles.

I suppose there is another scenario which can prove problematic. One where *both* sets of grandparents have, in your view, a too distant, too authoritarian, inconsistent or over-involved parenting style for the well-being of your under-three. When you are struggling to move on from these backgrounds towards a balanced parenting style, you may need to use *both* sets of tips I have just listed. It will be a time for you and your co-parent to really pull together as a couple in your determination to do better as parents than the older generation in the family.

As a very young mother myself, I found it quite taxing to manage my in-laws' dismissive attachment style because my own parents tended more towards the opposite, my mother especially. There are so many possible permutations, aren't there? Touchingly, my mother-in-law chose to call her grandchildren 'darling', an endearment sadly not used towards her own offspring when they were young, it seems. I also have a moving and enduring image of my father-in-law with our first child, when she was aged about six months, tenderly holding her in his huge hands and smiling at her. Otherwise they were both decidedly taciturn when it came to talking about feelings and I'm sure they found my emotionally expressive nature uncomfortable. My own mum and dad, in their turn, believed my husband to have an interaction style that was too distant. I comfort myself with the thought that, were we all to be of identical attachment patterns, it would be a pretty featureless world. I must admit I would rather be challenged than bored. On the other hand, when our parents are having trouble in assimilating the fact that we, their children, are now parents ourselves, we might wish for rather less variety in family relationships. Time now to turn our attention to the third common source of tension between the generations.

When Your Mum and Dad Don't Realise You're a Parent Now

Why might this happen? Could it be because your parents can't see you as anything else other than their 'child', no matter how old you actually are? Or maybe they themselves are finding it tough to accept they have now moved up a generation in the family. Perhaps they see it as tacit admission that they are getting old. I do know that not everyone is as thrilled as I was to become a nana. Perhaps the new grandparents aren't ready emotionally to enter what they might see as the 'gardening instead of sex' phase of their lives. In that case, someone should reassure them that gardening and sex aren't mutually exclusive – thank heavens!

Whatever the cause, you find that your mum and dad are still telling you what to do. Still telling you off. Still telling you about how they brought your wind up or dealt with your teething problems. It's as if they do not believe you're capable of independent thought or action, let alone keeping their adored grandchild safe and well. 'Duh!' as my teenage grandchildren would say.

Perhaps there's a parallel to be drawn here. Maybe your mother and father still see you as the adolescent they feared would never mature sufficiently to be trusted with adult responsibilities. I know that when I had my first baby, at the age of twenty, my parents had barely been able to concede that I might manage the task when they were then shocked to the core by my plan to live in India for two years. At the time I was quite scornful of their anxieties. Only since becoming a grandmother myself have I been able to appreciate their position. But that's central to the transgenerational problem, isn't it? We are all much better at hindsight than we are at expressing our approval of plans we are not sure are advisable. That applies to all of us, whatever stage of our development we have reached. Understanding this and trying to make allowances is obviously important, though you must always remember:

YOUR BOND WITH YOUR BABY AND TODDLER MUST BE TOP PRIORITY

That said, you are still left with the task of establishing yourself in your mum and dad's eyes as a parent in your own right, which can be a challenge, so here are some thoughts on how to tackle this transgenerational source of tension:

- Stand in front of your mirror and say out loud: 'I am the Mummy!' or 'I am the Daddy!' Look yourself in the eye and repeat this several times a day.
- Think of occasions when you can genuinely ask your parents for advice on bringing up babies. Let them know you are sometimes putting their ideas into practice.
- Sit down with your parents and share a coffee together. Then gently tell them that, while all their help has been a life-saver, you need to do things your way, just as they did with you as a baby.

- Make sure you and your co-parent support each other in your attempts, some of which are bound to miss the mark, to be independent parents. Use humour as it will help you maintain a healthy perspective.
- Be as assertive as you can when grandparents try to run the show on the grounds that they 'know better' than you. Say, 'We find it works best when we . . .' then describe your own parenting tactics as you simultaneously swing into action.
- Try a simple, 'It's all right, Mum/Dad. I can manage thanks', said in a friendly fashion. This allows grandparents to relax, without loss of face.

However devotedly you put these tips to the test, there is no getting away from the fact that coping with Grannies and Grandpas who don't appear to have a great deal of faith in your parenting abilities can be a tough call. In large part, that's because we ourselves aren't at all sure we can manage to successfully negotiate the many hazards of being a good-enough parent. In fact, as well as juggling with all the practical and emotional dimensions of parenthood, we might well be trying to steer a safe course through the anxieties associated with our very own set of Scary Lists. Take a look and see if any of these items ring a bell:

Across the Generations
OFFICIAL SCARY LIST

Her	Him
I might turn out to be just like my mum – too critical and impatient	There's no way I'll be like my father – distant and unaffectionate
My parents are much more loving to my baby than they were to me	My father thinks I'm spoiling my baby/toddler
It was always difficult to be close to my mother	I could never get close to my father or mother
My parents won't approve of how I'm looking after my baby or toddler	I don't expect my parents to approve of my approach

The Official Scary List is really about how we try to improve on our parents' style of raising ourselves and our siblings, but at the same time we can feel anxious that we might not manage to pull it off. We fear we may be trapped by our attachment history, which of course was mostly dictated by their style of interacting with us when we were little. There is also a worrying component regarding the inner conflict we might experience when wanting to be different from our mother and father, yet still earn their approval. For some of us, being an independent parent in our own right might involve having to acknowledge that, just like when we were children, our mum and dad will never be able to assuage our yearning for their praise.

Your best bet in such circumstances is to hold fast to the Parent/Baby Game principles and put all your efforts into making sure your own child does not suffer the same fate. Paradoxically, if we think our own mum and dad have been brilliant parents, we might still have an Official Scary List about disappointing them! I remember I used to criticise my own parenting efforts sometimes because I feared I was less patient, less inventive, less available and altogether a less loveable mother than mine had been. It can feel like a no-win situation sometimes, can't it? It can certainly seem like that when we are at the mercy of our Unofficial Scary List! Let's take a look.

Across the Generations
UNOFFICIAL SCARY LIST

Her	Him
I am *just* like my mum, critical and impatient	I'm *just* like my dad, distant and unloving
My mum and dad never really loved me	I never felt loved by my parents
Now, when I really need my mum, there's no love between us to draw on	I think I hate my father
It's too late to ever put things right between us	The gap with my dad will never heal.

It can be extraordinarily painful even to whisper these fears to ourselves, never mind actually saying them out loud to someone else. And yet this is where sharing your apprehensions with your partner can pay enormous dividends, so the sooner you get started the better for everyone concerned. I know facing up to things in this way is tough, but until you have managed it you will find it difficult to move on.

In the past you may have shied away from taking a good look at these transgenerational issues, your most private vulnerabilities. This may be partly because it was too painful and partly because you could not see any benefit in opening old wounds. What I am suggesting is that now, in your new role as parent, you are in a prime position to look forward. Your bond with your baby does not have to be a replay of your parents' mistakes. You can acknowledge that you cannot change the past *and* you can orchestrate a more secure bond with your baby and toddler. How? Well, I sincerely hope you have more ideas on that than when you started leafing through this book! If in any doubt, you could flick forward to the final part of the book, where I sum things up. But for now I want you to banish your fears by reminding yourself of the most important mantra of this book:

BE BABY CENTRED – BE BALANCED – BE BEAUTIFULLY BONDED

Here are six Golden Bullets to help you refresh your memory on the main issues covered.

GOLDEN BULLETS

- **No. 1. My Baby Needs . . . Sensitivity**
Being sensitively responsive to your baby and toddler means knowing how to interpret their emotional and physical needs, and respond appropriately. This includes *Ignoring Minor*

Naughtiness along with giving only a limited number of *Commands*, which must be clear, instead of *Saying No* and using *Fuzzy Commands*. This will increase the trusting nature of the bond between you and your under-three. Choosing to *Ignore* rather than give critical attention to annoying but not dangerous behaviours will still decrease their frequency. Ignoring 99 per cent of *Minor Naughtiness* will sweeten your bond with your baby and toddler. Use often. Give your toddler simple instructions on what to do. Only use when you intend to follow through. *Clear Commands* help your one- and two-year-olds to find security in your predictability. Use sparingly.

• **No. 2. What Not To Do: Don't Give Fuzzy Commands**
Non-specific instructions – *Fuzzy Commands* – set toddlers up to fail and can lead to anxiety where none is necessary. Avoid altogether if possible. *Saying No* to prevent, stop or threaten negative consequences for undesirable behaviour can actually prompt your under-three to do it all the more. It also damages their self-esteem and undermines your bond. Use very infrequently. *Saying No* and *Fuzzy Commands* should be kept to an absolute minimum because they create an environment of criticism and confusion around our under-threes. Don't undermine your baby and toddler's potential to become a balanced personality. Instead give them the benefits of *Ignoring Minor Naughtiness* and using *Clear Commands*. This will enable them to trust in your ability to keep them safe when their impulses threaten to overwhelm them. Baby Centred to Baby Directive ratio: aim for a consistent six to one ratio on *Ignoring Minor Naughtiness* versus *Saying No*. For *Clear Commands*, when you get a 75 per cent success rate, you are giving your under-three a positive emotional family environment.

• **No. 3. Special Feature: Displaying Physical Affection**
Staying physically in touch with babies and toddlers in a loving way is vital to every area of development, especially their bond with you.

• **No. 4. Special Feature: When Grandparents Undermine**
Having a baby affects all the generations in a family. Relationships with grandparents have to be renegotiated. Remember your baby and toddler will benefit from contact with their wider family, so keep communication channels open if at all possible. Don't let relationship problems with your own mother and father prevent you from becoming a more balanced mummy and daddy than they managed to be.

• **No. 5. Echoes From Our Past: Balanced Parenting**
Whatever sort of parent you may have had you can make progress towards being a balanced mummy and/or daddy who is fond, firm and fair in relating to their under-three. This will allow infants to develop a bubble of self-confidence that they can use throughout their lives. Nurture and stabilise the bond between you by frequently *Ignoring Minor Naughtiness* and giving a limited number of *Clear Commands* only. Cut down on *Saying No* and *Fuzzy Commands*. You and your baby and toddler will find your bond extremely rewarding when you can keep your balance and yet forgive yourself if you slip.

• **No. 6. What To Do Next: Troubleshooting**
Rising to the challenge of being sensitively responsive to your under-three can be exacting, as can staying in touch. Your baby and toddler will need you to constantly fine tune to their ever more complex development. Remember, balanced Baby Centred parents *don't* need to *Say No* or give *Fuzzy Commands* because they are too busy being fond, firm and fair.

Conclusion

Beginning Your Life Together

When I started writing this book, my aim was to spell out how putting the Parent/Baby Game principle into practice might help parents of under-threes meet their emotional needs and so forge a strong and mutually rewarding bond between themselves and their child from the moment of birth onwards. I only hope I have managed to achieve my goal, at least in part, and that you found what you have read so far useful. But before finally wishing you every good fortune in your challenging role as mummy or daddy to your under-three-year-old, I am going to leave you with just a few more lists.

The title above gives you a clue as to my aim here. I simply want to remind you of where we started out, which was with our babies and toddlers' psychological, emotional and social needs. These are very much more difficult to meet than the more material kind. While anyone could buy your baby nappies and night lights, you and you alone are in the privileged position to ensure your under-three learns the most important lesson of their lives, that they are loved and loveable. That, in essence, is what this book is all about.

Providing for babies and toddlers' psychological, emotional and social needs centres on their mothers and fathers' ability to form, and then maintain, a Secure Bond with their under-threes. It is a pretty daunting responsibility and not one that many of us feel fully prepared to tackle successfully. It is in order to lighten your load and guide your footsteps that I have written in such detail about how to achieve just such a truly beneficial relationship with your little one. Each of my comments is based on well-established psychological theories and therapies. I have included some personal reminiscences too, but I wouldn't want you to see these as anything other than simply the memories of someone who, like yourself, struggled to be the best parent possible to their under-threes. We are all bound to fall short of perfection. We are only human, after all. However, we can significantly increase our chances of being a good-enough mummy or daddy by focusing our energies – or what's left of them – on being Baby Centred and *not* Baby Directive.

Just to remind you of the difference between the two, here are the **DOs** and **DON'Ts**:

DOs	DON'Ts
Do give lots of *Attends*	Don't ask too many *Questions*
Do offer masses of *Praise*	Don't *Criticise*
Do provide miles of *Smiles* and *Positive Looks*	Don't, if at all possible, frown, scowl or look angry and frightening
Do make frequent use of *Imitation*	Don't spend too much time *Teaching*
Do dare to *Ask to Play*	Don't waste your time issuing unclear and unnecessary *Commands*
Do *Ignore* 99 per cent of all *Minor Naughtiness*	Don't overdose on *Saying No*
Do let yourself go with oodles of *Positive Touches*	Don't give in to the urge to use a *Negative Touch*. You will only immediately regret it

I know it's easy to write and even recite these **DOs** and **DON'Ts** and a million times tougher to come up with them on the spot. And that's right where we are, a lot of the time, isn't it? On the spot! The tears, the tantrums, the crying and the crises – and that's *before* breakfast! It takes amazing devotion, generosity, patience, humour, vigilance, good timing and fast footwork to be an OK mum or dad. Of course, it helps no end that we not only think our under-threes are adorable, we *know* they are the most talented and brilliant ever to be born. Naturally, they deserve the very best we can give them, and that very best is a bond with you secure enough to give them total reassurance that they are loved and loveable. Putting the ideas and techniques of the Parent/Baby Game into action at least half the time, much more if at all possible – remember the six to one Baby Centred to Baby Directive ratio – will see you well on your way to reaching that goal. Especially if you add in the following:

Additional Vital Points

Best Guess your under-three when they seem upset or distressed.

Remember: Mirror, Validate, Empathise and Resolve.

Using the Attention Rule will help you to be a balanced parent.

Praise and reward all good behaviour, *Ignore* 99 per cent of all *Minor Naughtiness* and only use punishment for dangerous behaviour.

Give *Clear Commands* that leave your under-three in no doubt you mean what you say and say what you mean.

Only give a *Clear Command* when you intend to follow through.

Don't Smack because it will harm the security of your bond with your baby and toddler. Remember: a parent who smacks has lost control of the situation.

Don't ever tell your under-three they are stupid because it will seriously undermine their self-confidence. And self-confidence is the bubble that keeps us afloat when life's troubles threaten to drown us.

Dislike the bad behaviour but never stop loving your baby and toddler.

We all need to know that we are loved and loveable, even when our behaviour is out of bounds.

I am going to finish off with some reminders on the benefits of making links between our own childhood experiences and the type of parent we have turned out to be. But first let's remind ourselves of those parenting styles and mantras:

I CAN BE BRAVE – BE WARM – BE HAPPY

This mantra is for those parents who feel they may be a trifle emotionally distant from their baby and toddler.

I CAN BE RELAXED – LET GO – BE CLOSE

This mantra is for parents who fear they may be emotionally over-involved with their under-threes.

I CAN BE CARING – BE CALM – BE CONSISTENT

This mantra is for the parents who believe they have improvements to make in being more consistent.

I CAN BE FLEXIBLE – BE FRIENDLY – BE FUN

This mantra is for parents who would like to be less authoritarian.

I CAN BE FOND – BE FIRM – BE FAIR

This mantra is for all parents trying to be balanced, a goal we all have in common.

Everyone who wants to *can* make progress towards nurturing a secure bond with their treasured under-three, by meeting their emotional needs. And the best way to do that? By being Baby Centred, of course!

So – how do you feel? Overwhelmed by the journey ahead? Pleased with the progress you have already made? Perhaps a little of each. After all, the fact that you have looked through this book means you are taking your role as a parent seriously and realise there is always more to learn about yourself and your baby and toddler. You may find the practical steps I have suggested the easiest ones to take, but don't neglect the more psychological ones. Talking to yourself, for instance, or even out loud, is a sign that you are beginning to move forward towards your goal of being a balanced parent, not proof of madness! Self-instruction has proved to be a powerful tool for tackling the emotional and relationship issues left over from our own childhood. Talking to trusted others and sharing our hopes and fears is also a very positive step in making changes in our own behaviour and feelings about ourselves. You may feel you would prefer to remain silent because of the fear you may be ridiculed. In fact, you'll generally find that once you open up, your chosen confidant follows suit – to the benefit of all involved. So be brave, the rewards of sharing your innermost thoughts and emotions usually far outweigh the risks.

In this book, I have tried to show what all babies and toddlers need from their parents. I hope I have also highlighted how the style of parenting we find ourselves using can be related to our own early lives. Acknowledging that our parents, despite wanting the best for us, could not quite meet our needs for warmth, approval, security, stimulation and sensitivity is a real step towards maturity. When we can remember without blame, we may have actually arrived! By making these links and then moving forward, we can begin to find some resolution of those left-over issues from our childhood. It is from such progress that we lay the foundations for the loving bond between us and our beloved baby and toddler. This is a bond that can allow us and them the freedom to trust that we are loved and loveable. A secure bond with you, their mummy and daddy, will enable your under-three to develop a clear sense of their own identity and become gradually, very gradually, more independent. Above all, they will learn to approve of themselves, which in turn will allow them to show love and affection to the important people in their lives and have the self-confidence to explore the world around them.

We can all work towards being a Baby Centred and balanced parent. Each step we take towards that goal will increase the likelihood that our young ones receive enough of our top quality attention to grow into an adult who can pass on all those benefits to their own babies, toddlers and children. Finally, we can enjoy the fun of being grandparents to tiny tots who will be truly delightful personalities. Their parents, our own children, will have been able to give to our grandchildren what we ourselves worked so hard to give them when they were babies and toddlers: the message that they are loved and loveable.

Further Resources

'ABC of Behaviour: Troubleshooting For Parents of Young Children. Getting Ready For School. Right from the Start', Right from the Start Publications, 1998. *www.rightfromthestart.co.uk*

'The Assessment and Treatment of Parenting Skills and Deficits, Within the Framework of Child Protection', Sue Jenner, in *Association of Child Psychology and Psychiatry Newsletter* Vol. 14, No. 5, 1992

'The Assessment of Parenting in the Context of Child Protection, Using the Parent/Child Game', Sue Jenner in *Association of Child Psychology and Psychiatry Review* Vol. 2, No. 2, 1997

Child Development from Birth to Eight: A Practical Focus, Jennie Lindon, National Children's Bureau, 1993

Early Childhood Education, Tina Bruce, Hodder and Stoughton, 1998

The Family Game, Sue Jenner, BBC Education QED programme, 1993. Available from The Family Caring Trust, 8 Ashtree Enterprise Park, Newry, County Down BT34 1BY

Helping the Non-compliant Child: A Clinician's Guide to Parent Training, Rex Forehand and Robert McMahon, Guilford Press, 1981

Parenting the Strong-willed Child: the Clinically Proven Five-week Programme for Parents of 2–6 Year Olds, Rex Forehand and Nick Long, Chicago Contemporary Books, 1996

Partners Becoming Parents, edited by Christopher Clulow, Sheldon Press, 1996

'Psychological Methods', Sue Jenner in *Standards and Mental Handicap; Keys to Confidence*, edited by Tony Thompson and Peter Mathias, Baillière Tindall Press, 1992

'Quantitative Assessment of Parenting', Sue Jenner and Gerard McCarthy in *The Assessment of Parenting*, edited by Clare Lucy, Routledge, 1995

Voices from Childhood, Susan Creighton and Neil Russell, NSPCC National Centre, 1995. Publications Unit, 42 Curtain Road, London EC2A 3NH

Why Love Matters: How Affection Shapes a Baby's Brain, Sue Gerhardt, Brunner-Routledge, 2004

The Science of Parenting, Margot Sunderland, Dorling Kindersley, 2006

The Parent/Baby Game: The Official Version

Here are the steps which would occur if you were participating in the full Parent/Baby Game treatment:

- Before-and-after recording of the parents' ratio of Baby Centred and Baby Directive behaviours.
- The baby and parent playing together for ten minutes in a room wired for sound and vision.
- During this ten-minute period the parent wears an earbug through which they can hear the therapist.
- Meanwhile, the therapist is behind a one-way screen prompting and rewarding the parent for being Baby Centred rather than Baby Directive towards their baby. It is known that one of the reasons for the technique's great effectiveness is the praise delivered to the parent via the earbug.
- Throughout the ten minutes, the baby cannot hear what the therapist says, though they know that the therapist is there behind the screen.
- After ten minutes' 'parent training' the baby has an hour for either play therapy or fun and games.
- During this time, the parent and the therapist work together on the daily home-based version of the ten minutes' Baby Centred input for the baby; on the parents' unresolved baggage; and on how best to tackle the 'problem of the week'.

Helpful Organisations

EXPLORING PARENTHOOD
4 Ivory Place, Treadgold St, London W11 4BP
Telephone 020 7221 6681
Exploring Parenthood is an organisation which offers help and advice to parents and runs an advice line during office hours.

FAMILY WELFARE ASSOCIATION
501–505 Kingsland Road, London E8 4AU
Telephone 020 7254 6251
Fax 020 7249 5443
Email *fwa.headoffice@fwa.org.uk*
FWA offers a variety of help to enable people to find the best solutions to their problems. FWA works with people to build confidence, self-esteem and enable children to have fun and excitement; lone parents to make friends; and mentally ill people to rebuild their life in the community.

PARENTLINE PLUS
520 Highgate Studios, 53–79 Highgate Road, Kentish Town, London NW5 1TL
Telephone 020 7284 5500
Helpline 0808 800 2222
Parentline Plus offers support for concerned parents in times of crisis, including through a confidential telephone helpline. There are local groups around the UK.

PARENT NETWORK
Room 2, Winchester House, 11 Cranmer Road, London SW9 6EJ
Telephone 020 7735 1214
Fax 020 7735 4692
Trains parents and professionals in offering accredited parenting skills courses. Parents, grandparents and carers are most welcome. Parent Network has local UK support groups.

NATIONAL CHILDREN'S BUREAU
8 Wakely Street, London EC1V 7QE
Telephone 020 7843 6000
Fax 020 7278 9512
NCB is a charitable organisation that acts as an umbrella body for organisations working with children and young people in England and Northern Ireland. Through working in partnership, sharing knowledge, resources and services NCB has created a powerful, authoritative and influential voice to improve the lives of children and young people. NCB has an extensive catalogue of texts relevant to parenting.

RELATE
Premier House, Carolina Court, Lakeside, Doncaster DN4 5RA
Telephone (UK) 0845 456 1310
Relate helps couples, or one partner only, where there are relationship difficulties. You may have to wait to see one of their specially trained counsellors, but it is well worth it.

Professional Help

If you would like to contact a professional, visiting your GP should be the first step if you need individual help. He or she can then refer you for counselling or therapy at a local resource centre for adults. Visiting your GP should also be your first move if you need help with family problems. Your GP will then refer you to your local children and families services.

Should you wish to contact me professionally, my details are: Sue Jenner BSc, M.Phil MAE, Independent Consultant Clinical Psychologist, 130 Island Road, Sturry, Canterbury, Kent CT2 0EG. Telephone 01227 710884; fax 01227 710894 and email *sue.jenner@talktalk.net*

I can provide:
- Individual Parent/Baby Game sessions
- Parent/Baby Game groups for parents
- Developmental assessments for adults
- Expert Witness court reports

Index

A NOTE ON THE AUTHOR

Sue Jenner is a distinguished clinical psychologist. She has worked with troubled children, parents and families for twenty-five years. While at the Maudsley hospital in London, she made several seminal documentaries for the BBC QED programme. She is the author of *The Parent/Child Game*, also published by Bloomsbury.

A NOTE ON THE TYPE

The text of this book is set in Linotype Sabon, named after the type founder, Jacques Sabon. It was designed by Jan Tschichold and jointly developed by Linotype, Monotype and Stempel, in response to a need for a typeface to be available in identical form for mechanical hot metal composition and hand composition using foundry type.

Tschichold based his design for Sabon roman on a font engraved by Garamond, and Sabon italic on a font by Granjon. It was first used in 1966 and has proved an enduring modern classic.